RADIO AND TELEVISION REPORTING

Roy Gibson

University of Utah

ALLYN AND BACON
Boston   London   Toronto   Sydney   Tokyo   Singapore

Series Editor: Steve Hull
Series Editorial Assistant: Becky Dudley
Cover Administrator: Linda K. Dickinson
Cover Designer: Design Ad Cetera
Manufacturing Buyer: Tamara Johnson

Copyright © 1991 by Allyn and Bacon
A Division of Simon & Schuster, Inc.
160 Gould Street
Needham Heights, MA 02194

Library of Congress Cataloging-in-Publication Data
Gibson, Roy
    Radio and television reporting / Roy Gibson.
      p.   cm.
    Includes bibliographical references.
    ISBN 0-205-12307-4
    1. Broadcast journalism. 2. Television broadcasting of news.
3. Radio authorship. 4. Television authorship.   I. Title.
PN4784.B75G5 1990
070.1'9--dc20   89-17861
                                                  CIP

Printed in the United States of America

10 9 8 7 6 5 4 3 2 1   94 93 92 91 90

Photo Credits
Pages 6, 24, 154, and 219: Courtesy of WORLD MONITOR; A Television Presentation of
The Christian Science Monitor. **Pages 16, 48, 69, 222, and 240:** Robert Harbison, photog-
rapher. **Pages 20, 120, 164, and 258:** AP/Wide World Photos. **Pages 101 and 217:** © The
Christian Science Monitor. **Page 126:** © The Christian Science Monitor—Neal Menschel.
Page 201: Paul Conklin, photographer. **Page 251:** © Frank Siteman 1989.

Text Credits appear on page 291, which constitutes a continuation of the copyright page.

CONTENTS

5 CHOOSING WORDS   92

__6 INTERVIEWING   114

__7 LOOKING FOR NEWS   135

PREFACE

The purpose of *Radio and Television Reporting* is to give its readers an overview of the spectrum of radio and television news. Few broadcasters are able to develop a high degree of proficiency in all of the skills they need to produce polished news stories for radio and television, but they become familiar with all facets of news production, possibly becoming experts in one or more skills. Successful news broadcasters are adept at one or more skills—writing, reporting, recording, photographing, editing, producing, performing—and they cultivate a sense of journalistic ethics and a knowledge of the laws that affect news.

This book is designed to introduce neophyte broadcasters to writing news for broadcast and to refresh the skills of experienced news broadcasters who want to improve their styles. *Radio and Television Reporting* is designed to give its readers an overview of news broadcasting and to encourage them to hone their skills and discover where they can adapt best to the process.

Reporting is a companion skill to writing. Broadcasters who can generate story ideas, interview newsmakers, cull records, and observe and absorb the atmosphere and actions that surround the events and newsmakers they cover will be able to interpret events clearly for their listeners and viewers.

Sounds and pictures are particular properties of radio and television news. Reporters who, with their specialized technology, can record and combine the voices and the ambience, the faces and the scenes that reveal information and emotions, can give human dimensions to their news. Broadcasters who cultivate talents to communicate ideas vocally and physically can enhance the understanding of their listeners and viewers. And practicing reporters need to be aware of how their work affects the people they report about and the people they report to. They need to develop their own ethical principles and learn their employers' ethical guidelines. They also need to know the legal limits of defamation, privacy, and federal regulations.

The people with whom I worked for twenty years in broadcasting and the people I have watched for fifteen years as a media critic have taught me much about broadcast news. My colleagues at the University of Utah encouraged me to complete this book and gave me helpful suggestions based on their expertise. Students and former students challenged my ideas and helped me to refine them.

I owe special thanks to the people who reviewed the text and suggested revisions: Bill Knowles, former Washington bureau chief for ABC-TV, now at the University of Montana; Craig Wirth, former feature reporter for KUTV, WWOR, and KNBC, now a freelancer; Christine Davidson, Syracuse University; Bob Farson, Pennsylvania State University; Thomas Grimes, University of Wisconsin–Madison; and Peter Mayeux, University of Nebraska.

Finally, lasting appreciation to my late wife Bena Le whose gentle prodding encouraged me to finish the manuscript.

R.G.

1

THE ROLE OF BROADCAST NEWS

What we've done is to create a vast complex of information machines, which are being fed by a storehouse of knowledge and entertainment of every conceivable kind. The endless mass of material is fed from diverse sources into the process, and it comes out the other end in a variety of ways. Technology is greatly increasing that variety every day.
—WILLIAM S. PALEY, "Press Freedom—A Continuing Struggle"

We've come a long way since November 2, 1920, when KDKA broadcast the *Pittsburgh Post*'s running tally of votes that saw Republican Warren G. Harding elected to the presidency.

We've come a long way since December 7, 1941, when WCBS-TV, New York City, broadcast news for nine consecutive hours about the Japanese attack on Pearl Harbor.

We've come a long way, but we didn't get here quickly. For 14 years after KDKA's pioneering public affairs broadcast, radio stations and networks did little more than read daily newspapers over the air. By 1934, however, newspaper publishers were angry. Realizing that radio stations were competing for advertising dollars, they voted to provide no more "free" news. Associated Press, United Press, and the International News Service adopted policies to allow only stations owned by newspaper publishers to buy short bulletins. That prodded CBS and NBC to begin to gather their own news, and they gave birth to original reporting in radio.

NBC introduced television at the 1939 World's Fair in New York. CBS also began telecasting in New York that same year. And a young inventor, Allen B. Dumont, put an experimental station on the air and marketed the first all-electronic receivers. But the government needed materials and factories for the production of military equipment for World War II, so it forced NBC to suspend television activity for the duration of the war.

Both radio and television have since expanded the reach of journalism. With the rise of Hitler in Germany in the 1930s, radio demonstrated its capability for instantaneous transmission of news. Beginning with its coverage of the 1948 national political conventions, television demonstrated its capability for live coverage of events that carried viewers to the scene.

Radio and television reporters adopted the principles developed by print journalists and expanded them to utilize sounds and moving pictures. Edward R. Murrow once pinpointed the growing pains of these broadcast media as they cultivated their skills as distributors of news: "One of the basic troubles with radio and television news is that both instruments have grown up as an incompatible combination of show business, advertising, and news. Each of the three is a rather bizarre and demanding profession. And when you get all three under one roof, the dust never settles."[1] The conflict among those three disparate functions still exists, but broadcast journalists have learned better how to let the three coexist and stir less dust.

WHAT IS BROADCAST NEWS?

The character of news in newspapers and on radio and television is distinct.

Newspapers can convey complex stories best; they have space available to provide needed background and clarification. They can explain, for example, the motives and maneuvers of defense and prosecuting attorneys who question potential jurors for a fraud trial.

Radio can convey breaking stories best. It can deliver news about a mid-air collision or a new legislative action almost as soon as its reporters can collect the basic facts.

Television can convey action stories best. It can show firefighters battling a fire, tax protesters staging a demonstration, or sheriff's deputies rounding up a herd of stray calves as soon as camera crews can get to the scene.

But none of these media is restricted to the narrow spectrum of news it covers best. All of them try to cover as much of the news as they have staff, space, and time for.

Newspapers may devote more resources to abstract news—budgets, taxes, inflation, public issues, and concepts. But broadcasters, too, try to simplify such news stories for their listeners and viewers. Radio and television can effectively transmit the conflict in a legislative debate or the impact of a cost-of-living increase upon consumers because the stories contain emotional qualities that listeners and viewers can absorb vicariously to enhance their understanding. And in longer magazine programs, documentaries, or interview shows, broadcasters can explore the abstract intellectual implications of such stories.

Many consumers avail themselves of more than one medium to get the news: they may hear it on radio or television first, then read newspapers to amplify their knowledge about stories that interest them. Because radio needs so little time to process its news, and modern television is so mobile and so convenient, they are often the first source of news for consumers.

Of course, reporters see events from different perspectives, the character of their medium often governing their perspectives. Since time restrictions force broadcasters to be selective in what they choose to air, they may devote only ten seconds to one story and a minute and a half to another. Newspapers can be more expansive; they can publish comprehensive detail on each story.

Conversely, broadcasters often cover whole news conferences and large segments of legislative or public hearings. They also interrupt scheduled programs for expanded live coverage of assassination attempts, unusual criminal trials, severe weather occurrences, and serious crashes or accidents.

So, while radio and television may seem more abbreviated than newspapers in one time period, they will be more thorough in another. In long form or in short form, broadcasters serve the information needs of their listeners and viewers.

WHO LISTENS? WHO WATCHES?

The Associated Press commissioned Reymer and Gersin Associates, a Detroit marketing research firm, to conduct a nationwide study of radio listeners and found that "the vast majority of all listeners surveyed say they need and expect news and information."[2]

- Eighty percent agree they "like listening at the start of the day because they get a variety of information in a short time."
- Seventy-three percent agree they "like to hear information because it gets them thinking."
- Sixty-nine percent agree that the "main reason they listen to radio is to keep up with the latest news events."
- Seventy percent say they pay as much or more attention to news and information as they do to music.
- Sixty-seven percent are more likely to listen to a station with news and information than one without.
- Demand for radio news "is highest from 6 to 10 a.m. and is also high during the rest of the day . . . including midday and 3 to 7 p.m."

The audience for radio is fragmented. Each station chooses a format and a news style to appeal to a specific segment of the available audience. It will choose the kinds of news, the length of newscast, the writing style, and the reading style to fit the tastes of that audience. For example, ABC Radio now has six distinct styles on six separate networks—the ABC Information Network, the ABC Contemporary Network, the ABC Entertainment Network, the ABC FM Network, the ABC Directions Network, and the ABC Rock Radio Network.

Orson Welles's October 30, 1938, radio broadcast of
The War of the Worlds *was believed by thousands to
be news, and was an early example of the potentially
galvanizing effect of the young medium of radio.*

In television, many local news programs draw audiences as large as some of the top-rated prime-time entertainment programs. The media surveys of The Roper Organization since 1959 have shown a continuing growth in audience reliance on television for news and no growth in audience reliance on newspapers. In the 1960s, 42 percent of Americans said they got their news from two or more sources. By 1987, only 16 percent said they used more than one source. The 1989 Roper survey shows that television has been the primary source for news since the early 1960s, and has "enjoyed at least a 20-point lead over newspapers since 1980." Additionally, Roper found that 65 percent of the public rely mainly on television for news, 42 percent on newspapers, 14 percent on radio, and 4 percent on magazines. (The figures total more than 100 percent because Roper allowed respondents to give more than one answer.)[3]

Professor Lawrence Lichty questions Roper's figures. Lichty says people only *think* they get most of their news from television. He cites the findings of the Simmons Market Research Bureau that say 68 percent of adults in the United States read at least part of some newspaper every day and that only 26.5 percent of them watch late night local TV news, the news programs most often watched. Lichty says, ". . . the audience for TV news fluctuates. It is far more fickle than the audience for newspapers or magazines."[4]

Nevertheless, the public has entrusted the news departments of radio and television stations with continually greater responsibility for informing their audiences, and newspeople are meeting the challenge.

NEWS DEPARTMENTS WITHIN STATIONS

Former ABC News president Elmer Lower remembers his initiation into broadcast news. He had worked 20 years in print journalism when CBS News hired him in 1953 to be chief of its Washington Bureau. He described those headquarters as follows:

> What I found was a garage, a ramshackle *old* garage. I looked around and noticed the leaky casement windows, the dirt and the leaves blowing in under the doors, pushed by a sharp autumn breeze. I said to the first person I met, assignment editor Don Richardson: "I'm looking for the CBS Washington Bureau." Don replied: "You're in it." Somehow it didn't have that certain element of class I had associated with CBS and William S. Paley.[5]

Many reporters and news directors at local stations can remember similar facilities—a news department located behind the scene shop, two desks and a telephone housed in a lean-to shack.

Program directors or sometimes station managers supervised news departments, but their knowledge of news was limited. They knew how to sell 5- to 15-minute segments of news to sponsors, and they knew where to place news in the program schedule so it distracted minimally from entertainment programs. But they thought about news as little more than a public service required by the Federal Communications Commission.

After more than four decades of growth, news programs have become important functions for broadcast stations. Most have not only stopped draining profits to pay for their operations, they now contribute to their stations' earnings, some substantially.

Well-produced, interesting local newscasts stimulate audience enthusiasm for the programs that follow. Program directors often schedule newscasts in time periods where they act as lead-ins to network newscasts or entertainment programs. Local news has thus become a springboard that may lead to a station's success or failure.

The volume of news programming has also grown through most of the 1980s. All-news radio stations have succeeded in large cities, and many stations in smaller cities have expanded the number of minutes they devote to news, particularly during the noon hour and morning and evening commuter times.

Many early evening television newscasts run for two hours, with new anchors every half hour. Early morning, noontime, and late night newscasts are commonly aired during daily program schedules.

Stations affiliated with networks have denied their requests for air time to expand their early evening newscasts, but ABC's "Nightline" and CBS's "Nightwatch" have demonstrated that news can succeed in the hours after the last local newscast has signed off. NBC experimented with an innovative late night news program, "Overnight," but abandoned it when it failed to attract the expected audience.

Whereas network executives and many local station managers have trimmed news expenditures, the climate for broadcast news is still bullish. Audiences have asked for greater quantity and more quality, and sponsors have been willing to support those demands.

Exercises

1. Talk to the manager of a local radio or television station. How important is news in the station's program schedule? Do news programs bring in more

Reporters at work in a modern television newsroom. One survey found that 66 percent of the public rely on television as their main source of news.

income than the news department spends? How does news programming enhance the image of the station?

2. Talk to the news director of a local radio or television station. How has news
   changed during his or her career in broadcasting? What are the news director's
   relationships with the station manager? The sales manager? The promotion
   director?

3. Talk to a reporter at a local radio or television station. How does his or her
   work differ from that of reporters in other media? Does a broadcast reporter
   have to adjust to the philosophy or programming style of a station? How?

4. Talk to the sales managers or program directors of at least three local stations.
   Where do their stations' newscasts rank in the ratings? How influential are their
   ratings when they try to sell commercial time? How do they think newscasts
   should adapt to fit the station's image?

5. Listen to the news programs of at least two local radio or television stations.
   How do they differ? What kinds of similar techniques do they utilize? Compare
   the newscasts of network-affiliated stations to the newscasts of their networks.

Notes

1. Edward R. Murrow, a speech delivered to the Radio-Television News Directors Association, reprinted in *The Reporter* (13 November 1958): 32–36.

2. Reymer and Gersin Associates, *Radio Power* (New York: Associated Press Broadcast
   Services, 1987): 5–6.

3. Television Information Office (TIO), *America's Watching: Public Attitudes toward Television* (New York: TIO, 1989): 14.

4. Lawrence W. Lichty, "Video versus Print," *The Wilson Quarterly*, VI, no. 5 (1982): 55.

5. Elmer W. Lower, "A Quarter Century of Television News: From Talking Heads to Live
   Moon Landings," *Television/Radio Age* (28 August 1978): 184.

2

THE BROADCAST REPORTER

A general journalist is what? He's sort of a jack-of-all-trades and a master of none, except the trade of being a jack of all. He's got to know a little about nearly everything. My head is really just a kind of medium-sized waste basket. There's quite a lot of stuff in there, but I have to rummage around to find it; there's no filing system. Maybe most of us are like that.
—ERIC SEVAREID, "A Conversation with Eric Sevareid"
An interview with Charles Kuralt on CBS-TV, December 13, 1977

Most reporters, particularly broadcast reporters, are generalists. Although some news directors do assign reporters to specialized beats—police, courts, government, politics, education, business, science and medicine, environment, the arts, and other subject areas—beat reporters are expected to be flexible enough to occasionally cover stories outside their specialty.

A RADIO REPORTER'S DAY

Radio reporters may be required to cover, by telephone and in person, 15 to 20 sources in a single day. News directors expect their beat reporters to telephone their key sources as many as four times during a shift to be sure they haven't missed any stories.

Reporters might begin their day by telephoning the highway patrol and city police dispatchers to find out how a severe rainstorm during the night has affected morning rush-hour traffic. A story on the wire says power lines are down in some parts of the city, so a reporter will call an electric company representative to ask about area blackouts. If power outages are widespread, officials and executives will call in to report that certain schools and industries will be closed.

Radio reporters will call fire department dispatchers to see if they're aware of any problems or disruptions, talk to transit officials about bus schedules and to airline officials about flight schedules, ask the National Weather Service's chief meteorologist in the region about rainfall, wind velocity, temperatures, causes of the storm, and how long the storm is expected to continue.

Furthermore, reporters may be able to call the city's flood control director or public works director for information about flooding or overtaxed drains. The city streets superintendent may know about passable traffic routes around trouble spots. The city may have an emergency management director who has been assigned to supervise potential evacuation of neighborhoods. That person can tell reporters if any neighborhoods are endangered. If farm or ranch areas are located beyond the city limits, the county sheriff's dispatcher may be able to report on how the storm has affected crops or livestock.

Amid the swirl of calls, radio reporters will choose segments from the voices they've recorded over the telephone. They call these segments "sound bites" and the voices of the newsmakers "actualities." They'll transfer such bites to cartridge tapes; in newsroom jargon, that's dubbing the bites to carts.

Reporters may tear copy from wire service printers for information they haven't been able to collect by phone. They can use it to flesh out their own reports or their narrative scripts to go with the sound bites. They'll call the stories, complete with narration and sound bites, "packages" or "wraparounds" or "wraps." They'll either pass the wraps to a newscaster or announcer or ad-lib their own stories on the air, inserting the sound bites at appropriate moments during their impromptu narration.

Story Ideas

On another, calmer day, radio reporters will choose more diverse sources and cover a variety of stories. They'll scan the wires, skim through current newspapers, and listen regularly to other radio newscasts or television newscasts to learn about interesting stories they haven't yet covered.

They must develop new angles, find new facts or opinions, and discover new sources who can help them expand such stories so they give their listeners new information. Information from other news agencies is only a foundation on which to build new stories. Newspeople ask themselves questions like: What is missing from the story that my listeners want or need to know? What is likely to happen next as a result of what has already happened? What caused this event or what motivated this plan? Who is this story likely to affect and how? These and other questions will help them think of new approaches and new sources.

The wire services also transmit day books—listings of events scheduled on that or the following day. Many news departments and reporters keep futures files—numbered one to 31 for each day of the month—where they file newspaper clippings, news releases, and notes about events scheduled for specific days. Some reporters keep "evergreen" files in which they save story ideas that will still be fresh a day, a week, or a month later.

Reporters also develop a list of reliable sources who can provide leads and ideas, not confirmed facts, for stories. They may be police or fire dispatchers, information officers for government agencies, clerks in local courts, receptionists in business offices, supervising nurses at hospitals, or other useful tipsters. Some reporters cultivate prominent sources who are knowledgeable in a variety of fields, utilizing not only their story ideas but also the background information they supply.

From Ideas to Stories

One reporter may learn from the police dispatcher that a rape has occurred, and detectives suspect the assailant is the man they've dubbed the "serial rapist." The reporter asks the dispatcher to radio the detective in charge of the investigation and ask him to call the newsroom. Within 15 minutes the detective calls. The reporter asks permission to record his voice and questions him quickly to learn the essence of the incident.

She decides to use his statement that the rapist's methods were similar to those in other rapes: the man knew the victim's name, her employer, and her working hours; he knew when she'd arrive home and when she'd go to bed; and he was well groomed and polite, even apologizing for molesting her. The detective said the apology was odd but true, and at least six other rape victims had received similar apologies.

The reporter then dubs the sound bite on cartridge tape, writes a lead-in and a tag to complete the story, and leaves the script and cart in a file basket for the next hourly newscast.

She answers the phone and learns from the mayor's news secretary that he has an appointment with the leaders of a group of property-tax protesters at 11 o'clock this morning. The mayor is not in his office, so the reporter questions the news secretary about the group's complaint, the specific levies they dislike, and the mayor's likely response. She decides she has enough information for a short "reader"—a story she writes for the newscaster to read—and drops that in the newscast basket.

She checks the wire service printer and reads that a local Catholic bishop is being transferred to another diocese. She knows he's presided over this diocese for at least 15 years and has been popular among Catholics in the community. She calls the church office but learns the bishop will be in conference for another two hours, so she calls the editor of the diocesan newspaper to ask for biographical material and anecdotes. The editor says he has some interesting clippings he will duplicate if someone can pick them up. The reporter says she'll come by in ten minutes, since the radio station is only two blocks from the church office.

As she walks back to the station, she reads the clippings and decides to use two anecdotes that seem to characterize the bishop and his relationships with area Catholics. Back at the station, she writes a story about the bishop's transfer that emphasizes his impact on the community. The story, which is told entirely in her own voice, is called a "voicer." She writes a lead-in for the newscaster and leaves it with her voicer in the newscast basket.

A TELEVISION REPORTER'S DAY

Television reporters usually begin their shifts by checking with their assignment editor. All reporters are expected to develop their own story ideas, which they usually present to their assignment editor for approval so he/she can keep a record of the stories that will likely be available by newscast time and can assign photographers when they're needed.

Assignment editors also keep their own lists of story ideas they may want to assign during the day. They have futures files and wire service day books. They have at least one television monitor, sometimes a bank of monitors, tuned to competing stations and some connected to the closed-circuit lines of the networks they're affiliated with or the video news services they subscribe to. They have conventional radio sets they can tune to local radio stations and a two-way radio to communicate with their reporters and photographers. Their telephones sometimes include a "hot line" that police and fire dispatchers use to alert broadcast stations and newspapers to breaking events.

The assignment desk is usually the center of newsroom activity. Some are enclosed in glass booths so the sounds from "scanners," the radio receivers that sweep across the police, fire, and other emergency frequencies, will be muffled in the rest of the newsroom. Other assignment desks may be on raised platforms, enclosed only by waist-high partitions, so the assignment editor has a view of the entire newsroom.

As they assign stories or accept story ideas from reporters, some assignment editors write story headings—slugs—on huge erasable wallboards. In adjacent columns they write the names of the reporters and photographers they've assigned and the times and locations of the stories. Producers of news programs can tell at a glance what stories will be available to them.

Huge street maps of the city, and sometimes maps of nearby cities, hang on the newsroom walls.

At least one wire service printer will be operating near the assignment desk. Assignment editors hang stories they've torn from the printers on hooks or clips under cards labeled "local," "regional," "national," "sports," "weather," "business," "features," or other categories of news. These categories make it easier for reporters, writers, and producers to find the information they need. Such wire service printers and wire story boards are missing in computerized newsrooms, where employees call up what they want on their own desk terminals.

Assigning Ideas

The reporter who covers state government has arrived at the governor's office to learn that he has scheduled a 10 o'clock meeting with health department supervisors to talk about a six-percent cut he's proposed in the state health budget. The reporter calls his assignment editor, says he expects the meeting to be tense because health department executives are resisting the cut, and asks if the assignment editor can send a photographer. The editor says she'll have the photographer meet the reporter in the governor's board room at 9:45 A.M.

The assignment editor has a note from her futures file that says seven local activists who have been in the Soviet Union on a "peace march" with a group of Soviet citizens will return to the city on a TWA flight at 9:33 A.M. She assigns a reporter and photographer to meet and interview them when they arrive. Because the marchers walked through cities and towns between Leningrad and Moscow that Americans rarely visit, they might have some unusual insights about the Soviet people. She further suggests that the reporter ask if the marchers sensed that KGB agents were among the Soviet walkers. The assignment editor asks the reporter to be sure to find out what the activists think they accomplished during their three weeks in the U.S.S.R. The reporter should also ask if the marchers have any still or motion pictures they'll allow the station to use.

The police-beat reporter says the sheriff, who was hurt in a bomb explosion two months ago, is back on the job today, and she'd like to talk to him about potential changes in security in his department. A defendant in a drug trial had carried the bomb into the sheriff's office in a briefcase, and it exploded when the sheriff asked to see what was inside.

The assignment editor asks her to call the sheriff and make an afternoon appointment; she wants her to spend the morning checking a new crime report the FBI has just issued and getting some comparative figures on major crimes from the preceding year. Although the FBI is unlikely to comment on the report, says the editor, if the reporter finds striking increases or decreases in any categories of crime, she can write a story for the producer to illustrate with computer graphics.

Searching for News

Whether or not the station has an assignment editor, the news director will expect all reporters to show enterprise and to develop story ideas. The first hours of every shift are crucial. Since they'll stumble onto stories infrequently, reporters must canvass their beats until they find something that will interest their listeners and viewers.

Such emergency stories as storms, blackouts, brush fires, earthquakes, airliner crashes, and mass murders don't happen every day. So reporters scour the station's futures file for hints of scheduled events that might produce significant news.

Perhaps the state Public Service Commission has scheduled a hearing to discuss a utility's proposal for a rate increase. The state Department of Transportation might be opening bids for widening an interstate highway that passes through a congested metropolitan area. The U.S. Energy Department will conduct a public briefing to tell residents and state officials about its plans for a nuclear-waste dump in the region. The Metropolitan Water District has scheduled a meeting to hear the request of a neighboring district to buy some of its culinary water.

Or perhaps the local Chamber of Commerce has invited a city planner to explain his proposal to remove marquees from the commercial buildings on Main Street. The state Industrial Development Commission might have called a news conference to announce that a new industry plans to build a plant in the area. An attorney might have invited reporters to hear him announce that he'll file a class action suit to try to recover the savings of residents who deposited their money in a thrift company that went bankrupt. Such scheduled events often generate important news, upon which a newscast will be based.

Reporters also know that public officials sometimes hide stories from them. A school board may call a private meeting to talk about closing a high school; a library board may hold a closed meeting to talk about firing a librarian; a city council may schedule a private breakfast to talk about possible tax increases. Whereas open-meetings laws in most states declare such meetings illegal, public officials nevertheless occasionally meet secretly to discuss sensitive issues away from the scrutiny of reporters. So reporters must cultivate sources in public offices who are willing to tell them what public officials are doing.

Small town radio reporters have just as much news available to them as metropolitan television reporters do, but its significance and scope may be narrower. Small town reporters may spend much of their time looking for deaths, births, hospital admissions and discharges, social events, new books at the library, church functions, Parent-Teacher Association meetings, high school sports events, county fairs, school carnivals, sewing bees, rummage sales, and holiday parades. Their audience will listen for the feature "Who's New in Pink and Blue" just as avidly as a metropolitan audience waits for the "Probe 5" investigative report.

THE REPORTER'S SENSORS

Good reporters have a feel for their audience—its interests and its needs. They listen to the people who live in their community as they ride the bus, shop in the supermarket or corner grocery store, eat in the coffee shop down the block or in the restaurant on Main Street. They mix with people at church, at public hearings, in clubs, and at banquets. They are friendly with public officials, but never too close. They talk to competing reporters without revealing more than minor fragments of information. They listen to people to discover what they think about current issues and what they worry about.

Good reporters occasionally scan the classified ads in the newspaper to see what people are selling or buying or trading. They browse through the city directory and the yellow pages of the telephone book to discover what kinds of jobs and services dominate their community. They skim neighborhood "shoppers" and "nickel ads" to find out what people are bartering.

They read, particularly the local news pages of their dailies and the letters to the editor. If someone in the city publishes a business newspaper, they skim its headlines. Their news director or station manager may subscribe to other daily or weekly newspapers within the station's coverage area and to city and regional magazines. A nearby college or university newspaper may include reporters on its mailing list, and local high schools that intermittently publish student newspapers may send them copies.

Broadcast reporters listen to their competitors, who frequently uncover stories that merit further investigation. They may find sources and develop angles the broadcast reporter didn't think of. Competitors may have discovered techniques for digging up information and presenting it that make their stories more vivid.

Good reporters don't imitate their competitors, they learn from them and develop their own resources and techniques to enable them to compete more effectively. Cities where vigorous journalistic competition exists are usually cities where audiences are best served by their broadcast reporters.

Good reporters learn as much as they can about as many things as they can and enjoy the mental challenge of the reporting process. Poor reporters succumb to the temptation to write their story even though their research has been sketchy and their interviews shallow. Good broadcast reporters may have to cover everything from a scandal in local government to surgery that separates conjoined twins, but they're willing to work and learn from each event.

QUALITIES AND TYPES OF REPORTERS

The Competitive Reporter

Broadcast reporting is dominated by men and women who need public recognition for what they do. They are egoists, in a sense, but their egoism is beneficial rather than harmful. It drives them to do well, and it gives them patience to wait until they have substantiated their facts before they rush onto the air.

Thomas Whiteside, writing about CBS's coverage of the 1968 Democratic National Convention and the violence outside the convention hall directed against the war in Vietnam, quoted Dan Rather: "Yes, I'm competitive, all right. When I go out there on the floor, I want to be on camera beating the other guy. I want in. I want to be the biscuit company."[1]

Reporters who lack competitive drive are too often ones who write around the gaps in their stories, who are too lazy to verify information they've been given, and who go on the air with information from only one source when they know a second source would give them a different perspective. They are little more than stenographers transmitting fragments of information to their listeners and viewers without attempting to evaluate their truth or significance.

Broadcast reporters are under greater pressure than print reporters because their deadlines are more frequent and their medium's demand for brevity is more constraining. Nevertheless, they must try to research each story as thoroughly as time allows. No formula exists to tell them when they have all the needed facts; they must be knowledgeable enough to make reasonable, intelligent judgments.

A former CBS News president, Richard Salant, said, "Our craft is not a science. We can't gather and report news and make our own news judgments by computer. Reporters—most of them—are human beings, fallible, dependent often on feel, on hunch born of common sense and experience."[2]

News directors prefer to hire experienced reporters. In large to medium-size markets, they require applicants to have two or three years of experience. In smaller

Carol Rissman, news director of radio station WBUR in Boston, signals an engineer in the booth.

markets, they first consider applicants who show evidence of campus broadcast experience or internship experience in professional news departments. They know that young reporters develop journalistic insight primarily through practical experience.

Researcher Jerry Hudson of Texas Tech University surveyed broadcast news employers at more than 240 radio and television stations across the country in 1980 and again in 1986. He learned that they prefer employees who can demonstrate skill "in gathering, writing and reporting news. Television employers rated video equipment skills much higher in 1986 than in 1980." [3]

He also learned that a "college degree in journalism or broadcast journalism is preferred by broadcast news employers. Other academic degrees receiving high ratings are political science, economics, history and business law. . . . Broadcast news respondents want employees who understand government, history, economics, business law, legal processes and personal health care." [4]

Finally, according to Hudson, both radio and television news employers listed reporting internships as most important after journalism and a liberal arts education. [5]

Television reporters must be on hand to cover stories as they happen and interview sources on the spot.

Many news directors also like applicants whose knowledge extends to such subject matter as public opinion, psychology and social psychology, sociology, persuasion, literature, and advertising. Both skill and knowledge, therefore, contribute to broadcast reporters' qualifications for employment.

Transient Reporters

Professor Vernon A. Stone of the University of Missouri surveyed turnover among radio and television news staffs in 1985, concluding, "Staff turnover in the 112 smallest TV markets was about twice as great as in the 50 largest. . . . Radio news staff turnover was greater in medium markets, where half of the staff typically were new from a year earlier."[6]

Whereas some reporters work at the same station for their entire career, earning promotions to assignment editors, executive producers, managing editors, assistant news directors, and ultimately news directors or station managers, other reporters may work for as many as a dozen stations over the course of their career.

Young reporters are more likely to find their first jobs at small-market television stations or at small radio stations. They learn all the basic skills because news directors require them to do everything—reporting, writing, recording, shooting, editing, producing, and on-mike and on-camera reporting.

Then they become mobile. As they gain experience, they move to bigger cities and larger stations. Each move is likely to bring a higher salary and a better job. The larger the market, the more stable the jobs seem to become.

A Reporter's Energy

Reporters who succeed in broadcasting usually do so because they have talent and energy. Their talent may be latent, but reporters who possess desire and drive learn to develop it and make it work for them. They are the ones who work and practice to improve their craft. And their pursuit of excellence is sometimes accompanied by long, irregular hours.

The producer of CBS's "60 Minutes," Don Hewitt, has said, "It is no coincidence that the four most popular news broadcasters in history are also the four hardest working."[7] He was referring to Mike Wallace, Dan Rather, Morley Safer, and Harry Reasoner. He said Morley Safer, for instance, spends only eight weeks at home during the year.

A radio reporter who works the morning shift might leave home at 5 o'clock. He stops by an all-night coffee shop and orders two cups of coffee to go. He drives to the public safety building and walks to the police dispatcher's office. One of the cups of coffee is for the overnight dispatcher.

That dispatcher is a valuable resource for the reporter because she knows what's happened through the night, and the coffee "bribe" encourages her to call the reporter immediately if any unusual emergency occurs. The reporter has pasted a big card imprinted with his name and home telephone number on the wall above the dispatcher's console. Many times because of that card he's scored beats on his competitors. His card made it clear he was willing to work during the night, and to him the satisfaction of being first with the news of a major fire or an unexpected narcotics bust balanced the discomfort of being awakened during a sound sleep.

A television reporter may have worked 70 hours during the week to cover the final actions of her state legislature, including a 15-hour marathon session that adjourned Friday at midnight. But she appears in the newsroom at 9 o'clock Saturday morning to work with a producer and videotape editor to prepare an hour-long summary of the legislative session that will air at 7 o'clock that evening.

She'll spend an exhausting day screening tapes, writing the script, recording narration that will be played over the video, and anchoring the program live. But when she goes home Saturday night, she'll know that she's given her viewers useful information and satisfied her news director's and her station manager's policy of serving their audience.

Successful reporters are exhilarated by the process of reporting. National Public Radio's Daniel Schorr has said, "Reporting meant, to me, getting to know things, or getting to understand better things already known. My own keenest enjoyments, I must confess, came from finding out something that people in power didn't want known and telling people not in power something they should know."[8]

For many reporters, the challenge of uncovering hidden information makes their craft worthwhile. They find something new in every story, and it seems that no two stories duplicate each other. Reporters who are not stimulated by the acts of interviewing, searching records, watching events unfold, and trying to interpret what they see will soon be former reporters looking for other trades to ply.

The pursuit of information may infect investigative reporters more acutely than it affects general assignment reporters, but the excitement of the chase is an undeniable characteristic inherent in all reporting.

The Reporter as Skeptic

Some newsmakers come to regard reporters as cynics—people who believe nothing they are told, who mock the beliefs of others, who sneer at creditable motives. Experienced reporters do sometimes adopt superficial attitudes of scorn or suspicion or indifference, but their attitudes grow out of a healthy skepticism.

Reporters are often thrust into scenes of tragedy and pain, and they're deeply affected emotionally. They unconsciously assume surface attitudes to veil their feelings and shield themselves from drawing too close to the victims they report about. They still feel the impact of events, but their poses of neutrality help them to see events in detail and to report those details dispassionately.

Because newsmakers provide information out of self-interest, reporters approach such information skeptically. They question newsmakers' claims, not to cast doubt on them but to validate them. They weigh information, test it against what they already know and what they learn from other sources, then try to report it from an accurate perspective for their listeners and viewers.

A reporter may be assigned to cover a group of radical environmentalists who are trying to disrupt operations at a lumber mill. He talks to the demonstrators and learns that they want the mill closed, because closure will force lumbermen to suspend their cutting. They'll refuse any compromise.

But their demands are too unyielding, so the reporter challenges their leader. He asks if they don't have another way to achieve their goals. What will they do about all the workers they will displace with their plan? What will they substitute for lumber to build houses and apartments? How do the demonstrators expect police and judges to react?

When he reports the story to his listeners and viewers, he may decide to tell them that the demonstration of scaling fences, cutting power lines, and burning stacks of timber was a deliberate attempt to attract media attention.

Another reporter may be assigned to cover an emergency. Police have reported that a pedestrian saw something that appeared to be the body of a child fall from the 12th floor of a downtown hotel. When the reporter arrives at the scene, she learns from police that they've found the bodies of a woman and six children in the street and on the sidewalk at the base of the hotel. Officers say eyewitnesses saw the woman push or throw each of the children over the balustrade of a narrow balcony that extends from a 12th-floor window. The witnesses say the woman climbed over the railing and jumped after she threw the sixth child over.

As soon as her photographer arrives, the reporter begins to interview eyewitnesses—a business executive who had just parked her car, a construction worker who was in an excavation across the street, a bank teller who stepped down from a bus at the corner, a shopper from down the block, a newspaper deliveryman who had stopped at the intersection. She questions all of them about what they saw and asks for detailed descriptions. People affected by sudden emotional stress may think they have seen things that didn't really happen. Or, faced with a television camera, they may exaggerate. So the reporter questions them at length for information they provide in common, then she can decide what's accurate and what she must discard.

A reporter who covers the legislature may learn that a state senator has introduced an amendment to the school finance bill that would limit spending increases to two percent. The governor has asked for six percent. The newsman approaches the senator to ask her to explain her amendment. He cites studies showing that classrooms are overcrowded, schools have too few textbooks to satisfy the needs of students, and teachers are leaving their profession because salary increases have been so meager. Why is the senator proposing budget limitations if the state is facing a school crisis?

She replies that school districts have wasted money on unneeded new buildings; they could reallocate their money if they'd close some of them. The reporter asks which districts have unneeded buildings. The senator tells him to check the capital

Reporters at a press conference in the Oval Office. Reporters who cover any beat—particularly at the national level—may face fierce competition.

city district. It could consolidate six high schools into four. Which schools does she think they should close? It doesn't matter; the student population of all of the city's high schools is 20 percent below capacity.

The reporter decides to check the senator's claims against those of school officials, so he talks to the city's school superintendent, who says the senator is wrong, and he gives the newsman a copy of a study just completed by a special task force. It shows that instead of underpopulated high schools, the city's classrooms are strained to capacity, and it projects that school populations will grow for another five years until the district needs at least one additional high school.

The legislative reporter

- Calls his assignment editor to ask for a photographer
- Videotapes the comments of the senator and the school superintendent
- Writes a wraparound script that explains the issue
- Juxtaposes the claims of the two officials
- Writes a tag to the story that includes graphics to illustrate the school population figures from the task force study

After he's helped the video editor complete the story, he learns that the state senator is a member of a group of business executives who have been campaigning against property tax increases. He includes that fact in a tag for his newscaster to read.

Healthy skepticism helps reporters get closer to the truth than many newsmakers will lead them.

REPORTERS AND THEIR AUDIENCES

Audiences for local radio and television newscasts are growing, perhaps because they perceive broadcasters to be more credible sources of news.

The 1986 study of television news conducted by The Roper Organization found that respondents rely primarily on television for seven of ten principal kinds of local news:

> Most people look first to television for information on: the weather; major local events such as strikes, fires, and accidents; environmental problems; developments in local government and politics; crime and police activities; consumer information; and health and fitness information.
>
> In the remaining three areas—information about local entertainment, local economic and business news and information of special importance to minorities in the community—more people turn to newspapers. Their edge over television in providing local business and economic news is a relatively narrow one: 44 percent usually get this kind of news from newspapers, while 39 percent get it from television.[9]

The Roper study also illustrates the trust viewers give their local television reporters:

> Americans are generally pleased with their local television reporters. When presented with a list of ten attributes, Americans say first that local news personnel are hardworking and professional. Local news reporters also receive very high ratings for their intelligence and their enthusiasm. And their reporting of the news is considered fair and balanced.[10]

In the last two decades, news staffs, along with broadcast audiences, have been growing. But in 1986, growth began to slow. Professor Stone, who also conducts annual surveys for the Radio-Television News Directors Association, says, "The typical news staff was trimmed last year at commercial radio stations, particularly in major markets, and at independent TV stations. Meanwhile, one person was being added to the news staff of the average affiliate of the three major television networks."[11] During that same period, the major networks trimmed news budgets and cut the numbers of news employees.

Nonetheless, studies show that local news has assumed a stature equivalent to that of network news, and broadcast stations should continue to provide their audiences with essential news.

Exercises

1. Talk to a local radio reporter. Approximately how many stories does he cover each day? How varied are they? What proportion of his stories does he cover by telephone? In person? How much pressure does he feel from deadlines?

2. Talk to a local television reporter. Approximately how many stories does she cover each day? How varied are they? How much time does she spend shooting and editing? How much time writing? Is it easy or difficult to work with other people such as photographers, editors, assignment editors, and producers?

3. Talk to a radio news director or a television assignment editor. What are some of their best sources for story ideas? How frequently do reporters suggest ideas? What percentage are accepted? Do they encourage their reporters to cultivate secondary sources such as receptionists, secretaries, mail carriers in public buildings, security officers?

4. Talk to local radio or television news directors. How much experience do they expect job applicants to have? What are their entry level jobs? Entry level salaries? What skills and knowledge do they expect from applicants? What are the rates of turnover in their news departments?

5. Listen to more than one local radio newscast or watch more than one television newscast on the same day. Compare their treatment of the same story. Which did you like best? Why? Which do you think served the audience best? Why? Which reporter do you trust the most? Why?

Notes

1. Thomas Whiteside, "Corridor of Mirrors," *Columbia Journalism Review* (Winter 1968–69): 41.

2. Art McDonald, "News Media Not Always Right—Salant," *The Editorialist* (July–August 1979): 1.

3. Jerry C. Hudson, "Broadcasters Want Experience, Skills and Liberal Arts," *Journalism Educator* (Winter 1987): 36–38.

4. Ibid.

5. Ibid.

6. Vernon A. Stone, "News Staffs Change Little in Size," *RTNDA Communicator* (March 1986): 15.

7. "The Man Who Makes '60 Minutes' Tick," *Broadcasting* (11 February 1980): 82.

8. Daniel Schorr, *Clearing the Air* (Boston: Houghton Mifflin Co., 1977): viii.

9. Television Information Office (TIO), *America's Watching: Public Attitudes toward Television* (New York: TIO, 1987): 6–7.

10. Ibid., 9.

11. Vernon A. Stone, "News Staffs Trimmed in Major-Market Radio and Independent TV," *RTNDA Communicator* (May 1987): 7.

3

WRITING THE STORY

. . . Big news is very often bad news. Leads on these stories need to be spare and [as] lean as possible. The viewer needs to know the facts, and needs a little time to let them soak in. It's one thing to pick up a newspaper, read of some calamity in the headline, and go on to read the story itself. It's another thing to watch a television news program. A reader can go at his own speed, but a viewer needs time to comprehend the news.
— JOHN CHANCELLOR and WALTER R. MEARS,
The News Business. (New York: Harper & Row, 1983), p. 22

News is something our listeners and viewers want to know and need to know. It's something they don't know now, but it's something they care about.

Therefore, you need to ask yourself first, "Who am I writing this story for?" You're not writing it for your colleagues or for your sources; you're writing it for listeners or viewers who tune to your news program because they want to learn what's been happening in their world.

There is no typical listener or viewer, but you might conjure one up so you'll have someone to talk to. Think about listeners and viewers who have reacted to stories you've written, people who were interested in what you said or what you showed them. What were they like? How much did they know? What were their interests? How much of what you told them did they remember? What details were most vivid to them?

One person will emerge from among the people who reacted to your stories, one who seemed most interested in what you had to say. That's the one for whom you need to write. Or maybe you have a friend who's curious about what you do and asks questions about stories you've reported. If you have such a friend, write for him/her.

You've read an ad in the classified section of the newspaper: "Refrigerator. Must sell. Need emergency oxygen. $150 or best offer. 972–5164."

A newswriter types his story into a computer terminal.

You call the telephone number listed in the ad and find that the man who wants to sell the refrigerator is 68 years old, lives alone, suffers from emphysema, and needs to replenish the oxygen tank from which he inhales regularly. He gets a Social Security check for 310 dollars each month, but he spends approximately 70 dollars a month for food, a year-round average of 95 dollars a month for heat, electricity, and water, 22 dollars a month for a telephone, and 106 dollars for the monthly mortgage payment on his small house. He exhausted his savings two years ago. He has no other income, doesn't qualify for Medicaid, and has no living relatives.

Is this a story your friend will want to hear? If it is, how much do you need to tell him to help him understand? Does he know what emphysema is, or should you explain? Does he know why an emphysema victim needs oxygen? Will you need to total the man's monthly expenditures and compare them to his income to help your friend see how close to the limit the man is living? Does your friend understand Medicaid? Does he need to know how the man can get along without a refrigerator? Does he need to know why the man has no other retirement income? Does he need to know if the man has sold anything else to buy oxygen? In short, what can you delete or simplify, and what do you need to add?

Now that you know who you're writing for and what he needs to know, you can choose the most pertinent facts. You can narrow your focus to the one most important idea, and that will be your beginning, your lead.

THE LEAD

Your lead can be one sentence, two sentences, three sentences, even four, but it must quickly reveal the essence of the story—the most important fact, the crucial element, the nature, the flavor, or the atmosphere. It should be the fact that will be explained by every other fact that appears in the story. You must eliminate any fact that does not clarify your lead.

Your lead must also stir the interest of you friend. Unless you attract him in the beginning, he will mentally tune you out and think about something more to his liking.

Ask yourself, How will this affect my friend? Maybe it will cost him more. Maybe it will take away some of his pleasures. Maybe he'll have to work harder to reach his goals. Maybe he's in danger. Maybe this will solve one of his problems. Maybe this will comfort him. Maybe this will make him feel good about himself. If you can find the element in the story that will make your friend feel rewarded because he heard it, you'll be able to write a lead he'll remember.

You may need more time to write your lead than to write the rest of your story, but if your lead sets the tone, the details should fall naturally into place.

Start thinking about your lead as soon as you finish your research. By the time you get to your typewriter or word processor, the lead may flow from the keyboard.

TENSE

Remember that you're writing for a medium that broadcasts the news live, so write your leads to sound as current as possible. Avoid naming the day of the week the event occurred, however. Do not write, ''The National Weather Service said Monday's storm dropped 14 inches of snow on the airport measuring station.'' Even though Monday may have been yesterday, your listeners often forget what day of the week today is, so you may force them to stop listening to calculate when Monday was.

Be sparing with words like today, tonight, this morning, yesterday, last week. They tend to date your stories unnecessarily. If you write a lead in the past tense, however, you must include the time element in the same sentence: ''The state Banking Commission declared a Farmington bank insolvent today.''

Whenever it sounds natural, write your lead in the present tense:

```
The Labor Department says unemployment is down to
nine percent.

The Civil Air Patrol is joining the search for a
missing light plane.
```

> Some administration officials concede they've lost
> the battle of the budget.

If the present tense doesn't sound natural, try the present perfect tense, which attaches the companion verbs *have* or *has* to the key verb:

> Striking telephone workers and American Telephone and
> Telegraph have resumed their bargaining session.

> Two election losers have asked for ballot recounts.

> The County Board of Equalization has given taxpayers
> a two-week extension for property tax appeals.

Occasionally, you'll be able to write a lead in the future tense:

> A man convicted of killing his stepson will spend at
> least 20 years in prison.

> A small helium leak will not threaten the launch of
> the space shuttle.

> The mayor will appoint a special prosecutor to
> investigate irregularities in the city's finance
> office.

Be honest about the time. If you have written your lead in the present, present perfect, or future tense, identify the time element in the second or third sentence:

> An accused murderer says he didn't intend to kill a
> 17-year-old jail inmate. Matthew Marks told the jury
> today he struck Paul Peters, but that was half an
> hour before Peters collapsed.

> The state senate has passed a stiff new drunken-
> driving bill. The senate voted 28-to-12 this
> afternoon to approve mandatory jail terms for
> motorists convicted of drunken driving.

> Illegal aliens will not get Social Security benefits.
> The Social Security Administration ruled yesterday
> that no one is eligible for benefits if he/she
> doesn't have permission to work in this country.

ELEMENTS OF THE LEAD

What Happened?

Avoid the summary leads you see in many newspaper stories. Don't try to include all of the story elements—the who, what, when, where, why, and how—in your lead. Be concise. Choose the one or two elements you think best contain the essence of the story and emphasize them in your lead.

Most of your leads will tell your listeners what is happening. The story about the emphysema victim might begin: "An ill, elderly man is trying to sell his refrigerator so he can pay for treatment." Then you can go on to tell your listeners who he is, where he lives, why he needs the treatment, and why he must sell his refrigerator to get it.

If a prison riot that has continued for three days is settled, you can get directly to the point in your lead: "The state prison riot is over." Then fill in the background:

```
One-hundred-forty inmates took over two buildings,
held 15 guards and prison workers hostage, and set
fire to broken furniture. They were protesting the
cancellation of their recreation schedule after an
inmate was stabbed during a prison baseball game.
They abandoned their strike after the warden sent a
suspect to solitary confinement and reinstated the
recreation schedule.
```

Sometimes, when what happened is either unconfirmed or in doubt, you may have to attribute the information before you detail what has happened. For example, if police tell you four students were stabbed at a local high school, but they've charged no suspects, you could lead your story

```
City police say four students have been stabbed
during a fight at South High School, and two students
have been arrested.
```

Then you can attribute the information to the officer who provided it and give the details of the incident:

```
Police Lieutenant Talley Keith says the fight
followed a South High basketball victory over East
High. The wounded students are South High
cheerleaders. All four are in satisfactory condition
at St. Mark's Hospital.
```

If you have the names of the cheerleaders, and their relatives have been notified, include them in your story. Don't imply that the attackers were East High School students, even though it seems likely. You can't be certain until police identify them.

If the information is reliable, you need not attribute your lead:

>   Nearly a foot of snow has fallen on parts of Kansas.
>
>   China, Russia, and North Korea have all denounced
>   military maneuvers in South Korea.
>
>   A mother and her two sons have been charged with
>   robbing an Atlantic City casino.

If you think two aspects of the story are equally important, try writing them both into your first sentence. Perhaps a serious traffic accident has hurt several people, and the wreckage is tying up traffic:

>   Highway patrolmen say a four-car accident early this
>   morning injured 12 people and blocked the icy
>   westbound lanes of Interstate 90 near Moses Lake,
>   Washington.

Read that sentence aloud. Does it read comfortably? Will your listeners be able to absorb both facts easily? If not, rewrite it as two sentences:

>   Twelve people have been hurt in a four-car accident
>   near Moses Lake, Washington. The wreckage has blocked
>   the westbound lanes of icy Interstate 90.

Then you can explain how the accident happened, where the victims have been taken, how serious their injuries are, how traffic has been affected, and how long police think it will take to reopen the highway.

You can find more than one way to write a lead to tell your listeners what's happening, but be sure you write the essence of the thought at the beginning. For example, this lead buries the essence of the story under a mountain of words:

>   Texas prison authorities in Huntsville have carried
>   out the state's sixth execution since the Supreme
>   Court reinstituted the death penalty in 1974, but the
>   inmate was the first in the United States to die by
>   lethal injection.

The last two words in that 37-word sentence contain the essence of the story, but don't risk tiring your listeners before you get to the point. Rewrite the lead to include the essence at the beginning:

```
A convicted Texas murderer is the first in the United
States to be executed with a lethal injection.

A convicted Texas murderer has been given a lethal
dose of sodium pentothal--the first such execution in
the United States.

The first lethal injection in the United States has
executed a convicted Texas murderer.
```

The fact that this is the sixth execution in the state since the Supreme Court reinstated the death penalty may be interesting, but you should delay it until you've laid out the heart of the story.

Who Did It?

Sometimes, if your story is about someone who is well known, your lead can emphasize who the focus of the story is or who the event has affected directly.

Familiar names will help to attract your audience's attention:

```
Pope John Paul has elevated 18 Roman Catholic church
leaders to the rank of cardinal.

Consumer advocate Ralph Nader says Congress is
misleading Americans about Social Security.

Basketball star Kareem Abdul-Jabbar's Los Angeles
home has been destroyed by fire.

The groundhog, Punxsutawney Phil, thinks we'll have
an early spring.
```

Note that you help to establish the name if you introduce it with a short title; if the name is widely known, however, you can use it without a title.

Some newsmakers become familiar because the nature of their deeds is striking and is publicized regularly. The first recipient of an artificial heart, Dr. Barney Clark, lived almost four months after doctors implanted his plastic heart, and he was the focus of national attention. An update on his condition often started with his name: "Barney Clark is joking with nurses, exercising mildly, and listening to choral music."

The first convicted murderer in the United States after the Supreme Court reinstated the death penalty was Gary Gilmore. He had killed two people and insisted that he deserved to die. The media covered him extensively for nine months. He attempted suicide twice while he was on death row. His name became so familiar that a story lead could say: "Gary Gilmore attempted suicide again today."

Often, titles alone can be the focus of your lead:

> The surgeon general says lung cancer among women has reached the epidemic stage.

> Even bureaucrats can change their minds. Social Security administrators did today and settled out of court with an employee who sued because he had been denied a promotion.

> A 21-year-old snowmobiler is alive and in good condition after spending a night in a blizzard.

> Granite District school teachers have been on strike and off salary for six weeks now, and parents are getting impatient.

When Was It?

You'll write most leads in either the present tense or the present perfect tense, but sometimes, when you want to emphasize how current an event is, stress when it happened or will happen. Start your lead with the time element:

> Just minutes ago, three mysterious explosions rocked a downtown hotel.

> At this hour, surgeons at Pittsburgh's Children's Hospital are beginning to transplant a liver into a four-year-old boy.

> Within the next hour, Eastern Airlines ground workers are expected to walk off the job.

> Tonight, Congress adjourns for a month's vacation, leaving behind the president's emergency funding bill.

Today, winter began, and several northeastern cities
are feeling the sting of its first storm.

Where Is It?

Occasionally, you can begin your lead sentence with the location of an event. The
location—the dateline—sometimes helps you make a transition between stories:

In Rhode Island, controversy is swirling around the
governor's office.

In Cincinnati, the Reds will open the baseball season
with a ball that has traveled 52-thousand miles in
the submarine *Cincinnati*.

In Washington, the Senate will finish their debate on
the Social Security bailout today.

Sometimes, you may need to start with the location to clarify immediately the
focus of the event:

In Anchorage, Alaska, snow has forced schools to
close for the first time in 14 years.

In Casper, Wyoming, part of the landing gear on a 737
jetliner collapsed today as the plane touched down.

In London, gold prices have slumped.

At times, the location of your story may provide an atmosphere that attracts
listeners:

The California hills just north of the Mexican border
seem lifeless during the day, but at night they're
alive with illegal aliens.

Guatemala City's streets are dotted with people
whispering to each other about today's bloody
military coup.

The natty, decorous crowd at England's Epsom Downs
stared silently as the American trainer in cowboy

```
boots and ten-gallon hat led his winning horse back
to the stable.
```

Why Did It Happen?

You'll rarely lead a story with why or how it happened, but once in a while, why it happened may be the element that will attract your listeners:

```
Many Iranian newspapers have been criticizing the
Khomeini government, so the Ayatullah is shutting
down 22 of them.
```

```
Thirty years ago, the Atomic Energy Commission
conducted a series of above-ground nuclear tests in
the Nevada desert, and today Nevada, Utah, and
Arizona residents who live downwind of the test site
filed suit against the government, contending that
fallout caused cancer and other diseases.
```

```
A mountain man who testified in court that he killed
two game wardens only because they threatened to kill
him has been acquitted by an Idaho jury.
```

Such leads are more likely to succeed if the story is familiar to your listeners.

How Did It Happen?

Most of the time, how an event occurred will be the background to what happened, so it will follow your lead. But how it happened may sometimes be so striking that it can be the heart of your lead. For example, suppose midtown Manhattan has been blacked out at midday, but no one has been hurt and nothing has been damaged. The incident is an inconvenience more than a hazard. Perhaps your listeners will be more interested in how the blackout occurred:

```
A broken water main under midtown Manhattan has
flooded some transformers and ignited a fire under
the garment district. A 60-square-block area is
blacked out, but officials expect no danger to
residents or workers.
```

If people are in danger, however, you'll want your lead to emphasize that facet of the story.

Forest fires are usually remote events, and their impacts on your listeners are delayed. Perhaps they're more interested in how such fires started:

```
Violent lightning storms have ignited a score of
forest fires in three northwestern states.
```

Listeners in the region can visualize lightning storms because they've seen dozens of them.

Football fans want to know quickly who won and who lost, but they're interested, too, in how a team with a long losing streak could win:

```
Northwestern quarterbacks threw five interceptions
and fumbled four times to hand Wisconsin a 42-to-21
victory.
```

When you begin with how an event occurred, don't delay too long in telling your listeners what happened, or you'll alienate them. They don't like to be held in suspense.

LOOK FOR VARIETY

You'll find many ways to tell your story, but look for elements that will attract your listeners and viewers, and make them want to hear what you have to say. When you have to write more than one version of a story for more than one newscast, perhaps what happened will work for one lead, who it happened to will work for another, where it happened will work for another, and so on.

Suppose you have a story about two teenage runaway girls who told a radio talk show host yesterday they were being held as prostitutes in a white slavery ring, and he asked his listeners for contributions to buy them plane tickets home. Now the runaways admit to the police that they invented the story. In one lead you could say: "It's a hoax—those claims that a white slavery ring is operating in the city." In another you could say: "Two teenage runaways admit they lied when they told a radio talk show host they were prostitutes in a white slavery ring." And in another you could say: "The radio talk show host who broadcast a story about a white slavery ring has conceded it was a scam."

No formula will help you write leads. Experiment with the important facts in each story until you think you have the right combination in your lead. Follow your instincts. How would you react to the lead if you were the listener? Would you listen more closely, or would you turn your attention to something else?

Don't let the music of your words overwhelm you; look for the idea that is the heart of your story. If there are words or phrases or rhythms that will make the idea more vivid, let them flow naturally; don't strain for them.

Read this lead aloud and listen to it:

> Lower the flag to half-staff. Lay out the wreaths.
> Ask the bugler to play taps slowly and the drummer to
> roll softly. After three decades of blood, sweat, and
> cheers, professional football in Baltimore is dead.

Imaginative, an interesting angle, but overwritten. The event was given more importance than it deserved. The demise of the football franchise generated anger among fans and a sense of loss but hardly an atmosphere of weeping and wailing. The last sentence alone would have been vivid: "After three decades of blood, sweat, and cheers, professional football in Baltimore is dead."

TYPES OF LEADS

Summary Leads

You'll write your lead most often to summarize the most important facet of your story, to highlight the one aspect that makes the story news.

A newspaper reporter might write this lead:

> Eight canoeists who are reported missing on Lake
> Okeechobee are the objects of an intensive search
> tonight as winds, gusting to 50 miles an hour, blew
> them away from shore and apparently stranded them in
> rough waters.

That's more than you can read in one breath and more than your listeners or viewers can absorb. And neither you nor your audience has time to study what the writer said.

Write a simple lead:

> Searchers are looking for eight canoeists stranded on
> Lake Okeechobee.

> High winds have blown eight canoeists away from the
> shores of Lake Okeechobee. They're still missing.

> Rough waters on Lake Okeechobee have prevented
> rescuers from reaching eight stranded canoeists.

Find the one aspect of the event that most accurately reflects what's happening, base your lead on that, then fill in the supporting details in subsequent sentences.

You can write the essence of most hard news stories to make concise, clear leads:

Cleveland is digging out of the worst snowfall in a decade.

New York City seems to be coping well with the heat wave.

Hurricane Dolores has been downgraded to a tropical storm.

If you have time, you can brighten even hard news stories with imaginative leads:

Dolls in toystore windows seem to be more comfortable than inhabitants during Cleveland's record snowstorm.

Fire hydrants and lawn sprinklers are making New York City's heat wave bearable—at least for youngsters.

Hurricane Dolores turned out to be no more than a windbag. Weather forecasters have downgraded her to a tropical storm.

Tease Leads

Often, you can tease your listeners or viewers to attention with a lead that sets the flavor of the story but doesn't reveal its substance. A good tease lead can alert your listeners or viewers and prepare them to hear the substance that will follow.
    For example:

The rumor mill is grinding, but no one knows whether John McEnroe will show up on Wimbledon's center court this morning.

It's happening again. A heavy snowmelt like the one that preceded last spring's floods is flowing down the slopes of the Rockies.

It's two down, one to go. Kentucky Derby and Preakness winner Secretariat needs only to win the Belmont Stakes to complete his sweep of the Triple Crown.

Write tease leads concisely and follow with substance immediately. If you delay the substance too long, your listeners and viewers will tire and perhaps tune you out.

Read this lead aloud:

> A year-long financial battle is over. The loser won a
> profit. The winner had to pay, but gained control of
> the industry. That's one way you could describe what
> happened today in the fight to acquire control of
> Outer World Thrift. Centennial Savings and Loan
> announced it had picked up control of 51 percent of
> Outer World's stock, then Interurban Savings decided
> to abandon the fight and sell its Outer World shares
> to Centennial at a profit of 14 million dollars.

The writer held back the essence of the story so long that his audience must have chafed in the confusion. He might have written more concisely:

> Both competitors won and lost today. Centennial
> Savings won control of Outer World Thrift, but to do
> it they had to buy out Interurban Savings stock at
> premium prices.

Then the writer could have filled in the financial detail.

Tease leads can occasionally brighten a newscast that is filled with many hard leads, but if you write tease leads too often, they may sound tedious. Be selective and be brief.

Umbrella Leads

At times, you'll have more than one story related to.the same subject, or you may have more than one story that originated from the same source. If you think they should be included in the same newscast, you should group them and cover them with one lead, called an umbrella lead.

If the state House of Representatives is rushing for adjournment and approves three controversial bills affecting young people, you could write a lead something like this:

> House members flexed their adult biceps today. They
> approved a minimum drinking age of 21, a sharp
> curtailment of extracurricular activities during
> school hours, and mandatory car restraint seats for
> children under six.

Then you could fill in the pertinent detail for each of the three bills.

An umbrella lead sometimes can help you set the tone of the story. For example, if violent weather has caused a variety of accidents and other incidents, you might say:

> The region has been anything but sunny today. A series of thunderstorms ripped up dozens of trees, blacked out wide sections of the city, and poured more than three inches of rain over residential neighborhoods.

Now you can fill in specifics that make each of the elements of the picture vivid.

Narrative Leads

Most of the time, you'll write leads that get to the heart of the news immediately, then you'll fill in elaborating detail. But some stories lend themselves to narrative, storytelling leads wherein you can delay revealing the essence of the story. Start at its chronological beginning and build to its climax.

> Joanne Field doesn't think she's unusual. She just happened to drive up to the State Street bridge a couple of minutes after a car crashed through the guardrail yesterday, and she saw the car fall into the 34-degree waters of the Hawes River.
>
> She saw a dozen cars parked alongside the road, their occupants standing on the bridge, staring into the river. The car floated on the surface for a moment, then it started to sink.
>
> Joanne remembers that nobody moved to help. Instinctively, she jumped into the icy water, swam to the car, and pulled open the driver's door. She saw a woman's head above the water, so she reached in, grappled with the seat belt to release its buckle, cupped her hand under the woman's chin, and pulled her free.
>
> When she reached the bank, several pairs of hands stretched out to her and her semiconscious burden.
>
> The woman, 23-year-old Dorine Davis, was treated for exposure at St. Mark's Hospital and released.
>
> Police officers say she almost certainly would have drowned if Joanne Field hadn't come along.

> They've recommended Field to the governor for the
> state's Medal of Valor.

Use such leads sparingly, because your listeners and viewers may grow impatient
if you withhold the outcome of stories too often. They want the news and won't
tolerate delay if your information fails to pique their curiosity.

Sound Leads

Shun most direct quotations, especially in leads. Newscasters are tempted to dramatize material they see in quotation marks, and too often their dramatization sounds
exaggerated. The hazard is evident in a lead like this:

> 'I pronounce this man dead.' Those were the words of
> the prison doctor assigned to the Texas execution of
> a convicted murderer.

The words of the direct quotation are so unlike the normal narrative style of a
conversational sentence that they will jar listeners and viewers and draw their
attention away from the essence of the story. They'll hear style instead of substance.

You can utilize the voices of newsmakers occasionally, however, to draw your
listeners into stories. If you find a short, provocative sound bite, it may intrigue
your audience. You could begin with the voice of a newsmaker saying something
like this:

> We can save the lives of teenagers if we get them off
> the bottle.

Then follow with your narration:

> The head of Mothers Against Drunk Drivers testified
> this morning in support of a House bill to raise the
> state's legal drinking age to 21.

In most cases, newscasters use sound-on-tape leads only in the lead story of
the newscast. They read their newscast opening first to prepare their listeners or
viewers:

> This is KLMN News on the Hour. I'm Charlie Fisher.
>
> (Sound on Tape) We can save the lives of teenagers if
> we get them off the bottle.

Without preparation, your listeners may be startled and miss what the voice says. They need a few seconds to adjust their thoughts from the entertainment feature or commercials that precede the news you want to give them.

Question Leads

Direct questions sometimes work in broadcast leads, but use them infrequently because they may give your news story the sound of commercial copy.

An effective direct-question lead must be provocative, concise, and answered immediately.

If rumors have been circulating that the mayor is thinking about resigning, you could write this lead:

```
Is he in, or is he out? The mayor isn't talking yet
about those rumors of resignation.
```

The direct question lends an air of suspense to a story that has been on the minds of your listeners and viewers, but because you answer the question quickly, you don't prolong the suspense and irritate them.

If the country has been suffering prolonged inflation, and the Department of Commerce releases figures that show an abrupt change, you could write a lead like this:

```
Did you hear what happened to prices last month? They
dropped slightly--for the first time in a decade.
```

They you can fill in the details to show what specific prices dropped.

When you write a direct question lead, read it aloud. Will it hook your listeners and viewers, or will it irritate them? If you're satisfied that it will work, use it. If not, rewrite it. Perhaps an indirect question will work better:

```
We're still asking if the mayor will resign, but he
isn't talking yet.
```

```
Some people have been wondering what happened to
prices last month. Well, they dropped--for the first
time in a decade.
```

STORY STRUCTURE

The classic inverted pyramid of newspaper journalism is useless to broadcast news-writers. It's structured to allow exit points for readers—points where they can leave the story whenever they have all the information they want. It's also structured so that the information declines in significance as you read deeper into the story.

Broadcast newswriters rarely provide exit points. They don't want their listeners and viewers to become bored or impatient, so they reserve throwaway lines for stories they may have to trim if their newscasts are running overtime. They write most of their stories intending to read *every sentence.*

Because your radio listeners and television viewers can't absorb much detail, limit your story to the one main idea that you decide is most important, then supplement it with only those subsidiary ideas that help to make that idea clear.

You can write some stories to be read aloud in as few as five seconds; others may require two minutes. But you must discipline yourself to expect that many television news stories will be shorter than one minute, and many radio news stories will be shorter than 30 seconds.

You'll have no formula for writing news, but you can develop an instinct for structuring facts into meaningful patterns. In radio and television, your instinct must include a sense of drama—a feeling for the emotion, the conflict, the suspense, and the human qualities that draw your listeners and viewers into events to experience them as if they were participants.

You'll present news in subtle contexts of entertainment, but you must remember that you're still dealing in facts, and your listeners and viewers expect accurate information without distortions. If you can cultivate a sense of logical, undistorted balance between information and entertainment, you'll become a master of the craft.

FOCUS THE STORY

Think about the information you've collected for your story. Choose the primary facts. Narrow your focus to the one most important idea. Eliminate the facts that don't contribute to that idea. Arrange the primary facts into a logical pattern. For some stories, the pattern may be chronological. You can tell your listeners and viewers what happened from the first action to the last.

For other stories, the pattern may be the order of importance of your facts. You can tell your listeners and viewers what the problem is, why it demands solution, how it affects them, and what solutions are available.

For still other stories, you may organize the facts on the basis of their relationship to each other. You can answer the questions of your listeners and viewers as you yourself raise questions in your presentation of the facts.

Decide what the pattern of your story should be, then test it. Write a story outline, or at least create a story outline in your mind. If the main idea reveals the essence of the story, and if each contributing idea elaborates on or enhances the essence, write the story. But if your outline shows only a jumble of vaguely related details, junk it and start again.

A written outline gives you a sense of organization, but gradually you'll develop instincts about organization that will help you to think through the facts and order them in your mind. Then you'll be ready to write when you get to your typewriter or word processor, and the ideas will flow spontaneously.

Your lead is the climax of your story. It tells your listeners and viewers about the change that has occurred that makes the story news:

> Forty-eight hours after the baseball strike began, players are back on the fields, and fans are back in the stands.
>
> Two Air Force military police officers have been removed from duty and accused of selling cocaine and marijuana.
>
> Russia's Communist party chief will meet the president in Stockholm next month.

If you were writing fiction, you'd save the climax for the end of the story. You'd explain the background and introduce the participants in the event, they you'd detail the conflict or the chronological sequence of events that led to the climax.

But listeners and viewers are impatient. They want to know immediately what happened. In most instances, they need to hear the story's climax before they'll focus their attention on your explanation of the background, introduction of the participants, and chronological detail.

You can still adopt a storytelling attitude to write most of your news, however. Radio and television are oral and visual media, and you can approach each story with the attitude that you have something urgent and exciting to say. With such an attitude, you can draw your listeners and viewers into the story, eager to hear its detail.

Think of many of your stories in this structure: climax followed by chronological narrative. Begin with the turning point, the change, then write from the beginning. Here's an example:

> *Climax:* A college student tried to re-enact a daredevil exploit from his high school days this morning and fell 200 feet to his death.
>
> *Chronological Narrative:* Twenty-one-year-old Rob White was at a party last night when one of his friends recalled how five of them crossed the steel waterline over the Snake River Canyon when they were seniors in high school. They decided to repeat the stunt.

Four men and a woman drove to the south rim of the
canyon at about 5 o'clock this morning. White and 20-
year-old Mike Adams started across the pipeline
first, walking on the steel pipe and holding onto the
suspension cables.

About 20 feet from the north end of the line, they
encountered a barrier gate that had been erected to
prevent such crossings. Adams swung around the gate
and scrambled back to the top of the line. White
started around the gate but apparently lost his grip
on a suspension cable and fell 200 feet to the rocks
below.

White's three remaining friends made their way
back to the south rim and drove to Ketchum to call
the sheriff.

When rescuers reached the bottom of the canyon,
White was dead. He suffered multiple fractures and
internal injuries.

This afternoon, White's friend Adams called it a
"stupid stunt."

Sometimes, a story doesn't lend itself to a chronological pattern; it may be
based instead on a group of important related facts. You must first decide which
are the essential facts—the ones that will help your listeners and viewers understand
the issue—then you must place them in the order of their importance.

The story will still begin with its climax or essence: The state's director of
disease control has warned parents to immunize their children against whooping
cough.

Now, ask yourself what your listeners need to know or want to know about
that fact. Three important questions arise: Why do children need to be immunized
now? How does the disease affect children? Is any cure available? Order them in
the sequence of their importance and write the answers:

Disease Control Director Roger Hudgins says 27 cases
have been reported to his office in the last two
months. That's one-third of all the cases reported in
the last five years. Hudgins thinks the growing
number of cases suggest a potential epidemic.

Whooping cough is a highly contagious respiratory
disease. Its bacteria can be transmitted through
coughs or sneezes or through contact with clothing or
toys.

It affects children, especially between two months

> and four years of age. It starts with sneezing,
> coughing, loss of appetite, and sometimes fever.
>   If whooping cough is not treated, the affected
> child may develop a severe cough, expel large amounts
> of mucus, vomit, and sometimes choke. It can be
> fatal.
>   Hudgins says doctors can treat the disease once
> they diagnose it, but parents would be safer to
> immunize their children now. He says 75 percent of
> the children who die of whooping cough are children
> under the age of one who haven't been immunized.

The way facts relate to each other may sometimes determine the structure of your story. When one fact raises another question, answer it immediately. As you write your story, ask yourself what questions your listeners or viewers are asking next.

The climax of your story may say:

> A North Terrace woman says she's lost all tolerance
> for teenagers who cruise Main Street on weekend
> nights.

Your listeners may be wondering who she is and why she's lost tolerance, so you need to respond to that question:

> Convenience store owner Marcie Madsen says cruisers
> use her parking lot as a meeting place and turnaround
> point.

Why does that trouble her?

> They leave empty beer cans and trampled shrubs in
> their wake, and sometimes they beat neighbors who
> complain about the noise and debris.

Has she done anything about it?

> Madsen says she's called police numerous times, but
> officers have been unable to control the problem.

Why not?

> Police Captain Ozzie Roberts says his officers lack
> the legal power to arrest the troublemakers.

Why?

> The parking lot is public, so the teenagers are not
> trespassing. Officers can cite teenagers for
> littering, but it's difficult to prove which
> teenagers are the litterers. Officers can arrest
> teenagers who assault residents, but most residents
> are afraid to sign complaints.

What else can officers do?

> Roberts says the city needs ordinances to control
> beer drinking in public places and to prohibit open
> containers of beer in public places.

Where is the trouble spot?

> Madsen's 'All-Night Shop' is located at 12 hundred
> Main Street, at the north end of the strip where
> teenagers cruise.

You may be able to draw your listeners and viewers into a story by letting them empathically feel what the participants in the story felt. That means you must utilize whatever emotion inherently exists in the event—sorrow, laughter, pathos, love, fear, anger. But remember, the emotion must be a natural, innate characteristic of the event. You cannot force emotion. You cannot inject it into the story artificially and expect your listeners or viewers to accept it. They sense the difference between genuine and artificial emotion, and if you try to color the narrative artificially, they'll feel only sentimentality. And sentimentality will affect them negatively.

A reporter or newscaster who first delivers a businesslike, direct report about the president's State of the Union speech, then delivers a story about six people killed in a head-on collision in a lower pitch, slower pace, and deliberate emotional tone, will only irritate listeners and viewers.

The reporter or newscaster who laughs openly when he delivers the punch line to a humorous story will probably antagonize his listeners and viewers.

Avoid temptations to write emotion into your stories. Like a drunk who gets teary when he remembers his misfortunes, your writing may sound maudlin. Utilize emotions that exist in the event—describe actions that show emotions, include the voices and pictures of newsmakers who show emotions—but resist the urge to be emotional yourself. Write your story straight, and read it straight.

NARRATIVE WRITING

Three elements exist in the narrative style of writing: the story itself, the storyteller, and the listener. Storytellers must draw their listeners into harmony if they are to tell their story successfully. They must relate all of the pertinent facts, but to affect the listeners in some way: to stir them, to provoke them, to entertain them, or merely to interest them.

This means that conflict will often be the core of the story. In conflict, protagonists oppose antagonists. The protagonists can be individuals, groups, or nations. Perhaps a local beauty queen has been threatened with expulsion from state competition by the state pageant committee. Perhaps a planeload of hijacked hostages is being held by half a dozen armed terrorists. Perhaps residents of an alpine village have been swept away by a flash flood. Perhaps a nation of blacks is protesting the minority whites' system of apartheid.

Av Westin, ABC's vice president for program development and a former producer of "20/20" and "World News Tonight," asked a series of questions to decide what was newsworthy, and they all suggest the element of conflict in news:

- Is my world safe?
- Are my city and home safe?
- If my wife, children and loved ones are safe, then what has happened in the past twenty-four hours to shock them, amuse them or make them better off than they were?[1]

If your world, city, or home are not safe, the force that disrupts your sense of security—the individual or group or natural force—becomes the antagonist. The individual or group or natural force that opposes the disruption becomes the protagonist.

The African "killer bees" that escaped from a research laboratory in Brazil in 1957 became instant antagonists. They've been antagonists ever since, wreaking havoc on the honey industry in Brazil and Venezuela, killing more than 150 people and uncounted animals. Each year more people become protagonists as the bees migrate northward through Central America and Mexico into the western United States. The conflict between people and insects keeps listeners and viewers focused on the progress of the bees.

Once in a while, a dead person becomes a protagonist, and bystanders become antagonists because they failed to help someone in trouble. In West Virginia, a 31-year-old man drowned because his friends simply watched as he cried for help. Someone pushed him off a float, but all his friends ignored his pleas because they didn't know he couldn't swim. The conflict between the helpless man and his unknowing, seemingly insensitive friends generated a sense of sadness and some anger among listeners and viewers.

Sometimes, an institution can become an antagonist and another institution can become a protagonist. For more than a decade, the United States government was unable to control inflation and therefore became an antagonist. One company stepped into a community to become a protagonist when it offered city dwellers the use of some of its land for garden plots. Company officials said they would loan 20-by-20-foot plots and provide free water to any family willing to spade the ground, plant the seeds, and tend to their plants.

Many combinations of protagonist-antagonist relationships exist, and you can employ them to make your stories interesting if you have a sense of how the events surrounding the protagonists and antagonists affect your listeners and viewers.

In some stories, you may not know who your listeners and viewers perceive to be the protagonists and who the antagonists. Strong feelings may exist on both sides of an issue. In such cases, let the characters in the controversy speak for themselves. You can write the background and summarize the debate, as in this story about a city council controversy:

> Reporter: City council members still disagree over the need for transient shelter to house homeless drifters during the winter. They debated a proposal tonight to lease a vacant West Side warehouse and furnish it with cots the Salvation Army offered to donate.
>
> But council member Nola Mulder leads a faction opposed to the plan.
>
> Mulder (on tape): You'll attract a mob of derelicts from every city within 500 miles when they hear how easy it is to freeload here.
>
> Reporter: Council member Bruce Esterhold says the local Rescue Mission has offered to feed the transients, and the warehouse owner will contribute the space without cost. But Esterhold has apparently opened old wounds.
>
> Esterhold (on tape): It won't cost the city a plug nickel, so why can't you give a little milk of human kindness.
>
> Mulder (on tape): You're asking us to open our arms to people who will steal the neighborhood blind, and that won't cost us?
>
> Esterhold (on tape): Aren't you the one who saw bogeymen last year when we wanted to tear down that warehouse and build a park?
>
> Reporter: Council President Wallace Darrell tried unsuccessfully to cool the debate, then recessed the meeting. He asked both factions to return next week with evidence to back their points of view.

When you report conflict that seems to represent no clear protagonist or antagonist, probe to see if more than two opposing points of view have surfaced. You should try to give each worthy viewpoint a hearing. Few issues are all black or all white. Some of the shades of gray may emerge as factors.

At times, the roles of protagonist and antagonist are clear. But when they're not, don't try to impose them. Try to understand even those people with whom you disagree. A woman who would abolish the First Amendment to protect children from what she perceives as the "evil" of cable television must be motivated by genuine feelings. Put yourself in her position. Imagine you are speaking in her voice. Ask yourself questions, and answer as if she were speaking. Why do you believe what you do? What motivates you to react as you do? Why are these people you oppose wrong?

This exercise may help you understand viewpoints you oppose. And it may help you report all viewpoints without coloring them. Remember that each character in your story has dignity, and you should not destroy it. Report what you see, let your sources talk for themselves, and the ideas, attitudes, and actions you reveal in the controversy will help your listeners and viewers see for themselves who is right and who is wrong.

A warning: Your stories will reveal protagonists and antagonists—that's drama. But resist the temptation to paint them as heroes and villains—that's melodrama.

WORKING WITH WIRE COPY

The wire services provide needed story material for radio and television stations, but they sometimes present special problems for broadcast writers.

Copy from the wires may be difficult to rewrite because:

- You'll be dealing with someone else's reporting, which has often already been through a rewriting process.
- You may be uncertain about how complete the reporting is.
- You may be uncertain about the story's accuracy.
- You may be uncertain how widely the story has been reported before the wire service picked it up.

Wire services, particularly broadcast wires, depend on newspapers and radio and television stations for much of their material. They have agreements with newspapers that allow them to rewrite stories that have been published already. They offer small fees to radio and television reporters who relay stories they have collected for their stations. So you need to be aware that some of the material the wire services transmit has already been made public by some other medium. Nevertheless, you'll need stories from the wires; they're useful resources. But find ways to make their copy fresh.

A reporter checks stories as they come in over a wire service computer.

"60 Minutes" correspondent Harry Reasoner remembers the experience of writing news for CBS Radio:

> The thing is, the first obligation of an hourly radio newscast, at least at CBS, was to assume that for some unknown percentage of your audience that was the only news they would hear that day. So in the ten minutes minus commercials (six minutes now, as, even at CBS, pressure from radio affiliates has steadily eroded news time) you wanted to make sure that you touched every major story of the day. And every newscast included at least one report from the field. So, ostensibly, there wasn't much time to fool around. But you can pack a lot of stories into two or three minutes, and along with the percentage of people who had heard no other news, you knew there were a lot of folks who had heard the same news a half-dozen times since they woke up that morning. So you found ways to keep from being bored yourself, without clowning, and in the process you hoped to keep some of the people out there in their cars and kitchens from being bored. . . . And you read the news wires carefully because sometimes the way you can make a story a little different is a nugget down in paragraph forty-two.[2]

Read all the way through wire stories, whether they're from the broadcast wire or the newspaper wire. Newspaper wire stories are usually written in the inverted pyramid style and may have all of the major facts in the first paragraph. But the scope of a story from the newspaper wire is probably broader than you'll need for a broadcast story. Because you'll need to write a concise story with a precise focus, choose details that fit your idea of a story that will be worth your listeners' and viewers' time.

Read through this story from the United Press International (UPI) newspaper wire:

> NORTHUMBERLAND, N.Y.--A PACK OF WILD DOGS--PROBABLY COYOTES--SLAUGHTERED 28 CHICKENS, CHASED A BOY UP A LADDER AND TERRORIZED A WOMAN IN A TRUCK BY GROWLING AND CLAWING AT THE VEHICLE, AUTHORITIES SAID FRIDAY.
>
> "IT WAS SCARY. I'M JUST GLAD IT'S OVER," SAID ANGIE SICKO, WHOSE FARMHOUSE A FEW MILES EAST OF SARATOGA SPRINGS WAS VISITED THURSDAY NIGHT BY THE WOLF PACK. SICKO AND HER SON WERE UNHARMED.
>
> STATE BIOLOGISTS CAPTURED ONE OF THE WILD DOGS TO DETERMINE IF IT WAS A COYOTE, A WILD DOG OR A "COY DOG"--A CROSS BETWEEN A COYOTE AND A DOMESTIC DOG. A PRELIMINARY EXAMINATION INDICATED IT WAS A COYOTE.
>
> THE INCIDENT BEGAN SHORTLY AFTER 6 P.M. WHEN SEVEN WILD DOGS, INCLUDING ONE PUP, CAME OUT OF THE WOODS AND BEGAN ATTACKING THE SICKOS' CHICKENS, AUTHORITIES SAID. THE PUP JUMPED INTO A PEN AND WAS BUTTED BY A GOAT. THE PUP WAS SLIGHTLY INJURED.
>
> THE DOGS RETREATED TO THE WOODS BUT CAME BACK A FEW HOURS LATER, APPARENTLY TO RETRIEVE THE PUP. IT WAS THEN THE ANIMALS CHASED SICKO'S SON, ROBERT CURRIE, 15, WHO ESCAPED BY CLIMBING A LADDER ONTO A SHED ROOF.
>
> "THE DOGS CHASED THE BOY UP ON TO THE ROOF OF A SHED," SAID CHRIS MORRELL, CHIEF DEPUTY SHERIFF FOR SARATOGA COUNTY. "THEN THEY ATTEMPTED TO CLIMB THE WALLS OF THE BARN TO GET AT THE BOY."
>
> SICKO GOT INTO HER TRUCK AND DROVE AROUND THE YARD BLARING THE HORN, TRYING TO SCARE THE ANIMALS AWAY. BUT THAT ONLY INCITED THE DOGS, WHO YELPED AND CLAWED THE TRUCK. "THEY LEFT SOME CLAW MARKS ON THE LEFT FRONT FENDER OF THE PICKUP," MORRELL SAID.
>
> THE DOGS EVENTUALLY TURNED AND SCATTERED INTO THE WOODS.
>
> "THERE'S SOMETHING WRONG WITH THESE COYOTES. THEY JUST KILLED FOR THE SAKE OF KILLING," SICKO SAID.[3]

You couldn't read that story as it's written. Read it aloud and you'll know it's not written in conversational style. Some of the sentences are too long and too complex to read with comfort and understanding. The lead alone requires at least ten seconds to read aloud.

The facts are organized erratically in places, and some are confusing. For example, the third paragraph about state biologists intrudes into the natural chronological flow of the narrative. And the writer confuses us by mixing "wild dogs," "coyotes," and "wolf pack" into the story as if they were synonymous. They aren't.

But it's an unusual and interesting story. You can rewrite and tighten it for broadcast.

First, since state biologists think the animals were coyotes, call them coyotes.

Second, since the deaths of the chickens are less important than the threat to the boy and his mother, ignore the chickens, at least in your lead.

Third, eliminate all direct quotations. None is colorful enough or important enough to appear as it is. The content of Sicko's statements is apparent in the narrative of the story, and you can restate the substance of Morrell's quotes indirectly in your narrative.

Finally, eliminate unneeded detail such as the number of chickens, the time of the incident, and even the name of the deputy sheriff, because he says nothing that needs to be attributed. Now write the story, climax first, followed by the chronological sequence of actions. Perhaps it would read like this:

> A mother and her son are frightened but unhurt after an attack by coyotes.
>
> Angie Sicko says seven coyotes killed some of her chickens last night on her farm near Saratoga Springs. They also chased her 15-year-old son Robert. He clambered up a ladder to the roof of a shed as the coyotes snapped at his heels.
>
> Sicko tried to chase the coyotes away with her pickup truck, but they howled and clawed at the truck.
>
> After a few anxious minutes, the coyotes retreated to the woods.
>
> Sicko and her son now venture into the farmyard warily.

The last sentence relates an idea not included in the wire story, but you can assume what the mother and her son are feeling.

You can read the story aloud in fewer than 30 seconds, but you still have its essence and emotion. If you have more time, you could add the detail about the injured coyote pup and the return of the pack.

Note, too, that you haven't copied any of the wire story's sentences verbatim, so your story will sound different than anyone else's version.

Read aloud this story from the Associated Press (AP) television wire:

VALENTINE, ARIZ.--MORE THAN 200 PEOPLE WERE EVACUATED
FROM THREE TOWNS IN NORTHWESTERN ARIZONA TODAY AFTER
A FREIGHT TRAIN CARRYING TOXIC SUBSTANCES DERAILED
AND CAUGHT FIRE, RELEASING CLOUDS OR POSSIBLY
POISONOUS SMOKE INTO SHIFTING WINDS, AUTHORITIES
SAID.

U.S. HIGHWAY 66 ALSO WAS CLOSED AS A PRECAUTION
AFTER 27 RAILROAD CARS DERAILED AND BURNED BETWEEN
HACKBERY [sic] AND VALENTINE, ABOUT 30 MILES
NORTHEAST OF KINGMAN, MOHAVE COUNTY SHERIFF'S LT.
CLARK MORRELL SAID. VALENTINE AND HACKBERRY ARE
LOCATED FIVE MILES APART.

THERE WERE NO IMMEDIATE REPORTS OF INJURIES.

CAUSE OF THE DERAILMENT WAS UNDETERMINED.

VALENTINE RESIDENTS WERE TAKEN TO TRUXTON, ABOUT
10 MILES FURTHER NORTHEAST, AND THEN THEY AND TRUXTON
RESIDENTS WERE EVACUATED TO PEACH SPRINGS, ANOTHER
SEVEN MILES TO THE NORTHEAST, WHEN THE WIND SHIFTED,
SAID CAPT. CHUCK OSTERMAN OF THE KINGMAN FIRE
DEPARTMENT.

HACKBERRY RESIDENTS WERE TAKEN TO KINGMAN.

OSTERMAN AND MORRELL SAID THEY WERE TOLD BY SANTE
[sic] FE RAILROAD OFFICIALS THE TRAIN WAS HAULING 46
CONTAINERS FILLED WITH VARIOUS HAZARDOUS CHEMICALS,
INCLUDING CYANIDE, FORMALDEHYDE, ALCOHOL, AMMONIA AND
SULPHURIC ACID.

SGT. ALLAN SCHMIDT OF THE ARIZONA DEPARTMENT OF
PUBLIC SAFETY SAID HE UNDERSTOOD THE FIRE WAS
RELEASING "SOME KIND OF TOXIC FUMES" BUT NEITHER HE
NOR THE OTHER OFFICIALS COULD SAY WHETHER THE
CONTAINERS WERE DIRECTLY INVOLVED IN THE FIRE.

OFFICIALS SAID EVACUATION OF HACKBERRY AND
VALENTINE INVOLVED ABOUT 125 PEOPLE. THEY WERE UNABLE
TO SAY HOW MANY MORE WERE INVOLVED WITH THE TRUXTON
EVACUATION, BUT SCHMIDT SAID THE TOTAL WOULD BE UNDER
500.[4]

The copy is loaded with broadcast style and punctuation and spelling errors, plus it's written in the inverted pyramid style. But it contains most of the basic information you need to write the story conversationally.

First, it contains too much detail for your listeners and viewers to absorb. You can eliminate all attribution if you drop or soften all of the information the sources are uncertain about. You can assume that police and fire officials have provided the basic information accurately.

The writer has made it clear that officials are uncertain whether toxic fumes really have escaped, so you can avoid exciting your audience if you eliminate phrases like "possibly poisonous smoke" and "he understood the fire was releasing 'some kind of toxic fumes.' " The potential hazard should be obvious to your listeners and viewers without your emphasizing it.

In the fifth, sixth, and seventh paragraphs, the complex description of shifting evacuees from town to town, the detail of specific chemicals, and the number of containers aboard is excessive information.

Also compare the first paragraph with the last paragraph. Since the figures in the last paragraph are unconfirmed, you might be inaccurate if you use the figure "more than 200" in the first paragraph. To be safe, lead with "more than 100" until officials can confirm the numbers.

Now check the spelling of *Hackbery* and the *Sante Fe Railroad*. You'll find that *Hackberry* and *Santa Fe Railroad* are correct.

The time of the accident is missing. You can call your local wire service bureau to ask if the writer knows the time. If not, you should probably say simply *today*.

Now you can write your story concisely, conversationally, and as much as possible in the active voice:

```
     Authorities have evacuated more than a hundred people
     from three small Arizona towns. They're afraid
     residents may be endangered by hazardous fumes from a
     derailed freight train.
         Twenty-seven Santa Fe Railroad freight cars jumped
     the tracks and caught fire about 30 miles north of
     Kingman today. Some of the cars carried hazardous
     chemicals.
         Officials have reported no injuries and have not
     yet determined the cause of the accident.
```

If you had accepted the original story as it came down the wire, you would have consumed at least a minute and a half to read it, and you would have confused your listeners and viewers with its detail and complex sentence structures. You can read the rewritten version easily and understandably in about 25 seconds.

When you're working with wire copy, protect yourself as much as possible. Be sure you know the essence of the story. Be sure you can enunciate the words easily. Be sure the copy is clear and accurate. And be sure it's organized logically.

If your station subscribes to two wire services, you can get a clearer view by reading both versions of a story. Here are two stories about a major airline crash that are dated within eleven minutes of each other. Both are follow-ups to breaking stories that appeared earlier.

The first cleared the UPI wire at 4:56 A.M., Eastern Daylight Time. Note that UPI utilized the understrike at the end of a phrase as if it were a dash and the ellipsis as if it were a comma:

RESCUE TEAMS DROPPED INTO A REMOTE, MOUNTAINOUS AREA
BY HELICOPTER HAVE FOUND AT LEAST FOUR SURVIVORS IN
THE SMOLDERING WRECKAGE OF YESTERDAY'S JAPAN AIR
LINES JUMBO JET CRASH.

THE SURVIVORS_ TWO WOMEN AND TWO GIRLS_ SURVIVED
IN THE TAIL SECTION OF THE PLANE FOR SOME 17 HOURS.

BUT AUTHORITIES FEAR THE OTHER 520 PEOPLE ABOARD_
INCLUDING AT LEAST TWO AMERICANS_ WERE KILLED.

THE BOEING 747 SLAMMED INTO THE DENSELY WOODED
MOUNTAINSIDE AND BURST INTO FLAMES SOME 60 MILES
NORTHWEST OF TOKYO. THERE WERE REPORTS FROM THE SCENE
OF MORE SURVIVORS . . . BUT POLICE COULD NOT CONFIRM
THEM.

J-A-L PRESIDENT YASUMOTO TAKAGI (YAH-SOO-MOH'-TOH
TAH-KAH'-GEE) MADE TWO PUBLIC APOLOGIES TO THE
FAMILIES . . . SAYING SIMPLY_ "I AM VERY SORRY. I
HUMBLY APOLOGIZE TO YOU ALL."

MORE THAN THREE-THOUSAND SOLDIERS WERE ORDERED TO
THE CRASH SITE TO HELP RECOVER BODIES. AIRLINE
OFFICIALS SAY THE PLANE WAS PACKED WITH BUSINESSMEN
AND VACATIONERS TRAVELLING DURING A RELIGIOUS HOLIDAY
WEEK . . . IN WHICH JAPANESE VISIT FAMILY HOMES AND
HONOR THEIR ANCESTORS.

A JAPANESE MILITARY SPOKESMAN SAYS SEARCH TEAMS
HAVE RECOVERED 52 BODIES SO FAR.

THE DEAD AMERICANS WERE IDENTIFIED AS EDWARD
ANDERSON SENIOR OF ENGLEWOOD, COLORADO . . . AND
MICHAEL HANSON OF AURORA, COLORADO. BOTH MEN WORKED
FOR THE STEARNS CATALYTIC CORPORATION OF DENVER AND
WERE IN JAPAN ON BUSINESS.

THE FLIGHT CRASHED ABOUT 45 MINUTES AFTER TAKING
OFF FROM TOKYO. THE PILOT REPORTED ABOUT 20 MINUTES
BEFORE THE CRASH THAT A RIGHT REAR PASSENGER DOOR HAD
BURST ITS SEAL AN[D] ABRUPTLY DEPRESSURIZED THE
PASSENGER CABIN. THE CAPTAIN SAID HE'D ATTEMPT AN
EMERGENCY LANDING AT A NEARBY U-S AIR FORCE BASE
. . . BUT THE PLANE VANISHED FROM RADAR SCREENS.[5]

The AP update moved on the wire at 5:07 A.M., Eastern Daylight Time:

(KITA-AIKIMURA, JAPAN)--OFFICIALS IN JAPAN NOW SAY
THEY'VE FOUND ONLY FOUR PEOPLE WHO SURVIVED
YESTERDAY'S JUMBO JET CRASH IN THE RUGGED MOUNTAINS
OF CENTRAL JAPAN.

THERE HAD BEEN REPORTS--BY THE JAPAN BROADCASTING
CORPORATION AND THE KYODO [*sic*] NEWS SERVICE--THAT AS
MANY AS SEVEN PEOPLE LIVED THROUGH THE CRASH. THE
REPORTS SAID RESCUE TEAMS HAD FOUND THREE SURVIVORS
IN ADDITION TO FOUR PEOPLE ORIGINALLY LOCATED IN THE
WRECKAGE.

NEITHER AUTHORITIES NOR A SPOKESMAN FOR JAPAN AIR
LINES WERE ABLE TO CONFIRM THE REPORTS. BUT THEY
SEEMED TO BE BORNE OUT BY A HOSPITAL OFFICIAL IN
FUJIOKA, WHO SAID THE HOSPITAL WAS AWAITING THE
ARRIVAL OF THREE SURVIVORS.

HOWEVER, IN A LATER INTERVIEW, THE HOSPITAL
OFFICIAL SAID THE REPORT OF THREE MORE SURVIVORS
APPARENTLY WAS NO MORE THAN A RUMOR.

MEANWHILE, POLICE SAY THEY CAN CONFIRM ONLY FOUR
SURVIVORS.

THE FOUR WHO LIVED THROUGH THE DISASTER WERE
IDENTIFIED AS TWO WOMEN AND TWO GIRLS: A 35-YEAR-OLD
WOMAN AND HER EIGHT-YEAR-OLD DAUGHTER; A 12-YEAR-OLD
GIRL WHO REPORTEDLY WAS FOUND IN THE BRANCHES OF A
TREE, AND A 26-YEAR-OLD WOMAN, WHO WAS IDENTIFIED IN
THE FIRST REPORTS OF SURVIVORS AS A YOUNG BOY.[6]

If you came on duty in the early morning hours and hadn't read earlier reports of the crash, you probably were confused. UPI says rescuers found "at least four survivors." Then it says, "There were reports from the scene of more survivors . . . but police could not confirm them."

AP reports officials saying "they've found only four people who survived," followed with: "There had been reports . . . that as many as seven people lived through the crash. The reports said rescue teams found three survivors in addition to four people originally located in the wreckage." And again, more confusion: "Neither authorities nor a spokesman for Japan Air Lines were able to confirm the reports. But they seemed to be borne out by a hospital official in Fujioka, who said the hospital was awaiting the arrival of three additional survivors." Still more confusion: "However, in a later interview, the hospital officials said the report of three more survivors apparently was no more than a rumor." Finally: "Meanwhile, police say they can confirm only four survivors." In the last line, AP adds one more element to compound the confusion: ". . . and a 26-year-old woman, who was identified in the first reports as a young boy."

Remember, the reports are coming in from various sources, and each wire service is trying to bring information up to date while simultaneously correcting earlier erroneous information. You cannot assume these stories to be readable on the air as they are; they'll confuse your listeners and viewers. You must take time to sort out the information and provide your audience with your best evaluation of what the confirmed facts are at the time you write.

After you've read the accounts on both wires, you may decide to say there are four known survivors and ignore the rumors about the others. But you should leave your story open to be amended if rescuers find more later. Perhaps you could write your lead:

> Rescuers have confirmed only four survivors from
> yesterday's crash of a jumbo jet in Japan. They
> assume 520 others died.

Now you can pick up other details about who the passengers were, where the accident occurred, and its potential cause.

You might decide to lead with the two known American passengers, especially if you work for a station in Colorado. AP ignored them in its morning story; UPI dropped them in the middle of a third-paragraph sentence, then reminded us of them again in the eighth paragraph. You could write your lead this way:

> Two Colorado men were among the passengers on the
> jumbo jet that crashed yesterday in Central Japan.
> They are presumed to be among the dead.

Then you can identify them and say what they were doing in Japan. Because you said, "They were presumed to be among the dead," you can go on to talk about the survivors.

Read all wire copy through before you write your story to be sure you have found the information that is most important to your listeners and viewers.

NEWS CAPSULES

Broadcast newswriters work under pressure. They must write quickly but accurately. Above all, they must write concisely. This is particularly true of the broadcast writer who writes news capsules, the short but informative news minutes that grew out of the "Bicentennial Minutes" of 1976 and such headline newscasts as "NBC News Digest" and "CBS Newsbreak."

Now each of the television networks, and many local television stations, produce news capsules during selected station breaks. Many radio stations similarly inject news capsules or abbreviated headline summaries into their program schedules.

Most are one-to-two minute capsules that usually include a brief opening and a closing and sometimes a ten-second commercial or promotion spot. The writer allows time for approximately 150 words of news.

Most news capsules contain four or five concise stories, because producers want to give their listeners and viewers a sense of a complete newscast of the day's news. The stories are, in essence, headlines, but they must sound like complete stories.

Assume that your opening and closing take five seconds each, and your commercial takes ten seconds; you have 40 seconds left for news, so each story must average no more than ten seconds.

You can write some stories in one sentence, but few one-sentence stories will sound complete because newscasters have trouble vocally making a concise single sentence sound conclusive. For example, you can write: "The governor says he won't run for a second term." That's the essence of the story, but it leaves a question in your listeners' and viewers' minds: Why not? So you'd do well to write a second sentence: "He says he needs time to resolve family problems."

That still may not answer many of your listeners' and viewers' questions, but you will have provided enough information to satisfy them until your next regularly scheduled longer newscast. Such a concise story will inform them, and it will also subtly promote your newscasts. Your listeners and viewers will expect you to pick up and expand the story later.

Also, you can read that two-sentence story in seven seconds, so you have given yourself a three-second bonus for another story that may require a little more time.

You need not automatically eliminate all one-sentence stories. Some may sound complete. That's particularly true of continuing stories. If your listeners and viewers have known for some time that a prominent former football star has been dying of Lou Gehrig's disease, they may already know how the disease affects the body and that no cure is available. You have told them in other stories about his football career and subsequent life. In a new story, it may be enough to summarize the current development concisely: "Former All-American tackle Joe Mandell died today in St. Louis."

That's a complete story. Few of your listeners or viewers will have questions.

But maybe you should also think about the impact of the single sentence. Since the football player was prominent, the news of his death will be important. Your audience may need a moment to absorb it. You can help by adding another brief fact: "He was 52."

Your listeners and viewers don't need that information, but the three added words will give them a chance to think and also give you an opportunity to diminish your vocal volume, slow your reading pace slightly, and close the story with a deliberate downward vocal inflection. Then you can pause for a second and attack the beginning of the next story with a stronger voice.

You can read that short story aloud in six seconds, with the slower pace and deliberate pause.

Interested listeners and viewers will expect an obituary story in your next news-cast, summarizing his life and his career highlights, but for the moment, you have given them the news.

You'll find it more difficult to write a complex story in capsule form. Study a complex story. Decide how much information your listeners and viewers will need to understand it. Estimate how much time you'll need to give them the essential facts. Then, if you think you'll need more than 15 seconds, you may be wise to eliminate it from your capsule.

Sometimes the story may be of overriding importance, however. If it is, you may be wiser to use more time and eliminate other shorter stories.

Perhaps you have a report from the state Bureau of Public Water Supplies that says 283 of the state's 722 community water systems have failed to meet standards for bacteria count. Most of the unapproved systems are in rural areas, and they affect only three percent of the population of the state. You've talked to a water quality engineer from the bureau who told you the state's disapproval doesn't mean the water is unsafe, but it does mean residents face potential health risks if they don't clean up their water systems. He also told you 197 of the unapproved systems have promised to act. The bureau will publish the names of the offending systems in tomorrow morning's newspaper. They'll appear in a public notice in the classified section.

You have more information, but those are the essential facts.

You face a dilemma. You can't name all of the 86 communities where water officials seem to be ignoring the problem, but if you don't name them. you may unnecessarily excite residents in communities who are unaffected. At the same time, the residents of those 86 communities need to know they live in affected areas, because they may need to pressure their water officials to act.

Maybe you can take the sting out of the story if you start with a qualifier:

```
No one's in danger yet, but some rural towns in the
state need to clean up their water supplies. Bacteria
levels in the drinking water of three percent of the
state's residents is higher than the law allows.
Names of the affected towns will be published in the
classified section of the daily newspaper tomorrow.
```

You've softened the story's impact, but you've alerted affected residents, and you've told them where they can find more specific information.

You can read the story in 16 seconds. That's a little longer story than you'd like in a news capsule, but since your first two stories ran seven and six seconds, all three total 29 seconds. You still have eleven seconds for one more story.

Maybe you can choose a light story or an off-beat story to please your listeners and viewers. Here's one with a touch of irony:

> Police have arrested a 14–year–old boy who tried to
> hijack a bus at scissors–point this morning. He told
> the driver he wanted to go cross–town to his
> grandfather's house because his mother made him get a
> haircut.

A longer story might tell your listeners and viewers the boy wanted his hair long, like that of his peers, but his mother wanted it short, like that of his father. She took him to the barbershop and stood over him while the barber cut his hair, but while she paid for the haircut, he grabbed the barber's scissors and ran out the door and down the street to the bus stop. The startled driver regained his composure three blocks down the street, wrestled the scissors from the boy, and radioed his supervisor to call the police.

The two-sentence story is intriguing, and it tells your viewers enough to satisfy them for the moment. You can read it aloud in ten seconds, so it fits comfortably into your news capsule. In a later newscast, you can flesh out the story.

Now write your opening and closing, and you're ready for the air.

STORY IMPACT

The most important element in the news you write is your audience. Without your listeners and viewers, you are the only person who benefits. So you must find ways to reach them and make them listen and watch. Ask yourself what this story means to them; then, early in the story, point up its significance so your audience gets a sense of its impact on them.

For example, if your viewers live in an earthquake fault zone, they probably know it. If they haven't felt the tremor of an earthquake, they've probably read or heard about it from someone else, and they have a sense of how it affects people.

One of your sources is a state geologist who has just completed tests on a local dam and determined that it would take an earthquake that measures at least seven-point-five on the Richter scale to rupture the dam. That's the heart of your story, but is it your lead? Maybe not. The fact is merely a figure, unrelated to the people in your audience.

So you interview the geologist:

> *How strong is an earthquake that would measure seven-point-five on the Richter scale?*
> "The strongest earthquake recorded in this area was in 1932, when a quake measuring seven-point-five, knocked most of the merchandise off grocery store shelves 20 miles from its epicenter, cracked the walls in a school building five miles from its epicenter, and left a rift nine feet wide and 12 feet deep at its epicenter, in an unpopulated area."

How far is the dam from the fault line?
"Six miles."

If the dam should burst when its reservoir is full, how many people would be affected?
"The rushing water would kill eight thousand people before we could warn them. Another 200 thousand would be affected to some degree. Others would die, of course, in fires, accidents, and diseases that result from the lack of water and sanitation. In the flood plain below the dam, residential and commercial property valued at 300 million dollars would be destroyed or damaged."

Why did you study the dam?
"Because city officials want to know what they can do to plan for growth, change building codes, and educate residents to protect themselves."

All of the geologist's figures are speculative but educated. You know your listeners will want this information, so your lead might say:

```
The odds are slim, but sometime in the next 50 years
an earthquake could shake the Swan Mountain Fault. If
it should happen, it could trigger the collapse of
the Bear Valley Dam and·kill as many as eight
thousand residents in this city.
    But experts say the earthquake would have to be
strong to be that damaging.
```

Then you could tell them about the state geologist's study, his estimates of earthquake force, damage, and the area most likely to be affected. You could also tell them why the study is significant to them. But most important, your lead has already told your listeners and viewers why they need to listen to the story—because they will be affected.

Try not to incite them, however. The story could rouse fear, or even panic, unless you caution your listeners and viewers that danger is only remotely possible, not imminent. Note that two softening phrases and one softening sentence were inserted in that short story.

You can personalize some stories that have universal effects on your listeners and viewers. Because radio and television are one-on-one media, a personal approach may draw them into your stories.

Perhaps all through the late spring and early summer you aired stories about a grasshopper infestation in farm areas. Now, in late summer, the Department of Agriculture has assessed the damage. It says the wheat harvest will be smaller because grasshoppers ate much of the crop, but the corn harvest will be good because it matured before grasshoppers damaged it. Use of a personal pronoun could personalize your lead:

> The grasshoppers have eaten their fill, but *we* can
> still expect to find plenty of sweet corn in grocery
> store produce bins.

Some newswriters prefer the personal pronoun *you* instead of *we*, but either may sound natural. Use the personal pronoun that sounds most comfortable in the context of the sentence and the substance of the story. It helps you draw your listeners and viewers into harmony with you; then you can give them enough detail to help them understand the effects of the infestation of grasshoppers.

Many stories will affect your listeners and viewers because they can empathize with the people who are affected. In such stories, the emotions of the people involved in the event must be clear.

Suppose you interview a young elementary school teacher who volunteers ten hours a week at a crisis center for abused children. You want to know why a teacher who spends five days a week with children would work for nothing to spend another day with them. You record her answer on tape:

> I sat down at lunch yesterday with a little girl who
> said she wasn't hungry; she didn't want to eat. I
> didn't say anything because I thought she was just
> being temperamental. But in a couple of minutes, she
> told me why she wasn't hungry. Her stomach hurt
> because her daddy punched her. I didn't feel like
> eating then either.

You haven't seen the abused girl; neither have your listeners and viewers. But all of you can visualize her through the words and the emotions of the volunteer teacher. Viewers can see the emotion in her face.

Write your lead to set up the story without taking away from what the teacher has to say:

> Some volunteer workers get more for their time than a
> certificate after a thousand hours and a gold-plated
> pin after five thousand. First-grade teacher Tammy
> Huber volunteers at the Child Abuse Crisis Center.
> Why?

Now you can play the audio tape or videotape. Her message will be clear, and your listeners and viewers will understand the human facets of the story.

Then you can tell them why the crisis center exists:

> The Community Services Council established the center
> to help potentially abusive parents. Staff members
> offer training for parents who don't know how to deal
> with their children and a nursery where parents who
> are angry and need time to calm down can leave their
> children.

The suspense lead, which delays the essence of the story, sometimes works well with a feature story like this, where the hard facts alone are unlikely to affect your listeners and viewers. If you get to the interesting sound bite early, it will hold your listeners and viewers.

THE HUMAN ELEMENT

In every story you write, think first about people—the people who will hear or see your story and the people who are participants in the story. Think second about ideas or objects, and include them in your story only as they relate to the people who develop ideas or the people who make objects.

Your listeners and viewers will relate to the people in your stories and understand what people in the news think or what they do because they can hear and see them talking, acting, and reacting.

In short, don't *tell* your listeners and viewers what people in the news are like; *show* newsmakers in action, and your listeners and viewers will know what they're like. The sounds and pictures of radio and television are the tools that make your stories vivid and human.

Exercises

1. Choose a story from one of the wire services or a newspaper. Write three different broadcast leads designed to attract your listeners and viewers to the story. Explain why you think your leads will attract an audience.

2. Develop a story idea and research it to find the information you need. Write the body of the story first without a lead. Now write three different broadcast leads that will fit the story. Evaluate them. Which is the best and why?

3. Record a story from a radio or television newscast. Choose a story from the newscast that particularly interests you. Analyze its structure. Did it follow a chronological pattern? A problem-solution pattern? A question-answer pattern? Explain why the story fit the pattern it followed rather than another pattern.

4. Develop a story idea in which conflict plays the primary role. Research it to find the information and opinions you need. Write it to reveal the conflict

without injecting your own point of view. Analyze your story. Did it reveal all of the relevant points of view on the issue or problem? Is it fair to all sides? Have you written a balanced story?

5. Read through some wire stories until you find one that seems to have omitted some important facts. Call the local wire service bureau and ask for the person who wrote the story. Ask for clarification on information you think is missing. If the writer is unavailable, call the newsmakers named in the story and ask them for clarification. Rewrite a corrected story.

6. Choose four or five stories from a wire service or from a newspaper. Rewrite them into a one-minute news capsule. Include an opening something like this: "Good morning. I'm (your name), and this is 'Newsbreak.' " Include a closing, too, something like this: "That's 'Newsbreak.' More news later on this C-B-S station."

   Allow ten seconds for a commercial, but do not write the commercial. Simply write a lead to the commercial, something like this: More news after this. . . . Read your capsule aloud and time it. Rewrite it until you can read it aloud at a normal pace to within two seconds of one minute total time, including the ten-second commercial break.

7. Develop a story idea and research it to find the information you need. Write your story to point up its significance to the listening or viewing audience in your area. Analyze the story. What facet of the story should have alerted your listeners and viewers to its impact on them? Did you make clear its effect on them? How?

Notes

1. Av Westin, *Newswatch: How TV Decides the News* (New York: Simon & Schuster, 1982): 62.
2. Harry Reasoner, *Before the Colors Fade* (New York: Alfred A. Knopf, 1981): 71–72.
3. United Press International, 1 August 1985.
4. Associated Press, 12 August 1985.
5. United Press International, 13 August 1985.
6. Associated Press, 13 August 1985.

4

BROADCAST WRITING STYLE

I have a theory that the quality of writing in broadcast journalism means a lot more to the success of your enterprise than anyone knows. . . . The audience may not be aware of bad newswriting, [but] they feel vaguely uncomfortable and turn away.

—HARRY REASONER,
"Newscasting: Cloaking Pitfalls in Smiles," *Time,* January 10, 1969, p. 39

Good writing flows onto paper as it flows from your mind—casually, informally, unpretentiously, conversationally. It conveys to its listeners a sense of spontaneity and energy. It is simple, direct, concise, positive, active, and clear. The spoken words fall gracefully from your tongue.

Journalist David Halberstam says Edward R. Murrow was a master of the kind of simplicity and understatement broadcasting demands:

> Murrow was not a trained journalist and that was an asset because there was a vast difference between the words and rhythms of print journalism and the words and rhythms of spoken English; he had nothing to unlearn. The spoken word is colloquial, print journalism when read aloud is by necessity stilted and forced.[1]

Broadcast writers know their listeners and viewers are often inattentive. Consequently, they must compel their audience to listen. They must attract and hold them long enough for ideas to be absorbed. So, most broadcast writers talk out loud as they write, their words spilling from their minds as if they had just witnessed events they must share immediately with their listeners and viewers.

Broadcast writers talk to one person, not to thousands. They know that radio listeners and television viewers are usually alone in their thoughts, if not in their physical space. They know that their audiences mentally shut out their surroundings and intimately exchange thoughts and ideas with the voices and faces transmitted by microphones and cameras.

SPOKEN LANGUAGE IS NATURAL

Broadcast writers who think they must impress their listeners and viewers may labor over their scripts, searching for sentence structures, words, and phrases that will sound important. When they do, their audiences will probably tune out, because they dislike the oratorical quality of pretentious speech and resist it.

Such writers would be wise to study their notes, organize the important details in their minds, drop their notes in a wastebasket, and ad lib their scripts as quickly as their fingers can encode the words.

By ad libbing their stories into tape recorders, then transcribing those oral stories, some broadcast writers have mastered this conversational quality. Such writers must polish their copy—substituting precise, active words, readjusting awkward phrases and sentences to eliminate confusion and wordiness, replacing generalities with specifics—but each time they ad lib their stories, their writing becomes more natural.

You may find another, more effective technique for learning how to talk to your listeners and viewers, but you must evaluate your progress by reading your stories aloud. If the copy flows easily off your tongue—without awkward pauses for breath, enunciation traps, confusing combinations of sounds, or distracting vocal pops and hisses—your listeners and viewers will probably understand what you say. But if you pause in places that seem to interrupt ideas, if you stumble over individual words or combinations of words, if you slur through phrases or whistle through your teeth, your listeners and viewers will probably be confused and discouraged.

Readjust sentences that trouble you when you read them aloud. Substitute or delete words that are difficult to enunciate. Most of all, when you listen to your oral story, listen for the ideas. Ask someone else to read your story aloud. Does that person understand the story well enough to convey the ideas you wanted to convey? If not, you have probably failed to write the story in a way that permits another reader to translate your ideas meaningfully. Rewrite your copy to allow the ideas to emerge.

Good broadcast newswriting attracts listeners and viewers in the same way that stimulating conversation attracts them. Well-written broadcast copy will flow into your listeners' and viewers' minds and be immediately understood.

Direct, Concise Sentences

A conversational sentence is a direct, concise sentence; usually, but not always, it flows from subject to verb to object. The sentence houses an idea, preferably only one, but it can contain several ideas if they are closely related. Don't force your listeners and viewers to struggle to unravel your meaning. Provide them with ideas in forms that make them easy to grasp.

"The wind blew sand" is a simple sentence—subject, verb, object. It evokes a memory from your listeners' and viewers' experience—a time when they stood on a beach or a plain and the wind whipped up clouds of sand or dust. But the idea is vague.

"The wind blew sand in his face" is more vivid. The sand now affects your listeners and viewers. They can feel it stinging their skin. But how do they react?

"The wind blew sand in his face, and he shielded his eyes with his hands." The idea is stronger still. The action stimulated an effect, then a reaction. You have written a compound sentence—two independent clauses, related closely enough that they can be joined by a conjunction. But since the ideas are written directly— subject, verb, object—and since they follow each other in logical sequence, your listeners and viewers will understand immediately. The first idea provides the foundation for the second.

You could have written the ideas in separate, simple sentences—"The wind blew sand in his face. He shielded his eyes with his hands."—but they might have sounded choppy and disjointed. The compound sentence structure ties them together comfortably. It breaks the monotony of consecutive sentences written in approximately the same length and rhythm.

Perhaps you have more information you want to include. For example: "The wind, which blew in from the south, whipped sand in his face." You've now written a complex sentence—you've added a subsidiary idea that interrupts the flow of the main idea, and you've given your listeners and viewers one more detail to absorb.

Maybe you have more to say: "The wind, which blew in from the south at 55 miles an hour, whipped sand in his face, and he shielded his eyes, already clouded with tears that rose to wash the grains away, with his hands." But the more ideas you pile into the sentence, the more you impede your listeners' and viewers' understanding. Most compound-complex sentences like that one hinder comprehension.

Some of the ideas in the sentence could be incorporated into the sentence more comfortably. For example, you could write: "The brisk south wind blew sand in his face, so he shielded his eyes with his hands," or "A brisk wind blew in from the south and whipped sand in his face, so he shielded his eyes with his hands." Either of those compound sentences is easier to understand than the complex sentence in which the subsidiary clause intrudes on the main idea. If you need to add something about the tears in his eyes, you could write that idea in a subsequent sentence: "Grains of sand lodged in his eyes, and tears welled up to cloud his vision."

Whether you write simple, compound, complex, or compound-complex sentences, write them so the ideas strike your listeners and viewers one at a time and usually in chronological sequence. Complete one idea before you begin the next.

Long, complex sentences can be clear, but only if the ideas are explicit and build upon preceding ideas.

A complex sentence that begins with a short introductory prepositional phrase may be clear: "After a five-month strike, workers are back on the job." The introductory phrase helps to prepare your listeners and viewers for the main idea because it recalls an event they've heard about continually.

A short introductory clause that anticipates an important main clause may build a sense of suspense that heightens your listeners' and viewers' interest: "As long as tax revenues lag, city services will be curtailed." The introductory clause provides the motive for the action in the main clause.

The longer the introductory phrase or clause, however, the more you risk confusing your listeners and viewers:

```
Suggesting that the president might veto the foreign
aid bill if it contains restrictions that might
reduce the amount of money available to Third World
countries, the secretary of state said the money is
vital to America's relations with underdeveloped
countries.
```

That sentence is so long that it clouds the idea the writer wants to convey. It would be better written as two direct sentences:

```
The secretary of state says the president might veto
the foreign aid bill if it restricts the amount
of money available for Third World countries.
The president wants enough aid to encourage
underdeveloped countries to support the West.
```

Phrases and clauses that hang at the ends of main clauses can be useful if they elaborate or build on the foundations provided by main clauses:

```
The young reporter likes to cover the hospitals, the
firehouse, and the police station -- all beats that
expose him to violence and death.
```

In that sentence, the main clause provides the conclusion, and the subordinate clause provides the motivation; the subordinate clause strengthens the main clause.

Nevertheless, long, complex clauses that hang on the ends of main clauses may confuse your listeners and viewers:

```
An Asian immigrant lost his footing and drowned today
while he fished in the Grand River as at least three
nearby fishermen stood by without any attempt to save
him.
```

Two subordinate clauses and a prepositional phrase encumber the end of that sentence and cloud its meaning. In addition, the most important fact is buried in the clutter. You can make the story clearer if you'll move the main idea to the beginning and break the long sentence in two:

> At least three fishermen stood by and watched as an
> Asian immigrant drowned in the Grand River today.
> None of them tried to save the immigrant after he
> lost his footing and slipped into the water.

The rewritten version requires five more words, but it helps the ideas to emerge clearly and gives the main idea additional emphasis.

The most difficult complex sentences to understand are those in which the main clauses are interrupted by long subordinate clauses. Sometimes, you'll need short restrictive clauses to identify nouns precisely: "No writer *who has talent* can ignore the rules of grammar." You need the restrictive clause because it identifies a specific kind of writer.

But you can eliminate most nonrestrictive clauses. You can write them as separate sentences without sacrificing clarity. Look at this example:

> The first space vehicle to carry geologic
> experiments, <u>selected from among more than 700</u>
> <u>proposed to NASA last summer</u>, will be launched in
> July.

Take out the nonrestrictive clause and rewrite the ideas in two sentences:

> The first space vehicle to carry geologic experiments
> will be launched in July. The experiments were among
> more than 700 proposed to NASA last summer.

Look again at every complex or compound-complex sentence and try to write a more concise, more direct version of the ideas. You should try to write each sentence so that it will catch and hold the attention of your listeners and viewers, and each sentence you add should make the story a little clearer. When you reach the end of the story, your listeners and viewers should feel they have a complete story without confusing lapses of information.

Active Voice

The active voice is the voice of news because it forms the natural, conversational structure of a sentence. The active voice also emphasizes people, and in broadcast news, people should be the focus. Most of the time, people are more important than their actions; their actions reveal their character.

Write in the active voice as much as possible because it is direct, strong, concise, and definite, whereas the passive voice is indirect, usually weak, often wordy, and frequently indefinite. In the active voice, the *actor* performs the *action:* "The policeman arrested the suspect." In the passive voice, the *action* is performed by the *actor:* "The suspect was arrested by the policeman." The active voice is direct, forceful, and sounds lively and urgent: "The storm slashed through the city tonight." The passive voice paints a less colorful picture, often delaying the important facts: "The city was sent reeling by the storm tonight."

The active voice encourages strong, active verbs: "The child *believes* the tooth fairy is real." The passive voice fosters weak, inactive verbs: "The tooth fairy is the object of the child's belief."

The active voice is concise: "Police will charge a local man for trying to elude them during a high-speed chase." The passive voice encourages wordiness and pomposity: "Charges are pending against a man who fled law enforcement officers after involving them in a high-speed chase."

The active voice clearly states who acts: "The company president insists that his employees start work on time." The passive voice can be evasive and secretive: "It is expected that company employees start work on time." Who expects it?

The passive voice combines some form of the verb *to be* with the past participle of a transitive verb: "He is taught." "He was taught." "He will be taught." "He has been taught." "He shall have been taught." It is an acceptable form if the group or person who performs the action is unknown or uncertain: "His hair must be cut before he appears on camera." Or the passive voice is acceptable if the action is more important than the group or person who performs it: "A tax cut has been approved by the legislature."

Be aware of other forms of the passive voice. Sentences that begin with such phrases as *there were, it was, the reason for,* and *the purpose of* are usually passive and wordy. The passive sentence "There is apparently no way weather experts can explain yesterday's freak storm" can be written actively: "Weather experts apparently cannot explain yesterday's freak storm." The passive sentence "It was fewer than 15 minutes before the board of directors approved plans for a new building" can be written actively: "The board of directors approved plans for a new building in fewer than 15 minutes." You can rewrite the passive, cumbersome sentence, "The reason for the delay in the completion of the new jail is because of the long bricklayers' strike last summer" as: "Construction crews have not completed the new jail because the summer bricklayers' strike delayed them." You can rewrite the passive sentence, "The purpose of the citizens' vote to consolidate city and county governments is to save tax money" as: "Citizens will vote to consolidate city and county governments. They hope to save tax money."

Some writers mistakenly write passive voice sentences with phantom, or implied, subjects. This sentence—"Drivers won't be allowed to exceed 55 miles an hour in urban areas"—is obscure. Who won't allow them to exceed 55 miles an hour? This sentence—"Playing baseball on a wet diamond is a worry"—is obscure. Who worries about playing on a wet diamond? The players? The umpires? League of-

Television news anchors usually read their stories from teleprompters mounted on studio cameras.

ficials? Fans? This sentence—"A distinction must be made between personal property and real property taxes"—is obscure. Who must distinguish between them? Legislators? Tax assessors? Tax collectors? Taxpayers? Don't force your listeners and viewers to puzzle over such sentences. Clearly identify the actor in each sentence.

But remember that some sentences sound more natural in the passive voice than in the active voice. "It's 3:30" is more concise and natural than "The time is 3:30" or "3:30 is the time."

Positive Sentences

Broadcast writers have little time to reiterate facts, and their listeners and viewers have little time to think about them. Reporters must speak their ideas clearly the first time. They should write their ideas forcefully and positively because negative ideas tend to confuse listeners and viewers. A positive sentence tells your listeners and viewers what *is* happening. A negative sentence tells your listeners and viewers what *is not* happening.

The play-by-play announcer who said, "The coach sent his 230-pound fullback into the center of the line, and he got absolutely not much," led us to believe he was praising the success of the play, then abruptly reversed his field and left us gasping. He would have been clearer if he had worded the last clause, "and he gained little," or, "he gained only one yard."

Most negative statements are indefinite: "The terrorist plot did not succeed." The writer should have shown us the certainty of the action: "The terrorist plot failed."

One reporter talked about a rock concert at which gunfire erupted and stray bullets killed two fans, then he concluded, "A police spokesman said that, considering the number of people in the stadium, things weren't all that bad." How bad were they? Specifically, how bad were they for the relatives and friends of the dead fans? The police officer probably intended to say that greater violence had erupted at earlier rock concerts, but the reporter carelessly painted him as an insensitive cynic. He could have written the last clause positively: "things could have been worse."

Positive statements encourage active verbs. The negative statement, "Economists will not speculate about how fast prices will rise," is clear, but it's less lively than the positive statement, "Economists refuse to speculate about how fast prices will rise."

Positive statements demand that writers be precise rather than evasive. The sentence, "The problem should not be all that difficult to solve," sounds like the writer is uncertain about how difficult the solution might be, and he's too lazy or too rushed to investigate it. So he hides his doubt in negative verbiage. He should have asked himself, "Will it be easy to solve? Will it require study? Or am I too blind to see the solution?" Then he could write something like this: "They should solve the problem easily," "They should be able to solve the problem soon," or "They should be able to study the problem briefly, then solve it."

Broadcast writers should also be aware of the confusion that double negatives can create. A sportscaster who said, "We shouldn't be in doubt that Alabama won't win the national championship," would have made a clearer statement this way: "Alabama is unlikely to win the national championship."

Not every negative sentence is weak, however. This sentence is probably stronger than any positive substitute you can write: "The president cannot deliver the speech." Or this sentence is just as clear as any positive substitute: "Middle-class voters no longer accept the way rich people evade taxation."

Think of the logic of what you write. Ask yourself, "Have I said it clearly? Have I said it actively? Have I said it precisely? Have I left no doubt?"

QUOTATION TECHNIQUES

Shun Direct Quotations

Broadcast reporters are storytellers; they tell about the fortunes and misfortunes of people their listeners and viewers watch or hear about. Since they seldom witness or participate in the events they talk about, newspeople collect information from others and relay it to others. They tell their stories as intermediaries, relating most information in the third person, infrequently using such pronouns as *I, we,* and *us.*

Actors, oral readers, and orators who perform for large audiences like to quote their characters directly. They try to recreate and project the physical and vocal characteristics of the people they represent. But reporters who tell their stories intimately would seem ridiculous if they tried to mimic their sources, so they quote them, for the most part, indirectly. They paraphrase and often condense what eyewitnesses and experts have told them.

A paraphrase of direct quotations requires some simple changes. Broadcast reporters change personal pronouns and possessive adjectives in the first and second person to the third person. Thus, the broadcast reporter who hears a political candidate say, "My opponent is a nice guy, but he lacks experience in solving our problems," would quote the candidate indirectly this way:

```
The candidate says his opponent is a nice guy but
lacks experience in solving the city's problems.
```

The reporter who hears a seismologist say, "We're not sure the tremor that registered on our instruments was an earthquake," would quote her indirectly this way:

```
The seismologist says she's not sure the tremor that
registered on her instruments was an earthquake.
```

Broadcast reporters also change adverbs and adverbial phrases and adjectives that designate time and place to indirect forms or to specific nouns or clauses. The third baseman who hit a double to bat in the winning run may say, "Right now, everybody knows me. Yesterday, I was nobody." A broadcast reporter will retell that quotation in this way: "The third baseman who hit the game-winning double says everybody knows him now, but no one knew him before he batted in the winning run." The police officer who gives you information about the arrest of a bank robbery suspect may tell you, "The officers who caught the suspect running out of here say they read him his rights right then," but you will repeat his statement indirectly: "The officers who caught the suspect running out of the bank say they read him his rights when they arrested him."

Too often, quotation marks tempt reporters and newscasters to dramatize the statements of their sources. If the mayor tells you, "My opponent is full of baloney," you might be tempted to imitate the mayor's vocal force if you quote him directly. If you overemphasize the quotation vocally, however, your listeners and viewers might take the words to be yours rather than the mayor's. You may want to use the mayor's colorful words, but to eliminate doubt about who said them, flag the words to make their source clear: "The mayor says his opponent is—and these are the mayor's words—'full of baloney.' " If a resident tells you, "The city council is made up of a bunch of petty thieves," you can remove yourself from the direct quotation if you write indirectly: "Mrs. Brown says the city council is made up of—and this is her phrase—'a bunch of petty thieves.' " If you're giving the story to someone else to read, enclose the strong words in quotation marks to call that reader's attention to the specific words, but quote everything except the strong words indirectly.

Sometimes, you may want to include a complete-sentence direct quotation. To do it, some newscasters still use the "quote . . . unquote" or "quote . . . close quote" phrase to set off such quotations, but that technique often sounds hackneyed and unnatural. Utilize it only when it seems to fit naturally into the context of the sentence, and if the direct quotation is short, flag it at the beginning but not at the end: "The governor says, quote, 'The legislature should fish or cut bait.' " Your listeners can sense when such a short quote ends. If the direct quotation is long, however, you may have to flag it at both the beginning and the end: "The neighborhood city council leader says, quote, 'I'll call down thunder and lightning if the sanitation department doesn't damn soon haul away that stinking heap of garbage,' unquote."

You'll use direct quotations best if you've recorded them on audio or videotape and let newsmakers state them in their own voices.

Attribution

Whether they're quoting directly or indirectly, broadcast writers usually attribute information to their sources before they quote it. Reporters are seldom experts, except perhaps at gathering information. They seek out experts who know the issues, the concepts, and the programs that are making news, or they search for eyewitnesses who have seen events occur. Then they attribute the information to the sources who have provided it. Attribution helps to establish the credibility of information or opinions.

When you name the source of your information at the beginning of a sentence, you give your listeners and viewers a foundation for believing or rejecting it. If you report that "the incumbent governor is leading his challenger in pre-election polls," your listeners and viewers will have no reason to believe you're telling them the truth because they know you're not a pollster. But if you report that "pollster Dan Jones says the incumbent governor is leading his challenger in a pre-election poll," your listeners and viewers who have heard of the pollster will remember that he has an established reputation for scientific polling and that his findings are usually reliable.

If you allow attribution to dangle at the ends of sentences, your listeners and viewers may miss it. Too often in oral language, the information at the end of a sentence seems to be only incidental to the principal thought. So if you report, "It doesn't matter whether Congress balances the budget, says a prominent Republican leader," your audience may hear only that a balanced budget doesn't matter, and they may even assume that you expressed your own opinion, not that of a political leader. Don't risk such misunderstanding. Attribute the statement clearly at the beginning of the sentence where it will get enough vocal emphasis to be heard: "A prominent Republican leader says it doesn't matter whether Congress balances the budget." Now your listeners and viewers will be alert, waiting for you to identify the prominent Republican.

Attribute a quotation at the beginning of the sentence, especially when it is striking or controversial. If you say, " 'The rumors that I have been unfaithful to my wife are false and scurrilous; they're damned lies,' the vice president told a news conference this afternoon," you're likely to lead your audience to believe you're rebutting allegations against you personally. Attribute the statement first, then remove further risk of misunderstanding by quoting indirectly: "The vice president has told a news conference that the rumors he had been unfaithful to his wife were, in his words, 'false and scurrilous.' He called them lies."

Occasionally, when you need variety, you might be able to attribute a direct or indirect quotation in mid-sentence, but be careful not to interrupt the flow of the main idea. For example:

```
The convicted murderer accepted the death sentence
calmly. "I'm not going to appeal," he told the judge,
"but you'll have to accept the guilt for my death."
```

When you interrupt the main idea for attribution, you may jar your listeners' and viewers' attention and force them to think about your technique rather than the idea. If you think that's possible, rewrite the sentence with the attribution at the beginning.

Sometimes, attribution will fit naturally between the subject and predicate of a sentence:

```
Health officials have asked residents to boil their
drinking water because it may be contaminated. A
sample of water taken at city hall, they said,
revealed an unusually high concentration of bacteria.
```

But don't wait too long to attribute. The attribution in mid-sentence in that example may be clear only because you've also attributed in the first sentence. Be sure to attribute before your listeners and viewers tire of waiting to hear the source.

Once in a while, you can dangle attribution at the end of a quotation, but only if the quotation states an idea that is generally accepted or an idea that is short enough to keep your listeners' and viewers' attention until you name the source. For example, you might utilize an indirect quotation in your lead to attract attention:

```
Three-fourths of the state's residents believe the
oil industry is contriving the gasoline shortage,
according to a statewide opinion poll.
```

If you have stated an opinion that seems to be shared by many of your listeners and viewers, then you've helped to stir their interest in the story and you've quickly added the attribution to make it clear that your source is reliable.

When you dangle attribution, choose words and phrases that sound natural, as the phrase *according to* does. Beware of newspaper styles of attribution that sound awkward when they're spoken: "One of the benefits of being mayor is immunity from parking tickets, Mayor Jerry Jacobs said today." Orally, that sentence may sound like one complete sentence followed by the beginning of a second sentence because the newscaster or reporter who reads it must vocally close out the quoted sentence. Read this sentence aloud: "The mayor interfered with police officers when they tried to close a downtown bar last weekend, says Police Chief Charles Mandel." The inverted attribution—predicate preceding subject—sounds unnatural because oral readers normally deemphasize attribution verbs vocally. Attribution verbs are merely connecting words, so they almost fade into obscurity when you speak them.

Listen, too, for the sound of monotony in your attribution. If your sentences are alike, following similar rhythmic patterns because your attribution appears too often at the beginning of a sentence, then attribute some sentences in the middle, or even at the end. Wherever you place attribution, however you phrase it, read each sentence aloud to be sure it sounds natural and reads comfortably.

You can also develop a sense of how frequently you need to attribute. No one can write a rule to guide you. You must listen for the sound of monotony, which will occur if you attribute every sentence, but you must also listen for potential confusion that may occur if you attribute too infrequently. Listen to your writing, and ask others to listen to it, so you can develop a sense of how often to attribute.

Don't strain for attribution verbs. *Say* is a small, common verb that almost disappears into the context of an idea. You'll be more conscious of its repetition than your listeners and viewers will, so attribute with *say* most of the time.

Longer attribution verbs may sound strained unless they fit into the contexts of sentences naturally. Whenever you choose a longer attribution verb, be certain you know its meaning and you're using it in a way that fits its meaning. Many attribution verbs sound pompous unless they fit into the contexts of ideas naturally. *To declare* is *to make known publicly or formally, to proclaim,* so it's unlikely that anyone would declare anything in an intimate setting. *To assert* is *to affirm positively, assuredly, plainly, or strongly,* so it's unlikely that an offhand or casual comment can be an assertion.

On the other hand, *to mention* is *to note or call attention to in a brief, casual, or incidental manner. To state* is *to recite, report, set forth*—the verb suggests that the speaker is reading or repeating from memory in a formal or pretentious manner. *To claim* is sometimes defined as *to assert with conviction and in the face of possible contradiction or doubt,* so it suggests that you are casting doubt on the statement of a newsmaker if you say, "He *claims* he has discovered gold."

Dozens of attribution verbs are available, but be cautious about the verbs you choose. Choose attribution verbs you would use in conversation, avoiding ones that may seem pompous. If you're in doubt, choose *say*. It's simple, straightforward, and unpretentious.

NAMES AND TITLES

To paraphrase Shakespeare, a good name is a jewel. Broadcast newswriters should remember that. The owner of a name holds a proud possession, and if you distort it, you'll offend him/her.

Utilize names respectfully: spell and pronounce them correctly, and employ them conversationally, but not frivolously. A radio station that, during the Nixon administration, instructed its announcers to call Secretary of State Henry Kissinger "Henry the K" may have entertained its listeners, but it also diminished the stature of the secretary's office.

Avoid beginning stories with unfamiliar names. Attract your listeners and viewers to the story with some of its flavor and essence, then introduce newsmakers by titles that generate interest or show that they have special knowledge about events, issues, concepts, or plans in the story. Unfamiliar names confuse us; we stop following the story line while we try to recall whether we've heard the names before. Titles, however, give us information that enables us to judge the expertise or qualifications of newsmakers. If you cite someone by only his name, John Smith, you won't identify his expertise, but if you cite security guard John Smith, you identify someone qualified to arrest suspected shoplifters or to protect property against burglars or vandals. The name Jack Horner may remind us only of the nursery-rhyme boy who sat in a corner, but Deputy City Attorney Jack Horner is a man who can tell us whether the city council can legally bar the public from one of its meetings.

Familiar names, on the other hand, may attract attention by themselves. For example, if you start your story, "Robert Redford is standing on a traffic island in the middle of Main Street, waving at passing motorists," you may intrigue your listeners and viewers. They'll probably stay tuned until you tell them why Redford is standing in such an unlikely place—because he is helping a political candidate conduct a "honk-and-wave" campaign.

Most of the time, you can eliminate middle initials and middle names. Most people can be identified easily without them. Retail merchant Henry Smith is not the same person as smelter worker Henry Smith, so you don't need to identify the retail merchant as Henry X. Smith and the smelter worker as Henry Y. Smith. You'll sound natural and conversational if you identify Richard M. Nixon as former President Richard Nixon and Eugene G. O'Neill as playwright Eugene O'Neill. Most people use their first and last names only, except on formal documents.

Some people, however, want their middle initials or middle names treated as importantly as their first and last names. Heavyweight boxing champion John L. Sullivan was never known as John Sullivan. Civil rights leader Martin Luther King was never known as Martin King.

Others adopt their first initials and middle names. Oil billionaire J. Paul Getty might not be recognized if you called him Paul Getty. Atomic scientist J. Robert Oppenheimer always affixed his first initial.

Still others, of course, prefer only their initials. We know former baseball pitcher James Rodney Richard only as J.R. Richard, and poet e.e. cummings not only preferred his initials, he always wrote them in lower case.

Avoid nicknames unless you know that newsmakers prefer them. Former President Carter preferred Jimmy Carter rather than James Earl Carter or James E. Carter or even James Carter. Former House Speaker Tip O'Neill was rarely known as Thomas P. O'Neill Junior.

If you're aware of how other reporters and newscasters read prominent names, you can follow their style; if you're unfamiliar with names and can't determine how newsmakers prefer them read, use first and last names and eliminate middle initials. But, if a name is listed with a first initial and a full middle name or with initials only or with three full names, read such names as they appear. You can check telephone books, biographical dictionaries, almanacs, or encyclopedias to see how they list names. If names have appeared regularly in the news, wire service pronunciation guides will list them every day.

Of course, when you need initials or full names for precise identification, use them no matter what the newsmaker prefers. If someone has been charged with a crime or has been seriously hurt or killed or has been named in a sensitive context, you must use an initial or a second name to distinguish that person from anyone else who might have a similar name. Often, you must identify such people by their ages and addresses, too.

Everyone has some kind of title, formal or informal. Informal titles help your listeners and viewers judge people just as much as formal titles do. "University student," "attorney," "writer," "truck driver," and "welder" are just as important in the news as are "president," "mayor," "general," "police chief."

When you choose an informal title, select one that either most closely fits the newsmaker's primary activity or most closely relates the newsmaker to the story. For example, "truck driver Alex Brown" fits the context of a story that says Alex Brown's truck rammed a compact car, but "protest leader Alex Brown" fits the context of a story that says Alex Brown led a group of angry citizens into a public hearing.

In broadcasting, titles usually precede names. If newsmakers' names are unfamiliar, titles identify their competence to talk on issues or concepts in the news. We can visualize architect Gregory Gregson as a person who knows something about the design of a new city hall, nursing supervisor Maybelle Mays as one who can give an accurate report on the condition of a hospitalized accident victim, and disc jockey Dave Davidson as one who knows what records are popular this week. But without titles, we may visualize Gregory Gregson, Maybelle Mays, and Dave Davidson as unknowns without reliable knowledge.

Also, if you place titles before names, you can write sentences that flow more conversationally. Thus, "Willenston Mayor Will Wilson resigned today" is a sentence that flows naturally without pauses, but "Will Wilson, the mayor of Willen-ston, resigned today" demands brief pauses where the commas appear and gives the oral sentence a staccato sound.

In most cases, broadcast writers eliminate the articles a and the before titles. Rather than "the speaker of the House, Henry Henderson," they say "House Speaker Henry Henderson." Rather than "a convicted strangler, Rusty Rufener," they say "convicted strangler Rusty Rufener." When they write titles without articles, they need no commas around them, and because they eliminate the commas, they eliminate unneeded pauses.

If a title is long and cannot be simplified, however, you may be able to write a sentence with more natural breathing spaces if you include the article before the title: "A suspect accused of threatening to bomb a bus station, Matthew Mathias," is much easier to enunciate and to understand than "bus station bomb threat suspect Matthew Mathias." Converting natural prepositional phrases into adjectives and stacking them in front of the name only complicates understanding. Whenever you place an article before a title or place a title after a name, commas must surround the name.

Simplify titles. Write them so they're easy to understand. "Two university fresh-men who have been studying astronomy for only two months" is cumbersome. Perhaps you can simply label them "two novice astronomers." "A representative of a mining company that has adopted new uranium mining techniques" is complex and vague. The title "a uranium industry representative" is clearer. Drop the other information into the story later if you need it.

Some titles of people in governmental agencies and industrial firms are written long deliberately to cover broad areas of authority. For example, "Tri-Cities Inter-national Airport Operations, Management, and Facilities Superintendent George Brown" may accurately reflect the title on Brown's letterhead stationery, but it is so unwieldy that it may bore your listeners and viewers. Simplify the title to reflect the substance of the story, and split it up, placing part of it before his name and part of it after. If your story is about some aspect of airport operations, call him "Operations Superintendent George Brown of the Tri-Cities International Airport." If your story details some proposed improvements in airport facilities, call him "Airport Facilities Superintendent George Brown." Experiment orally with cum-bersome titles to find natural ways to say them without losing their value for identification.

Write only one title at a time. If the newsmaker holds more than one title, choose the one that connects him most appropriately with the substance of your story. Since most university presidents are Ph.D.s, they can be titled either "pres-ident" or "doctor." But if a university president named Garry Garrison speaks for the university, refer to him as "University President Garry Garrison" rather than "University President, Doctor Garry Garrison" or "Doctor Garrison." Laurence Olivier was knighted. In your first reference to him, therefore, you should say "actor Laurence Olivier" rather than "actor, Sir Laurence Olivier." In a subsequent ref-erence, you might want to call him "Sir Laurence."

Sometimes, names may be unnecessary. Titles alone may carry all of the information your listeners and viewers need or want. This is particularly true when events are interesting but remote. If, for example, a Romanian poet who is little-known in America should arrive in Chicago, where his daughter lives, so that he can be treated for cancer, your listeners may never remember his name. So, rather than identifying him as "exiled Romanian poet Vasile Posteuca, who is dying of cancer," simply say, "an exiled Romanian poet, who is dying of cancer." Of course, if you were broadcasting from a Chicago station, you would probably want to identify the daughter, and perhaps the poet, by name.

Reporters often ignore the names of juveniles who are involved in such sensitive matters as misdemeanors, sexual abuse, or court proceedings. Court officers believe juveniles should be protected from potentially harmful publicity unless they have committed major offenses against society. Reporters can, however, give them titles that may be based only on their ages and home towns. Our listeners and viewers need some identifying information to accept the story as credible. You might lead a story involving a juvenile this way: "A 15-year-old local girl has filed a suit claiming that a state law that denied her an abortion is unconstitutional." This issue is more important than the identity of the girl, but her age and local residence add significance to the story.

Use your judgment about how you use titles after your first reference. Most style guides suggest that you eliminate courtesy titles on second reference and use last names only, irrespective of gender. But at times, you may think a newsmaker or his/her position deserves the dignity of a title. If you do, use the title with the last name alone. If you think the individual or his/her profession deserves special attention, you can write, "Mr./Mrs. Anderson says his/her fellow attorneys are wrong." But if a jury has convicted a felon of a heinous crime, you can ignore the courtesy title and write, "Anderson has been convicted of first-degree murder."

Sometimes, your listeners and viewers may be offended if you ignore the title of a prominent resident. For example, if the wife of a prominent merchant is the recipient of the city's "Humanitarian Award," you might sound disrespectful unless, on second reference, you call her "Mrs. Elmendorf."

Avoid Sexist Titles

Reporters still struggle for solutions to the problems of how to title women, and broadcast reporters find that struggle even more difficult because many of the proposed substitutes for stereotypical male titles sound ponderous and unnatural.

Chairperson, for example, is a title a minority of both women and men like. *Chair* is an awkward substitute for *chairman,* too, because it traditionally has been a noun for a piece of furniture. Unless such titles are in common usage in your region, find simple, natural substitutes, which are usually available.

A *chairman* could be a *presiding officer,* a *leader,* a *director,* a *committee head,* or a *department head.*

A *spokesman* could be a *representative,* a *designate,* an *advocate,* a *proponent* or, sometimes, a *messenger.*

A *newsman* could be a *reporter* or a *correspondent.* An *anchorman* could be a *newscaster.* A *cameraman* could be a *photographer* or a *camera operator.* A *weatherman* could be a *weathercaster* or a *forecaster* or a *meteorologist.*

A *councilman* could be a *council member.* A *congressman* could be a *representative* or a *member of Congress.* An *assemblyman* could be a *representative* of a district. A *statesman* could be a *diplomat,* a *political leader,* or a *world leader.*

A *fireman* could be a *firefighter.* A *policeman* could be a *police officer* or simply an *officer.*

A *foreman* could be a *supervisor* or, sometimes, a *boss.*

A *salesman* could be an *agent* or a *sales representative* or a *clerk.*

A *craftsman* could be an *artisan.*

A *repairman* could be specifically titled according to expertise: a *carpenter,* an *electrician,* a *plumber.*

You can find many natural, conversational titles to substitute for titles that are sexist or pompous or both. You need not strain for titles.

Lady and *gal* appear occasionally; many women are offended to be called *lady golfers* or *lady lawyers.* They've earned status alongside men who are called simply *golfers* and *lawyers.* The correct title of the LPGA is still the *Ladies Professional Golf Association,* however, and some women's gymnastic teams still accept the title *lady gymnasts.* If that's commonly used in your area, adopt it.

Gal, however, is a denigrating term you should excise from your vocabulary. You may need to distinguish between the *women's basketball team* and the *men's basketball team,* but you need not call the outstanding female player the top *gal* athlete. After all, you don't call the outstanding male player the top *guy* athlete.

And colleges no longer admit *coeds;* they admit *students.*

Some broadcast reporters have been forced to break habits formed in traditional classrooms, but with a little thought, you can treat both sexes fairly in the way you write about them.

Direct Questions

Use direct questions sparingly. In oral language they often sound superficial or frivolous.

Commercial writers employ direct questions to attract attention: "The heartbreak of psoriasis?" Political orators utilize direct questions to stimulate emotional responses: "And what, I ask you, has my opponent done to curb inflation?" But commercials are repeated so often that listeners and viewers frequently respond to their direct questions with silent, or sometimes vocal, ridicule. Listeners and viewers of your newscasts are likely to react in similar ways if they hear direct questions in your stories because direct questions suggest you are selling something or trying to persuade them to accept some point of view.

A direct question, therefore, must be provocative enough to compel your listeners and viewers to wait for the answer. Ask them concisely and answer them immediately. The answers in the following example create an intriguing contrast:

```
After eight months of investigating the sniper
killings of two young blacks, F-B-I agents have
arrested a suspect who claims to be a neo-Nazi.
  Is he a racist? He says, "Yes."
  Did he kill the blacks? He says, "No."
```

In most instances, indirect questions seem more natural, and they may even be more concise and to the point than direct questions. Compare the following approaches to the same idea:

```
Are New Jersey parents aware of the drug crisis? A
state health official asked that question today.

A New Jersey health official is asking parents if
they're aware of the drug crisis.
```

(The first example requires two more seconds to read aloud than the second example.)

When you think about writing a direct question into a news script, remember that your conversation with your listeners and viewers is one-way. They can't answer you directly, so don't write the kind of question that will give them a chance to answer you flippantly.

NUMBERS AND OTHER DETAILS

In oral language, meaning must emerge immediately, and it must be unmistakable. Statistics and complex details impede understanding. Our ears are too seldom alert to oral details, so we tend to screen out particulars and rely on impressions.

Broadcast writers must find ways to write information that will leave their listeners and viewers with impressions of events that don't demand their recall of all the complex specifics.

To illustrate, television weathercasters who cover their maps with numbers want to provide temperatures for as many of their viewers as they can, assuming that individuals will focus on the section of the country that interests them most. But those same weathercasters would be foolish to call direct attention to more than a few selected temperatures.

The following newspaper story is packed with information that readers can browse and select from, but if you were to read the story aloud, you'd find that most of your listeners and viewers would remember only one or two details:

> Indiana's energy coordinator has predicted that the impact of the winter's cold -- which drove the mercury to a record eleven below zero in Indianapolis Monday -- will be felt long into the future.
>
> Dubuque, Iowa, had its 43rd day this winter of zero temperatures and below. Chicago was rounding out its 42nd straight day of freezing weather. Record lows included 17 below at Moline, Illinois, zero at Charleston, West Virginia, 19 at Wilmington, North Carolina, 21 at Charleston, South Carolina, and 27 at Jacksonville, Florida.
>
> The administrator of the National Oceanic and Atmospheric Administration in Washington has warned that heavy flooding could come in March or April.

Your listeners and viewers will probably remember the last fact—we can expect heavy flooding in March or April—perhaps one of the temperatures, and maybe the fact that some city has been through 43 days of below-zero temperatures. But most of the story is wasted—its details are too numerous for the ear to absorb.

Avoid offering such lists of numbers; they'll only confuse your listeners and viewers. Instead, give them selected details that leave them with impressions of lingering cold and caution them about potential flood waters that may follow when temperatures rise again.

You rarely need precise numbers. If an earthquake registers seven on the Richter scale, your audience may learn from that figure because they'll remember that earthquakes seldom register higher than five or six. But if 52 people were killed and 211 others are missing, round off the numbers, leaving your audience with a general impression: "More than 50 people have been killed, and more than 200 are missing."

You rarely need precise times. The fact that the earthquake struck at 5:33 A.M. will be harder to remember than the fact that it struck just before dawn or just before the city's residents awakened. The fact that the last major earthquake in this city occurred on August 31st, 1927, will be harder to remember than the fact that it occurred more than 60 years ago. The fact that the seismograph recorded minor shocks three days ago, on Monday the 27th, will be harder to remember than the fact that the seismograph recorded minor shocks earlier this week.

Broadcast writers also try to interpret large numbers for their listeners and viewers. The amount of the federal budget, for example, is almost incomprehensible. Half-a-trillion dollars means little more than a long string of zeros separated by commas into groups of threes. But CBS correspondent Roger Mudd said some reporters have found ways to interpret the significance of such figures:

> Every year about this time, America's journalists find it harder and harder to make the federal budget come alive and seem real. Like how far those dollar bills would reach around the world or how many times they would reach the moon.
> This year's prize goes to Robert Glass of Associated Press, who had discovered that the administration's budget would buy everybody in Minnesota a Rolls Royce or make every man, woman and child in Atlanta a millionaire.[2]

Images like those make complex figures vivid.

You can often eliminate address, age, room, and telephone numbers. If you've reported an upcoming concert at the civic auditorium, assume that interested listeners and viewers will know they can call the auditorium box office to ask for ticket prices and concert times. If you've told your listeners and viewers they can ask the tax assessor to explain their increased property values, assume they can find the assessor's office in city hall.

Only when you need numbers to identify newsmakers, or when you need to pinpoint precise locations, will you need to include ages and addresses. But write them in conversational ways. Instead of writing, as newspaper reporters do, that "Billy Brown, 5, is missing," write "Five-year-old Billy Brown is missing." Instead of identifying, as newspaper reporters do, "Harry Harrelson, 1325 W. Center St.," check the city directory or telephone book to see if they list other similar names; if no other Harry Harrelson lives in the same neighborhood, identify this one as "Harry Harrelson of West Center Street."

You should also write numbers informally if they don't need emphasis. Instead of *one-hundred,* write *a hundred.* Instead of *two-thousand-500,* write *25-hundred.* Instead of *one and one-half,* write *one and a-half.* Instead of *12-point-five percent,* write *12-and-a-half percent.*

Nevertheless, if you need to emphasize a number, write it formally. "*One thousand* motorists were killed in traffic over the holiday weekend" is more forceful than "*a thousand* motorists were killed in traffic over the holiday weekend."

Help your listeners and viewers calculate the differences between numbers. If you tell them Candidate A has polled one-million-327-thousand-916 votes and Candidate B has polled one-million-332-thousand-427 votes, your listeners and viewers will probably be unaware of who's winning, even if they see the figures on a television screen. Tell them, instead, that Candidate B is leading by about 45-hundred votes.

If you tell your listeners and viewers that today's high temperature was 92 degrees, and the normal temperature for the date is 87, help them place the information into understandable perspective by adding that today's temperature was five degrees above normal.

If you show your viewers the results of a public opinion poll and tell them that 48 percent of the respondents answered "yes" and 43 percent answered "no," add that nine percent were undecided, and that will explain why the figures on the screen do not total 100 percent.

Too many facts, other than numbers, can also muddy your listeners' and viewers' perceptions. In newspaper stories, details provide interesting profiles and backgrounds to events because readers can study them. But those same details in broadcast stories encumber your audience's understanding. Instead of listing the occupations of all 12 members of a jury, simply say the jurors work at such diverse jobs as housekeeper and used-car salesman. Instead of listing all of the experts who will appear at a public hearing on hazardous waste, choose one or two of the most prominent and say something about them. Instead of naming every play the community theater company will produce in the coming season, name only the first one, and say the company will present five others during the year.

You need specific details to make your stories believable, but choose the most important specifics and ignore the rest. Provide your listeners and viewers with enough information to help them remember the story, but don't burden them with details that may distract them from the main idea.

THE IMPORTANCE OF CLARITY

Avoid Stacked Modifiers

Too many newswriters think they can save words and time by stacking adjectives in front of nouns, but in most such instances, they merely add to the confusion of their listeners and viewers.

Stacked phrases range all the way from supposedly simple combinations like "the then district attorney" to complex combinations like "the Halloween-night multiple-gunshot killing of a 30-year-old woman."

The "then district attorney" is presumably a person who was district attorney at that time, and the murder must have occurred on Halloween night when someone shot a 30-year-old woman several times.

But the combination of "th" sounds in the phrase "the then" is so difficult to enunciate that your listeners and viewers may not hear what you say, and the profusion of facts contained in the other phrase is more than your audience's ears can absorb.

Such stacked modifiers are piled into sentences like damaged canned goods in supermarket bargain baskets. You must sort through the confusion of dented cans and torn labels to find something you can use. Unfortunately, other bargain hunters may elbow you aside before you have time to look at everything in the basket.

Newswriters who adopt this technique sacrifice clarity and may not save time. They certainly lose conversational flow in their language, replacing it with a clumsy, staccato rhythm. Concise prepositional phrases and subordinate clauses are usually more neutral.

Consider a sentence like this: "Wall Street closed a losing week by talking about the Federal Reserve Board's three-point-seven-billion-dollar money-supply calculating mistake." Even after study, you know little of what was said. Apparently, the Federal Reserve Board vastly underestimated the amount of money available to borrowers and thus frightened investors into selling many of their stocks. But few people would know that unless they were trained in mathematics and economics.

Consider the clarity of such compounds. You may be writing lucidly when you say "president-elect," but you may be clouding your meaning when you say "treasury secretary-designate."

Most qualifying words and phrases fit naturally *after* their nouns, but few fit naturally *before*. The sentence, "The state no longer has a custody-interest in the children," can be rewritten, "The state no longer wants to keep the children in its custody." The sentence, "Editors can ask just-as-tough questions as their reporters can," can be rewritten, "Editors can ask questions just as tough as their reporters can." The sentence, "He cites rising salary costs as budget-increase reasons," can be rewritten, "He says the budget keeps growing because salaries keep rising."

Ask yourself, "What do I want to say?" and "How can I say it naturally?" Then write to transmit the idea directly and clearly.

Verbs or Participles

Newswriters use participles to make their writing more concise, but they need to be aware of the hazards that participles pose. They can lead to confusion or lack of precision. Often, simple, straightforward active verbs are clearer than participles.

Participles are verbs transformed into adjectives or adjectival phrases. A present participle is a verb that appends the letters "ing" to assume the function of an adjective: "The *falling* oak crashed down on the road." A past participle is the third principal part of the verb: "The *fallen* oak blocked the road." The perfect participle adds the words *having* or *having been* to the past participle: "*Having* fallen, the oak was removed from the road," or, "*Having been* felled, the oak was removed from the road."

Straightforward present participles can be clear: "The *losing* team left the field first." Straightforward past participles can also be clear: "The *beaten* fighter left the ring first." Simple adjectival phrases formed with participles can be clear, too: "Some homeowners leave their lights on all night, *wasting energy*," or, "He assumed the leadership of the group, *chosen by his peers*."

Long, complex adjectival phrases, however, might be clearer if they were restructured as independent clauses. For example, the sentence, "The tropical storm dumped heavy rain on Texas today, *causing an estimated 750-million dollars damage along the coast*," might be clearer and stronger rewritten as two sentences: "The tropical storm dumped heavy rain on Texas today. Officials estimate damage along the coast to be 750-million dollars." The sentence, "The retired general has decided not to run for the presidential nomination, *saying it's too late to enter the crowded Republican field*," is cumbersome. It might be easier to read if it were rewritten in two independent clauses: "The retired general has decided not to run for the presidential nomination. He says it's too late to enter the crowded Republican field."

Avoid dangling participles. The sentence, *"Citing a prejudicial story in the morning newspaper,* a mistrial was granted in the rape case," dangles the participial phrase at the beginning of the sentence without any clear relationship to the main idea. It seems to say the mistrial cited the prejudicial story. It ignores the judge, the thinking human being who is capable of evaluating the effect of a newspaper story. Correctly written, the sentence might say, *"Citing a prejudicial story in the morning newspaper,* the judge granted a mistrial in the rape case," but the sentence will probably be still clearer if you were to move the main idea to the beginning of the sentence and follow it with the clause that justifies it: "The judge granted a mistrial in the rape case because he saw a prejudicial story in the morning newspaper."

The sentence, *"Introduced during a recession,* automobile connoisseurs say the Edsel was a good car that arrived at a bad time," seems to say that automobile connoisseurs, not the Edsel, were introduced during a recession. Correctly written, the sentence might say, *"Introduced during a recession,* the Edsel was a good car that arrived at a bad time, according to automobile connoisseurs." But that's still a cumbersome statement. It might be more clearly written, "Automobile connoisseurs remember that the Edsel was introduced during a recession, so they call it a good car that arrived at a bad time," or, "Automobile connoisseurs say the Edsel was a good car that arrived at a bad time. They remembered that Ford introduced it during a recession."

Watch out for fused participles, too. "The picture of the governor *barring the classroom door* is still vivid," fuses the participle *barring* with the noun *governor.* The sentence is clear because the idea emphasizes the governor rather than his action. The sentence, "The head of the campaign committee discounts the senator *wanting the nomination,"* is flawed, however, because it emphasizes the senator when it intended to emphasize his action. You can correctly fuse the participle by changing the noun to a possessive adjective: "The head of the campaign committee discounts the senator's wanting the nomination." But that sentence still risks confusing your listeners and viewers when it's spoken, so it might be better to restructure it: "The head of the campaign committee doesn't think the senator wants the nomination," or, "The head of the campaign committee doubts that the senator wants the nomination."

Unravel complexity. Each sentence must contain enough information to make its main idea clear, but beware of subtle mergers of words that cloud rather than clarify meanings.

Avoid Confusion

Many kinds of confusion create fuzzy ideas. Be certain your sentences say what you want them to say; open your senses to detect misplaced words and phrases. Be particularly aware of pronouns, which must clearly refer to their antecedents.

Look at this sentence:

> The man says he took his children out of the public
> schools because they are immoral and drug-ridden.

Is the man complaining about his children or the public schools? You can clarify the idea if you repeat the applicable noun:

> The man says he took his children out of the public
> schools because the schools are immoral and drug-
> ridden.

Consider this sentence:

> One city council candidate promised businessmen he'd
> hire more garbage collectors if they'd support him in
> the election.

Does he want businessmen or garbage collectors to support him? You could clear up the confusion by writing,

> One city council candidate promised to hire more
> garbage collectors if businessmen would contribute to
> his campaign.

Sometimes, by juggling words, we inadvertently disconnect appositives from the names they identify. In the sentence, "An aide to the governor, Merlin Melville, resigned today," Melville might be mistaken for the governor. You need to rewrite the sentence so the correct title appears alongside the name: "One of the governor's aides, Merlin Melville, resigned today."

Occasionally, punctuation causes confusion about an appositive. For example, in the sentence, "When the deputy secretary learned that his telephone had been bugged, he sued the president, the attorney general, his former boss, the secretary of state, and the White House chief of staff," the writer intended to say that the secretary of state was the deputy secretary's former boss, but he wrote the sentence to say the former boss was either a fifth defendant or the attorney general. Confusion could have been avoided by moving the words "secretary of state" and "former boss" to the end of the sentence: "When the deputy secretary learned that his telephone had been bugged, he sued the president, the attorney general, the White House chief of staff and the secretary of state, who was his former boss."

Sometimes, we confuse our listeners and viewers when we juggle the sentence syntax: "The law keeps young people in schools six to 18 years old." The writer meant to say, "The law keeps young people six to 18 years old in school," or, "The law keeps 6- to 18-year-olds in schools."

This writer apparently wanted to sound poetic when she wrote, "The carolers sang and the eggnog drank." She meant to say, less poetically but more accurately, "The carolers sang and drank eggnog."

You can always profit by reading your copy aloud. You often find errors when you read aloud that you may miss when you read silently. Or, better still, ask someone else to read your copy aloud to you. One of you may hear the errors before they reach the air.

Trim Wordiness

Broadcast news is casual, but it should never be careless. A good broadcast news-writer learns to be ruthless with copy, to slash the padding from sentences, and to speak ideas concisely.

For example, why should you write, "The senator will speak at the student council meeting," when you can write, "The senator will talk to the student council"? Why should you write, "The protesters will continue to remain where they are," when you can write, "The protesters will stay where they are"? Why should you write, "The opinion of the teacher is that everyone can learn to write," when you can write, "The teacher believes everyone can learn to write"? Why should you write, "It was argued by him that we shouldn't have taken action," when you can write, "He argued that we shouldn't have acted"?

Sometimes, wordiness is mere sloppiness. "The sheriff has not been able to confirm as of yet whether or not the suspect will be charged" travels unneeded detours to get to the point that "the sheriff doesn't know whether he'll charge the suspect."

Sometimes, we're wordy because we're afraid we'll misquote official sources. "The police chief says the suspect has been charged in connection with the shooting death of the victim" is gobbledygook that we should clarify: "The police chief says he's charged the suspect with shooting the victim to death."

Often, we feel impelled to tack abstract nouns on the ends of sentences, so we may say, "Residents have decided to do something on a local basis," when we could have said, "Residents have decided to do something locally," or, "Residents have decided to do something themselves."

And, frequently, we transform strong verbs into nouns and attach weak verbs. For example, "The truck came to a stop at the railroad crossing," is a weak substitute for "The truck stopped at the railroad crossing."

British television commentator Alistair Cooke has said about Americans, "Among all the English-speaking countries, we are the one that the others fear will drown in an ocean of verbosity."[3]

Politicians and sociologists contribute to that image, but so do newswriters when they take too little time to think about the quality of their work.

Incomplete Sentences

Some radio and television newswriters like to write incomplete sentences. They write some sentences, particularly leads, in headline style because they like concise statements that reveal the substance of stories quickly. Whereas you can write incomplete sentences occasionally, don't write them so often that they sound monotonous, and be sure you eliminate only those words that are clearly understood.

Usually, you can eliminate verbs, particularly forms of the verb *to be* that accompany other verbs. For example, you can write, "President hospitalized at Walter Reed Medical Center" instead of "the president has been hospitalized at Walter Reed Medical Center." You can write, "Transient found dead near railroad tracks" instead of "a transient has been found dead near the railroad tracks."

Sometimes, you can eliminate both the subject and the predicate of the sentence in a lead. You can write, "Another hat in political ring" instead of "another senator has thrown his hat in the political ring." You can write, "Bad news for wage earners" instead of "we have some bad news for wage earners." Of course, such vague sentences demand that you follow immediately with clear explanations: "Bad news for wage earners. Congress has approved another increase in the Social Security tax."

Occasionally, you can give ideas greater impact within the body of your stories by eliminating words that are understood:

```
Winter is a nightmare in the West. Reno had its worst
day today -- six inches of snow, ten-thousand homes
without power, schools shut, highways closed. The
forecast -- more snow.
```

In such a story, the short, incomplete clauses give the story a sense of urgency.

DEVELOPING A STYLE

Your Personal Style

Print news is often cold and impersonal. Broadcast news should not be. Because broadcast reporters present their news personally, they often become familiar "friends" in the homes of their listeners and viewers. Therefore, they can utilize the unique vocal and visual qualities of radio and television to draw their audience in to share the news.

You can generate warm, personal relationships with your listeners and viewers if you report your news in person-to-person language that shares information with them. Usually, you can create a sense of sharing by writing with such personal pronouns as *we, us,* and *our.* When you use personal pronouns, however, the substance of your story should have a fairly general impact on your listeners and viewers. Rising consumer prices, changes in postal rates, strikes that interrupt transportation schedules, tax increases, governmental actions that will affect many residents, crime or tragedy that occurs close to home, unusual weather, the fortunes of sports teams that number your listeners and viewers among their fans—all such stories can help you establish links with your audience.

David Brinkley effectively blended third person nouns with first person pronouns in a story gleaned from Census Bureau figures:

> The Census Bureau has run through its masses of
> figures and published some observations about the
> American people.
>   We are richer, live longer and are more educated,
> at least in years spent in classrooms, but many
> so-called educated people have very little practical
> knowledge. Twenty percent of American adults are
> functional illiterates, and fewer than half of us can
> deal with ordinary complexities of daily life, such
> as filling out forms. In short, we go to school more
> than earlier generations, but we do not learn more,
> and, often, less.
>   But, it says, 98 percent of us do have indoor
> plumbing.[4]

Very often, second person pronouns like *you* and *your* help you establish a sharing relationship with your listeners and viewers. You might attract your audience with a lead like this:

> If you thought your paycheck was smaller this
> month, you were right. The government took another
> half-percent of it for Social Security taxes.

You could suggest to your listeners and viewers that you have them in mind with a lead like this:

> Your bus may be late tomorrow. The Transit Authority
> is trying to save money by cutting back the number of
> buses that travel from the suburbs to the city each
> day.

Be sure you use personal pronouns to set up your relationship with your listeners and viewers, not to establish your relationship with other employees in your news department or station. The editorial *we* should have no place in newswriting. The editorial statement, "We believe the tax increase imposed by the state legislature is too severe," should be replaced with a statement such as: "We have a good idea how much the state legislature is going to raise our taxes."

Such a reference as, "The police chief told *us* reporters that *we* couldn't look at the scene of the crime," suggests that the chief affronted you personally. But a statement that says, "The police chief says that if too many of *us* know the details of the crime, we might jeopardize the case when it gets to court," suggests that you are sharing the responsibility with your listeners and viewers. "*Our* reporter says the city council will close the zoo," sounds self-serving and promotional, but "The city council will close *our* zoo," makes the issue a close, personal one between you and your audience.

Of course, an attempt to sound impersonal with a statement such as, "A witness told *this reporter* . . ." now sounds old-fashioned. Instead, you can say "A witness told *me* . . .".

You can often draw your listeners and viewers into your story by refreshing their memories about a common experience. ABC's Bob Hardt did that when he explained a substance that was the focus of a story about a chemical hazard:

```
The government warns today that undertakers and
other people using the chemical formaldehyde wear
protective clothing and have enough ventilation
in their work areas to avoid breathing the stuff.
Formaldehyde is the same stuff used to preserve those
frogs you dissected in biology class back in school.[5]
```

Personal pronouns establish broadcast reporters as people who care about their listeners and viewers because they talk to them one on one.

A Natural Style

You'll communicate best through radio and television when you develop a writing and speaking style that is natural and conversational. Remember that you are talking to each of your listeners and viewers individually, so your language must be casual and unpretentious. Resist temptations to *impress* your audience; *talk* to your listeners and viewers as you would to a friend. They should remember your voice or your face more readily than they remember the language you speak or the nuances of your reading style. Your audience will accept you more quickly if you talk like one of them, directly but correctly.

Exercises

1. Interview a newsmaker. Do not record the interview, but take notes. Decide what the essence of the story is and what your lead will be. Write some

abbreviated notes that contain only key words, not complete sentences—just enough to suggest what the ideas will be. Organize your notes. Then try to ad lib your story and record it on audio tape. Transcribe the story. Is it conversational, natural, and informal? Do you seem to be talking to your listeners or viewers? Evaluate your story; how would you change it to make it more conversational?

2. Choose a newspaper story or a wire story. Rewrite it to: (a) eliminate complex sentence structures; (b) change the passive voice to the active voice; (c) move needed attribution to the beginnings of sentences; and (d) shift titles to precede names. Read the story aloud and decide whether you should make other changes. Evaluate your finished story. Is it better than the original?

3. Choose a newspaper story or a wire story that's filled with detail—perhaps a story about the results of a public opinion poll or about crime statistics or about a government budget. Rewrite it to focus on only the most important details and to translate those details for your listeners or viewers so they can understand them immediately. Read your story aloud to someone else, then ask that person to repeat to you what he or she remembers about the story. How effective was your story? How interesting was it?

4. Tape record three news stories from a radio or television newscast. Transcribe them. Edit the stories to eliminate unneeded words and phrases. Rewrite sentences that are awkward. Evaluate your edited story. Is it still clear? How much were you able to cut?

5. Tape record a complete radio newscast or at least 15 minutes of a television newscast. Choose three stories that you think could be rewritten in a more personal style. Rewrite them, and read them aloud to someone else. Ask that person if he or she is comfortable or uncomfortable with your story. Do not tell your listener what you're trying to do, but if he or she mentions any of your personal pronouns, ask why. What is your listener's reaction?

Notes

1. David Halberstam, *The Powers That Be* (New York: Alfred A. Knopf, 1979): 40.
2. Roger Mudd, "CBS Evening News," 23 January 1978.
3. "America May Drown in an Ocean of Verbosity," *National Observer* (21 September 1974): 9.
4. David Brinkley, "NBC Nightly News," 28 December 1977.
5. Bob Hardt, "ABC Contemporary Radio," 22 August 1980.

5

CHOOSING WORDS

Words are clumsy tools, and it is very easy to cut one's fingers with them, and they need the closest attention in handling; but they are the only tools we have, and imagination itself cannot work without them. —FELIX FRANKFURTER

Broadcast writers must have a feeling for words; they must know what words mean, for both themselves and their listeners. Words distinguish a memorable story from a forgettable one. If your words are casual and unpretentious, specific and vivid, precise and active, and short enough to be enunciated clearly, then most of your listeners will understand and remember them.

And your listeners must understand you at once. They'll have no time to look up words in a dictionary; they'll have no time to study what you've said; they must hear you and know immediately what they've heard.

Talk the words onto the page, then read them aloud. Test your words; if they don't sound right, substitute others. Our ears are sensitive, but not as sensitive as our eyes. Unless the sounds of words trigger appropriate mental and emotional responses, our listeners will forget what we've said. Words need to be clear, concise, colorful, conversational, and subtly colloquial.

SIMPLE AND PRECISE WORDS

We tend to pose in public. We think we'll be more likable if we dress up and move in ways that enhance our attractiveness; we think we'll impress strangers if we use intellectual words. Instead of being ourselves, we pretend, assuming formal, pompous attitudes.

When we write, we pretend, too, so we search for words that sound erudite. We seek words of more than two syllables because smaller ones seem too common. We write down to our listeners when we should be talking to them.

Sit down with a group of friends. Start a conversation. Then watch them and listen to how they talk. Their movements are animated, their words lively. Their ideas excite them, and their words pour out enthusiastically. They don't worry about the polish of their words or the timber of their voices; they talk because they have something to say and they want you to hear it. They are natural and unpretentious.

Study your friends. Remove their slang, vulgarity, and excessive colloquialisms, and polish their ideas a little to make them clearer. Their language is the language you should bring to your writing.

You'll rarely hear your friends say, "The stench is allegedly emanating from the compost pile." They'll most likely say, "The pile smells." You'll rarely hear your friends say, "The suspect administered the fatal shots at close range." They'll more likely say, "The gunman was only a few feet away when he shot the man," or, "The man was within arm's length when he shot."

Yet, too many newscasters say, "The senator will opt for the nomination," instead of, "He'll run"; "The agency wants to obtain public comment," instead of, "The agency wants to know what people think"; "The determination of the cause of death pends toxicology tests," instead of, "They'll look for traces of poison before they decide what killed him."

Newscasters too often say *currently* instead of *now, inebriated* instead of *drunk, blaze* instead of *fire, halted* instead of *stopped, position* instead of *job, extinguished* instead of *put out,* or even *quenched.*

Certainly, you don't need to eliminate all words of more than one syllable. Some polysyllabic words carry a more exact meaning and state ideas more vividly. The newscaster who says, "The president skewered Congress for its failure to act," creates a clear, colorful image to help us remember the idea.

Syndicated columnist Sydney Harris has said:

> The art of clean and honest expression lies precisely in knowing which functions are best performed by short words, and which by longer terms. A good speaker or writer will use short ones in reference to the perceptual world. He will call a "lie" a "lie," and not a "terminological inexactitude"; by the same token, he will not use the generic short word, "dope," to refer to the whole spectrum of narcotics, from marijuana to heroin.
>
> It is not a matter of English, of grammar or style, but of intentions. If we want to communicate, we use the exact word, long or short; if we want to persuade, to befuddle, to conceal, to inflame, we squeeze or stretch the language to fit our own dark and devious motives.[1]

Too often, radio and television reporters choose words merely to impress their listeners and viewers. They should remind themselves that, although "sesquipedalian" and "polysyllabic" are synonyms, and one word may sound more musical than the other, their audience will recognize one more quickly than the other.

SPECIFIC WORDS

Generalities are the quicksands of writing. They swallow meaning before it has a chance to show itself. They suck understanding down into the bog of imprecision.

Such a common word as "people" can often veil the concrete image a writer hopes to create. Who are the people you write about? Are they football fans, meat-market customers, bidders at an auction, worshippers at a shrine, revelers at a party, tourists at a monument, picnickers in a park, protesters at a sit-in? When you say 50-thousand people watched the parade, your meaning may be clear, but when you say only two people showed up for a doubles match, are you talking about the players or the spectators?

If you write, "Officials knocked down the building for reasons of safety," do you mean they were afraid the building might collapse and hurt someone? If you write, "The senator conducted a hearing on toxic chemical allegations," do you mean the senator wanted to know if the chemicals were poisonous? If you write, "Students who live in dorms learn social skills," do you mean they learn how to talk to each other, how to cooperate, how to be polite?

Abstractions demand study. They force your listeners to think and imagine and paint their own pictures of the scenes you want them to see. But radio and television audiences have no time to study. You must give them specific details that keep them looking ahead to the next idea, rather than looking back to the last one.

If you write about inflation, write about the rising prices consumers have had to pay for food and clothing and gasoline. If you write about an infestation of fruit flies in California, write about potential shortages of oranges, lemons, and tomatoes. If you write about a proposed increase in Social Security taxes, write about how much it will bite into typical paychecks. Apply abstract concepts to the people they affect. Draw your listeners into the news by giving them concrete evidence of how they are a part of it.

LIMIT ADJECTIVES AND ADVERBS

You'll put vigor in your writing by using precise nouns and active verbs and limiting adjectives and adverbs to those nouns that need to be refined and those verbs that need to be enriched.

Follow this rule: Choose adjectives and adverbs that clarify nouns and verbs. Reject adjectives and adverbs that merely attempt to strengthen nouns and verbs.

"He gagged as he swallowed the goldfish" is vivid. "He swallowed the goldfish haltingly" is hazy.

Some reporters are tempted to embellish their ideas, as this one does:

> The president held a wide-open, no-holds-barred news
> conference. It was the kind of give-and-take
> question-and-answer session reporters have been
> demanding for six months.

"No-holds-barred" defines the news conference well. The reporter needs no more emphasis. "Wide-open," "give-and-take," and "question-and-answer" are adorning phrases.

Many reporters fall back on weak adjectives. One may describe the president's speech as interesting but fail to explain what made it interesting or why. Another may tell us the governor has accomplished much during his first three months in office but fail to list the accomplishments. Another may tell us traffic this morning is not all that bad but fail to tell us whether it's heavy, moderate, or light.

Weak adverbs are also useless. One reporter says the woman protested emphatically, but he doesn't say whether she ranted, shouted, cried, or pleaded. Another says the legislative debate will be prospectively long but doesn't say why or how long it might last. Another says voters reacted typically to the election but doesn't say what percentage of the electorate voted.

Here's a story that's more impassioned than informative. The writer dismisses specifics and relies on vague adjectives and adverbs.

> The dramatic entrance of the once-illustrious civil
> rights leader into the city's child-killings case is
> the latest in a long list of causes the man has
> embraced.
>
> With characteristic flair, the leader denounced
> the killings, but one of the mothers of the dead
> children predictably reacted that he was an outsider
> involved in a publicity grab.

> The civil rights leader angrily responded that his
> intrusion was a symbol of his organization's
> grassroots rebellion and its clearer purpose to move
> in one direction instead of many. He said his group
> is ready to fight a prolonged battle to unmask a
> police coverup.

The story says nothing, but it probably stirs emotions from its listeners. A demagogue might choose similar adjectives and adverbs to sway his/her audience.

Reporters who persistently use such excess endanger their credibility. Their listeners need specific information to help them recreate the event.

Writer Richard Powell has metaphorically talked about adjectives:

> In trying to make magic with words . . . it is wise to beware of the adjective. Nouns are good words to use in sentences. They are the bones, providing the needed skeleton. Verbs are good words. They are like muscles, providing the action. But adjectives are in most cases merely the clothing or ornaments of a sentence, and it is easy to overdress a sentence.[2]

Ornamentation in oral language is especially stark. It jars your listeners and viewers and diverts their attention from the ideas to the words themselves.

SHUN SUPERLATIVES

Lazy writers adopt superlatives as shortcuts to make stories seem important. Adjectives like *most, least, greatest, smallest, best, worst, highest, lowest, nearest,* and *farthest* abound. Absolutes like *perfect, pure, unique, complete, excellent, only, first,* and *last* appear as often in news stories as they do in commercials. Compound adjectives like *history-making, record-breaking, wide-ranging,* and *first-ever* recur incessantly.

We all know sportscasters who try to make records of every event. One such person interviewed a football coach:

> *Coach, did you know that if your team wins next week, it will be the first time in history you've won the first five games of the season?*
> "Wonderful. All we need is another piece of trivia to keep the pressure on."

You should excise such artificial details from your newswriting. Too many accident victims *narrowly escape* injury. Too many news sources *flatly deny* accusations. Too many critics *sharply criticize* proposals. Too many taxpayers become *increasingly concerned* about the rising cost of government.

And miracles occur too often: "*Miraculously,* no one was caught in the tornado."

"An investigator says it's a *miracle* the pilot survived the crash." "The Jets *miraculously* came from behind to win in the last two minutes of the game." According to Webster, a miracle is "an accomplishment or occurrence so outstanding as to seem beyond human capability or endeavor." Its use by reporters is presumptuous.

The former executive editor of *The New York Times,* Turner Catledge, gave this good advice to young reporters: "Play it straight, keep it short and never use the word 'unprecedented.' "[3]

REJECT EUPHEMISMS

Too many of our news sources try to soften the harshness of events and ideas by speaking in euphemisms—inoffensive substitutes for words or phrases that might be disagreeable or negative—rather than plain words. Merchants sometimes dress their products in euphemisms: a used-car dealer might want his merchandise known as *previously owned* cars; a second-hand furniture dealer might advertise *reconditioned* furniture; an undertaker might want you to remember him as a *funeral director* who takes people to their *last resting places.* But we aren't obligated to repeat their euphemisms.

Broadcasters similarly camouflage facts. The announcer who explains a program interruption using the phrase, "We are experiencing temporary technical difficulties," might discover that an engineer pulled the wrong patch cord or that a backhoe sliced a transmission line between Des Moines and Omaha. The announcer who warns, "Due to the nature of this program, parental discretion is advised," may mean the program is violent, sexually suggestive, vulgar, or tasteless. And the game show announcer whose program tag reads, "Promotional consideration furnished by such-and-such airline," means that the airline gave the program's producers free rides in exchange for the plug.

Newswriters should reject such attempts to soften information. They should remember that *honest toil* is *work,* an *underprivileged person* is *poor,* an *inebriated man* is *drunk, undocumented workers* are *illegal aliens,* a *management risk* is a *worker who cheats,* and a *passenger vehicle* is a *car.* They should remember that to *economize* is to *save money,* to be *deceased* is to be *dead,* to *claim the life* of someone is to *kill,* and to *be blessed with beautiful weather* is to *enjoy sunshine.*

You can sometimes have fun with euphemisms, however. Walter Cronkite once tagged a story about an expensive European car: "According to Rolls Royce, its cars don't break down; they fail to proceed."[4]

RESIST JARGON

We keep reminding ourselves that we must talk plainly to our listeners, but too often we're tempted to borrow an idiom or technical terminology of experts in specialized fields. It sounds impressive, so we imitate it. Or, we repeat it, even though we don't understand what it means. But if it's jargon, it will usually cloud ideas or encumber sentences.

Too often, jargon merely disguises meaning. For example, *conceptualizing* is a veiled way of forming ideas, *normalizing* relations between governments is a smoke screen for reducing tensions between them, and *finalizing* arrangements for a championship fight is a pretentious way of signing contracts.

Some jargon phrases come into vogue because public officials repeat them and reporters imitate them. They distinguish between the *public sector* and the *private sector* instead of between government and industry. They set up neighborhoods of loosely related people such as *academic communities, business communities, women's communities,* and *legal communities* in place of teachers, businessmen, women, and lawyers. They inflate *coming* events to *upcoming* events, *demolished* cars to *totaled* cars, *shortages of money* to *revenue shortfalls.*

Police officers are notorious for their straightforward language, but when reporters interview them, they shift to obscure jargon. They may say, "We rendered the suspected object inert," instead of, "We handcuffed the man," or, "We exited the structure and proceeded to incarcerate the suspected individual," instead of, "We took the bandit from the bank and booked him in jail." Too often, broadcast reporters repeat such bloated ideas rather than interpret them.

Because some jargon sounds colloquial, reporters adopt it as a device to help them sound informal. You're likely to hear the suffix *-wise* attached to all kinds of good words: "*Eastboundwise,* traffic is moving smoothly," instead of, "*Eastbound* traffic is moving smoothly." "*Temperaturewise,* it's warm today," instead of simply, "It's warm today." "The missile is not practical *costwise,*" instead of, "The missile will cost more than it's worth."

Some jargon sounds chic, but it's merely imprecise. Such phrases as "at this point in time" and "as of yet" are wordy ways to say "now."

We may use jargon to skirt facts about which we're uncertain, we may adopt jargon as a form of rhetoric designed to impress our listeners or viewers, or we may merely drop jargon into our ideas because it sounds erudite and conveys the impression that we're part of the in-group. But jargon is infectious. It's too easy to absorb it into our writing without being aware that we've stopped talking plainly to our listeners.

SPARE SLANG AND COLLOQUIALISM

We want our listeners to be comfortable with us, so we try to sound natural and informal. An occasional slang word or colloquial phrase may help, but we need to be sure it doesn't obscure the sense of our ideas.

Too often, slang is the language of a clique that adopts a special vocabulary to shut out nonmembers. Many radio and television slang terms grow out of the specialized technology of the industry, and reporters adopt them because they want to sound knowledgeable. But reporters who use such in-house terms are unlikely to contribute to their listeners' and viewers' understanding. A radio newscaster may apologize for why an actuality failed to appear on cue with broadcast slang: "I'm sorry, but the cart machine jammed." A television newscaster explaining why an erroneous superimposed name appeared on screen may apologize with television slang: "I'm sorry, but the super was wrong." Neither will add to his or her listeners' and viewers' knowledge.

Reporters sometimes adopt confusing slang terms from the beats they cover. The state government reporter might call the governor the "guv" and the attorney general the "A-G." The police reporter might call the police department the "P-D" and FBI agents the "feds." The education reporter might call the board of education the "ed board" and a court ruling on desegregation a "deseg ruling." The social services reporter might call detoxification centers "detox centers" and workmen's compensation "workmen's comp." But each reporter who adopts such slang risks failure to communicate with his or her audience.

Some slang terms belittle the people reporters apply them to. Police officers are offended by the word "cops." French people dislike being called "frogs." The stature of the presidency is diminished if you call the president "the pres."

Some reporters adopt slang terms merely because they're too lazy to look for precise words. "A thug ripped off the supermarket," doesn't tell us whether the incident was robbery, burglary, or theft. "Two kids have been picked up for vandalism," doesn't tell us whether they were children or teen-agers.

Some slang terms may be offensive. "A car mowed down a mother and her daughter on a downtown street," seems insensitive to the feelings of the victims' family. "The fire chief whom the city council canned last month says now he'll run for a council seat against his former bosses," may imply that the fire chief deserved dismissal. "When reporters pressed the sheriff for an explanation, he clammed up," may seem to degrade the sheriff's motives.

If a slang word or phrase will be understood and add flavor to your story, use it. You might say, "The governor has kept silent about whether he'll veto the tax bill, but if he's mum for one more day, the bill will automatically become law," and your audience will probably understand both the meaning and your informal approach. Such slang terms as "disc jockey," "the G-I Bill" and "the tube" are generally accepted now, but don't belittle your own industry by adopting "boob tube."

Unlike slang, colloquialisms are usually acceptable because they're casual, informal terms from conversational language. Such clipped words as "exam" and "quote" will be understood, and sports fans all around the country probably know that "stats" are statistics. Such colloquial words and phrases as "O-K," "flunk," "nix," and "in a jam" are accepted now in informal contexts.

Of course, you should avoid tasteless and obscene slang.

In general, use slang rarely, colloquialisms infrequently. But if you think you can acquire a specific, meaningful effect, use either.

CURB CLICHÉS AND JOURNALESE

We can't ban clichés. Some are colorful. Many are natural. Most are short. But since clichés are created because they suffer repetition, they become stale. Limit them. Use those that create metaphors and images, but abandon those that are tired and wordy.

Some clichés are journalese, that is, words reporters have adopted as substitutes for common simple words. We hear such tired nouns as "hikes"—wage hikes, price hikes, tax hikes. We hear often about "boosts"—salary boosts, budget boosts, unemployment boosts, revenue boosts—and we find halts—traffic halts, spending halts, battle halts and, of course, grinding halts—everywhere. Most fires seem to be "blazes."

Among verb journalese we find "mark"—we mark anniversaries, birthdays, openings, ground breakings, ribbon cuttings, and holidays. Public officials "call" often—for actions, decisions, votes, solutions, savings, and halts. Councils, commissions, and committees "air" things—opinions, feelings, differences, and facts. Public agencies "move" continually—to consider action, to act, to stop action, to react. And they "slate" meetings, hearings, study sessions, and votes.

Wordy clichés and journalese show up everywhere.

- Opposing parties rarely agree; they hammer out agreements.
- Long-lived people and events rarely celebrate anniversaries; they reach milestones.
- Investigators rarely find solutions; they find definitive answers.
- Plans rarely evolve; they take one step closer to reality.
- Self-reliant people are fiercely independent.
- Opponents are diametrically opposed.
- People in quandaries are caught between rocks and hard places.
- Agencies that delay killing proposals give them new leases on life.

Clichés are numerous, and they're convenient. Some newswriters argue for clichés because they know that their listeners and viewers will understand them. But clichés can destroy the freshness of ideas and they too often sound artificial.

Adopt a cliché if it gives you an interesting effect, but look for new images and metaphors, too.

RESTRAIN REDUNDANCY

Redundancies fall in news stories like dead wood falls in dying forests, and they are principal sources of wordiness.

Redundancies are unneeded repetitions of ideas. They can be as long as phrases—"Parolees are often forced to defend themselves *without any legal as-*

*Former ABC Sports reporter and commentator
Howard Cosell was known for his very colorful use
of language.*

sistance whatsoever"—or as short as words—"Passengers are getting to their *final*
destinations."

Most redundancies are superfluous adjectives or adverbs attached to nouns and
verbs that carry the meaning alone—*fatal* death, *new* innovations, advance *forward,*
cooperate *together, originally* begun, *completely* new, *fully* engulfed, *totally*
submerged.

Some redundancies occur because their writers are unaware of the meanings
of words.

- The reporter who writes, "They rallied together," apparently doesn't know that
  to *rally* is to *assemble.*
- The reporter who writes, "The union walked out of the negotiation talks,"
  apparently doesn't know that *negotiation* is *discussion.*
- The reporter who writes, "The victim was electrocuted to death," apparently
  doesn't know that *electrocution* is *death.*

Some redundancies occur unknowingly and leave their writers sounding foolish. If a sportscaster says, "The basketball player is in his first year as a freshman," he's unwittingly predicting that the player will fail his first-year classwork. The reporter who says, "The plane crashed on impact" is obviously unaware that she is stating the same idea twice. The sentence, "The river is contaminated by impure water" shows that the reporter didn't know that pure water cannot contaminate.

Sometimes, reporters insert synonyms for emphasis, but they waste words if one of the synonyms can carry the meaning alone. Such waste appears in these sentences:

The suspect has been *apprehended* and *arrested*.

Observers were *dumbfounded* and *astounded*.

The company gave the union its *last* and *final* offer.

Here, reporters should choose the strongest, clearest word and delete its synonym.

Occasionally, redundancies are included for emphasis, but be sure you need such emphasis. For example, to *alter* is to *change*, but if you want to show striking change, you could say, "The earthquake *permanently altered* the face of the mountain." If you need to emphasize the thoroughness of a presentation, you could say, "The architect missed not *one single* pertinent detail."

Use redundancies carefully, however; if your ideas are clear and strong without them, pare the excess.

CHOOSE ACTIVE VERBS

Choose verbs that show movement and force, that will stand alone without weak helping verbs or unneeded nouns.

Too often, newswriters rely on wordy predicates because they forget to think of active verbs. Forms of weak verbs such as *to be, to have,* and *to make* usually encourage wordy predicates. Such a sentence as, "Bulldozers *are being used to cut* fire lines," would be stronger as "Bulldozers *are cutting* fire lines." "The mayor *will have the budget completed* tomorrow," would be stronger as "The mayor *will complete the budget* tomorrow." "Geologists *have made* a major oil find," would be stronger as "Geologists *have found* a major oil deposit."

Active verbs such as *spark, defend,* and *appeal* are frequently transformed into nouns that take weak verbs: "The quarterback *was the spark* for the team," instead of, "The quarterback *sparked* the team." "Supporters of the plan *will have their defense ready* next week," instead of, "Supporters *will defend* their plan next week." "The convicted murderer *will make an appeal* to the Supreme Court," instead of, "The convicted murderer *will appeal* to the Supreme Court."

Sometimes, writers create wordy, inactive predicates. It takes longer to say, "His company *will be losing* a billion dollars this year," than to say, "His company *will lose* a billion dollars this year." It's wordier to say, "The tax limitation issue *will be confronting* voters," than to say, "The tax limitation issue *will confront* voters." You gain only two syllables in each sentence, but you've written livelier sentences and saved a second or two of reading time.

The passive voice also generates wordy, inactive predicates. The passive, "Indictment on the theft charges can result in a felony conviction for the suspect," is less forceful than the active, "The suspect could be indicted and convicted of theft." "The abolishment of the Commission on the Status of Women can be done by denying it money," is weaker and wordier than, "Congress can abolish the Commission on the Status of Women if it denies the commission money."

Sometimes, writers mistakenly rely on weak verbs alone to carry ideas. "The patient is out of surgery and recovering slowly, but *progress is there,*" states the idea indefinitely. He could have written, "The patient is out of surgery and recovering slowly, but *he's progressing.*" The writer who says, "The hearing *will be* next week," may be misunderstood. Does he mean the hearing *will begin, will be completed, will be conducted?* "Goblins *are* in the nightmares of children," could mean, more specifically, "Goblins *appear* in the nightmares of children," "Goblins *recur* in the nightmares of children," or, "Goblins *infest* the nightmares of children."

Avoid weak colloquial verbs. The weathercaster who says, "Some hailstorms *are going on,*" ignores the action of the hail *falling, pelting,* or *pummeling* the region.

Choose verbs that show precise actions. If a candidate speaks to an audience, he might *shout, demand, denounce, decry, murmur, whisper, harangue, lecture, preach,* or *talk.* But be sure to choose the verb that accurately describes the speaker's attitude. If none of the strong verbs applies, *talk* is a good neutral verb. The president of a baseball team may *fire* his manager or *dismiss* him, *discharge* him, *cast him off, turn him out,* or even *purge* him. A tornado might *slice* through a town, *slam* into it, *smash* it, *crash down* on it, or even *uproot* it if the force has been destructive enough.

Help your listeners and viewers to hear, see, and feel the event through your accurate choice of verbs.

DON'T MANUFACTURE VERBS

Headline writers and bureaucrats habitually manufacture verbs by converting nouns, adjectives, and adverbs. Headline writers save space when they transform a sentence such as, "The president *plays host* to the prime minister," to, "President *hosts* prime minister." Few usage experts accept *host* as a verb, but readers do understand the word. Bureaucrats find it fashionable to order their subordinates to *concept* the project when they want a preliminary idea of what the project will look like, but *concept* has yet to be accepted as a verb.

Newswriters sometimes fall into similar traps. The word *up* is an adverb in "He came *up* for air." It's an adjective in "Your time is *up*." And it's a preposition in "He walked *up* the street." Language experts now accept it as a verb—"The dealer *upped* the ante." But it's a weak verb. You'll write more forcefully if you say, "The governor will *raise* his budget request,"—or *enlarge, expand, increase* it—rather than, "The governor will *up* his budget request."

Jumped is a similar verb. Used in the active sense—"He jumped off the ladder," "She *jumped* rope," "He *jumped* when the horn honked," "He *jumped* on the bus."—it's natural and lively. But when you adapt it to mean *increase*, it sounds strained—"The death of the three-year-old-boy *jumped* the city's death toll to 15."

Manufactured verbs sound unnatural, but they abound in news: "Rioters *torched* more than a dozen houses." "Congress may *sunset* the cabinet department out of existence." "Police *shotgunned* the bandit to death." "The bandage failed to *cohese*." "The crowd *spectated* the game." Avoid such usage, or your language will sound contrived.

Occasionally, a writer will mistakenly combine a verb and an adverb. "The rain *poured down*," may appear as "The rain *downpoured*." Verbs like this do not exist. Reject them. They'll taint the quality of your language.

NATURAL CONTRACTIONS

Radio and television announcers enunciate clearly but casually, as most of us do in conversation. We blend vowels and eliminate difficult consonants because we don't want our language to sound stilted.

We often convert *want to* to *wanna* or *wanta*—"The Danes *wanta* delay action." We sometimes contract *would* to *d*—"He said *unemployment'd* hit six percent." We frequently contract *has* to *s*, as if it were a possessive—"The *president's* appointed a new adviser." We regularly contract *will* to *ll*—"The *plumbers'll* strike at midnight." We often contract *are* to *re*—"*There're* no restrictions." We don't write such contractions into our copy because they look unnatural in type and might force our newscasters to stumble; we let them contract such combinations in their own ways.

But we *do* write natural contractions—*isn't, aren't, hasn't, haven't, don't, won't, wouldn't, shouldn't*—into our copy. Avoid them when you want to emphasize the negative, however: "The Soviet Union surprised the United Nations and did *not* reject the Security Council resolution." You can call your newscaster's attention to the emphasis if you underline *not*.

Many pronoun-verb combinations contract naturally—*I'm, he's, she's, we've, they've, he'll, she'll, we'll, they'll, I'd, he'd, she'd, we'd, they'd, we're, they're, who's, who'll, it's. It'll* sometimes sounds awkward when it's enunciated alone, but in the context of most sentences, it sounds natural: "The senator says *it'll* take three days to finish the debate."

Some adverb-verb combinations contract naturally, too—*there's, where's, what's, when's, why's.*

Look at the contraction in print. If it's unlikely to confuse your newscaster, contract it. Read the contraction aloud in the context of your sentence, or ask someone else to read it aloud. If it sounds right, contract.

SOME SUPERFLUOUS THATS

Conversational English frequently gives us opportunities to omit words and still be understood. The conjunction *that* is a word you can often omit. You can leave it out when you don't need it for the sense of the idea. For example, "The news program *that* we watched last night . . ." could be clearly written, "The news program we watched last night. . . ." "The Senate has approved a budget *that* the House can accept," could be clearly written, "The Senate has approved a budget the House can accept."

You can also eliminate the conjunction *that* after many verbs of attribution, particularly after *say:*

```
Medical researchers say (that) we're unlikely to
check the disease soon.

The police chief says (that) all of his officers are
first aid experts.

The governor announced (that) he'll demand budget
cuts.

The director insists (that) she'll resign next week.
```

In such cases, you can write a stronger, more concise sentence without the conjunction.

Some verbs of attribution in some contexts, however, may need the conjunction *that* for clarity. "The justice declared the law unconstitutional" suggests that the justice issued a legal opinion. But "The justice declared *that* the law is unconstitutional" suggests that he publicly expressed an informal opinion.

Other confusion is possible when you eliminate *that.* If you say, "Council members are arguing an ordinance would regulate prostitution," you imply that council members support the concept of regulation. But if you say, "Council members are arguing an ordinance *that* would regulate prostitution," you imply that they are debating the merits of the proposed ordinance. If you say, "The defense attorney says in addition to overemphasizing the confession, the prosecutor is misleading the jury," your listeners may assume the defense attorney is over-emphasizing the confession. But if you mean the prosecutor is overemphasizing the confession, insert the conjunction *that:* "The defense attorney says *that* in addition to overemphasizing the confession, the prosecutor is misleading the jury."

You'll probably need the conjunction *that* when time is an element in the sentence. If you write, "The chief said at 8:30 A.M. the fire was out," do you mean the chief spoke at 8:30 A.M. or the fire was out at 8:30 A.M.? Place the conjunction in the sentence where it clarifies your intent. Write either, "The chief said *that* at 8:30 A.M. the fire was out," or, "The chief said at 8:30 A.M. *that* the fire was out." If you write, "He estimated today he could pay his debts," do you mean he estimated it today or he can pay his debts today? Place the conjunction *that* where it clarifies your meaning: "He estimated *that* today he could pay his debts," or, "He estimated today *that* he could pay his debts."

You can often omit the conjunction *that,* but sometimes you'll need it. If you're uncertain, leave it in.

THAT OR WHICH

As a relative pronoun, *that* is more conversational than *which,* but many grammarians suggest that you distinguish between the two. Use *that* to introduce a restrictive, or essential, clause. Use *which* to introduce a nonrestrictive, or nonessential, clause.

A restrictive clause cannot be separated from the main idea without changing its meaning. It defines the main idea: "The building *that* looks like an elongated pyramid is the TransAmerica Building." You need the clause to specify which building, so you introduce it with the pronoun *that* and do not set it off with commas.

A nonrestrictive clause can be eliminated from the sentence without losing the meaning of the main idea: "The TransAmerica Building, *which* looks like an elongated pyramid, is located in San Francisco." You don't need the clause to complete the main idea, so you introduce it with the pronoun *which* and set it off with commas.

A restrictive clause will flow with the rhythm of the sentence: "The officer ticketed the car that is parked in the red zone." A nonrestrictive clause will jar the rhythm of the sentence: "The officer ticketed the car, *which* is parked in the red zone."

WATCH FOR PRONOUN CONFUSION

Pronouns are useful substitutes for nouns. They help you avoid the monotony that grows out of repeating nouns. But if you're careless about pronouns, you may mislead your listeners and viewers.

Sometimes, you may need to repeat a name immediately after a pronoun to avoid confusion: "Former infantry soldier Alex Christian testified that his commanding officer, Captain John Jasper, beat him up while he, Christian, was a prisoner in the camp stockade."

Watch for misplaced relative clauses, too: "He gave his brother the sandwich that was lying on the floor." If the brother was lying on the floor, rewrite the sentence this way: "He gave the sandwich to his brother, who was lying on the floor."

Avoid the impersonal pronoun *one;* it sounds pedantic: "The chief of detectives warns that *one* should keep *one's* eyes on *one's* children when *one* takes them to the amusement park." That's unlikely language for a police officer, and it should be unlikely language for you. Be personal whenever you can: "The chief of detectives warns *us* to keep *our* eyes on *our* children when *we* take them to the amusement park," or, "The chief of detectives warns *you* to keep *your* eyes on *your* children when *you* take them to the amusement park."

LET PRONOUNS AGREE

Most of the time, pronouns must agree with their antecedents in number. But sometimes, we can relax that rule and write colloquially. For example, if you think of a collective noun as a unit, use a singular pronoun: "The *city council* voted *its* unanimous approval of the ordinance." If you think of the collective noun as a group of individuals, however, use a plural pronoun: "The *majority* of the city council voted *their* approval of the ordinance." You'll sound natural if you say, "The school's football *team* won *its* fifth straight game." But you'll also sound natural if you say, "The school's football *team* got permission to take *their* midterms early."

Remember that such pronouns as *each, either,* and *neither* are singular and demand singular companion pronouns.

> *Either* of the candidates to head the Women's Legislative Council must be able to complete *her* [not *their*] term in office.
>
> *Neither* the judge nor his bailiff could keep from chuckling to himself [not *themselves*].

Antecedents of mixed or indeterminate gender still call for masculine pronouns. We'd sound stuffy if we said, "Every *juror* in the box raised *his or her* right hand to take the oath." Until we find more comfortable genderless pronouns, we'll keep using masculine ones: "Every *juror* in the box raised *his* hand to take the oath."

If, however, you feel uncomfortable about using masculine pronouns with mixed or indeterminate gender antecedents, you might be able to change both to the plural:

> All the *jurors* raised *their* hands to take the oath.

> *All* of them can be heard if *they* talk loudly enough.

> *All* the members of the assembly will be allowed to explain *their* votes.

TRIM UNNEEDED PREPOSITIONS

In conversation, we tend to use prepositions indiscriminately, but in writing conversational language, we should pare those that are deadwood. For example, "We need to *pare out* the deadwood," should be, "We need to *pare* the deadwood." "The mayor wants to *consult with* party leaders," should be, "The mayor wants to *consult* party leaders." A basketball team shouldn't *win out over* its opponents when it can simply *beat* or *defeat* them. A candidate shouldn't *face up to* the issues when he or she can directly *face* them. Mechanics shouldn't *test out* a car's engine when they can quickly *test* it. Strikers shouldn't set up picket lines *outside of* the plant gates when they can set them up *outside* the plant gates. The emergency shouldn't be *over with* when it can simply be *over*.

You don't need to ban all double prepositions. Some may be natural. If you say an employer wants to *check up on* his employees, you make it clear that the employer wants to see if his employees are working or loafing. If you say the senator lives *over in* Virginia, you make it clear that she lives on the other side of the Potomac. It sounds natural to say the fighter wants *to come out* swinging, the retiring congressman wants *to stay out of* political activities, and the millionaire wants *to buy out* the resort's owner.

Nevertheless, some combinations of prepositions are simply wordy substitutes for a clear single preposition. Such inflated phrases as *in order to, with respect to,* and *in the case of* are lifted from the jargon of business letters. Say, "He's an expert *in* taxation," or, "He's a tax expert," rather than, "He's an expert *in the field of* taxation." Say, "He stopped *for* the red light," rather than, "He stopped *on account of* the red light."

Remember, too, that the rule that says you should never end a sentence with a preposition is not a rule at all. If a preposition dangles naturally at the end of a sentence, leave it there. "The witness couldn't remember the man he gave the gun *to*," is comfortable; "The witness couldn't remember *to whom* he gave the gun," is not. "The coach violated a contract he was two years *into*," might, however, be more clearly written, "The coach violated his two-year-old contract."

Think about the spontaneous, informal nature of speech, but think, too, about the clarity of the idea.

LISTEN TO WORD SOUNDS

Broadcast reporters might unknowingly sacrifice clarity by forgetting to listen to the sounds of their words. We enunciate many English words similarly, though their spellings differ.

Most of the time, we write words that sound alike in contexts that clarify their meanings. The difference between a *principal* stockholder and an ethical *principle* is clear. The difference between a *horde* of refugees and a *hoard* of stolen property is clear. The differences among a *vain* attempt, a *vein* of ore, and a weather *vane* are clear.

But if we fail to listen closely to the context in which a word appears, we may mislead our audience. If you're reporting on a potential strike of air traffic controllers and say, "Many passengers have *reservations*," some of your listeners and viewers might think you've said many travellers have guaranteed themselves seats, while others might think you've said many travellers are hesitant to buy airline tickets. If you say, "One of the resort's most popular ski hills has been *illuminated*," some of your listeners and viewers might think you've said the hill has been *eliminated*. If you say, "Seismologists say we'll get another earthquake *someday*," some of your listeners and viewers might think you've said *Sunday*. If you say, "Salvage crews plan to *raise* the ship," some of your listeners and viewers might think you've said salvage crews will *raze* the ship.

Many times, you can help your listeners and viewers distinguish between sound-alikes if you enunciate clearly. For example, most dictionaries accept *PRESS-ih-denss* as the pronunciation for both *precedents* and *precedence*. But you can distinguish between them by adopting the *preferred* pronunciation for each: *PRESS-ih-denss* for *precedents* and *pruh-SEED-uhnss* for *precedence*. Make the subtle distinction between *loathe* and *loath*, too. Enunciate *loathe*, meaning to detest or abhor, with a long vowel sound—*LOWWTH*. Enunciate *loath*, meaning unwilling or reluctant, with a short vowel sound—*LOHTH*. Distinguish between the noun *convict* (*KON-vikt*), a person found guilty and imprisoned, and the verb *convict* (*kon-VIKT*), to find someone guilty of a crime, by emphasizing the appropriate syllable.

Include a pronouncer—a phonetic spelling of the word—above or after the word to be sure your newscaster, too, understands which word you intend.

Sometimes, we mistake dissimilar words. *Washington Post* columnist David Broder once phoned in a story about a presidential speech in Los Angeles. He said, "The president *arraigned* the legal community for failing to serve the cause of social justice," but the person in Washington who transcribed the story heard the word *harangued*, and the *Post* published the story with the sentence, "The president *harangued* the legal community for failing to serve the cause of social justice.''[5]

SHRINK FROM SIBILANTS

Sibilants, those hissing consonant sounds such as *s, sh, z,* and *zh,* create a myriad of enunciation problems. You cannot avoid words that contain these sounds, but you can unravel many of their awkward combinations.

Read aloud the diction exercise, ''She sells seashells by the seashore,'' and you'll taste the enunciation traps that lie in wait among sibilant combinations. The Social Security System is difficult to enunciate, but add the word *statistics*—Social Security System statistics—and you'll find you have a tiger by the tail. Add the word *successes* to Selective Service System—Selective Service System successes—and you'll hear a mushy monster. You probably can't find an adequate substitute for Social Security, but you can delete System and substitute figures for statistics, and then talk your way through the idea clearly. You can substitute *draft* for *Selective Service,* and *gains* or *achievements* for *successes,* and then say something your listeners will hear and understand.

Many sibilant words are easy to enunciate when they stand alone, but you'll discover they're vocal hazards in some contexts. Such words as *enthusiasts, experiences, necessitates, seethes, youths, assistance, supercede,* and *seizures* will frequently force you to stumble. Be aware of them; read them aloud in their sentence contexts, and if they are troublesome, substitute synonyms. Some weathercasters have shortened *precipitation* to *precip* because they stumble over the polysyllabic word, but they could just as easily substitute *rain* or *snow.*

CHECK WORD MEANINGS

Too often, we adopt words without understanding what they mean. They sound right, so we drop them into our copy without checking their meanings, thus transmitting errors to our listeners and viewers. Eventually, after persistent misuse, dictionary editors adopt our errors as accepted usage.

Decimate is such a word. It sounds strong, almost absolute, so some reporters have substituted it for *demolish* or *destroy*—''The invaders *decimated* the village.'' Originally, to *decimate* meant to kill one in ten, but now Webster accepts it to mean ''to destroy a considerable part of.''

We hear too often that police are looking for a *light-complected* man. *Complect,* in its formal sense, means to *intertwine* or *interweave.* Webster now accepts *complected* as a synonym for *complexioned,* but we'd be more precise if we'd say *light-complexioned.*

Sometimes, we hear that cars crash into *cement* abutments, but *cement* is the powder mixed with water and gravel to make *concrete*.

Sportscasters sometimes tell us that players are *livid* about referees' penalty calls, but *livid* is *pale, ashen,* or *black and blue.* An angry athlete is more likely to be *flushed, red-cheeked.*

You may hear a newscaster say a flood has *inundated* the city. To *inundate* is *to submerge, to cover, to swallow up.* The flood may have inundated sections of the city, but it's unlikely that it swamped it entirely.

To *electrocute* is to *kill with electric shock;* to *drown* is to *suffocate in water;* to *suffocate* is to *die from being unable to breathe;* to *strangle* is to *choke to death.* So it's redundant to say the victims were electrocuted *to death,* drowned *to death,* suffocated *to death,* or strangled *to death.*

Sometimes, we confuse words that sound similar. A weathercaster may tell us to expect a *climactic* change—a triumphant change—when he or she means a *climatic* one—a change in the condition of the weather. A sportscaster may tell us the college coach is *disinterested* in the outcome of the Super Bowl—not rooting for either team—when he or she means the coach is *uninterested* in the outcome— indifferent to it. A newscaster may tell us the union was *enervated*—weakened— when the company refused to honor its demands, whereas he or she means the union was *invigorated*—strengthened—by the company's action.

BEWARE OF LOADED WORDS

Some words carry innuendo; they subtly suggest that you are biased.

Claim is such a word. It implies that the speaker doubts the honesty of the statement. If you say, "The landlord *claims* he paid the gas bill," you suggest that you have reason to doubt him.

Admit is another such word. It suggests that the speaker has confessed to some hidden sin. If you say, "The butcher *admits* there's more fat in pork this year," you imply that he's been trying to hide that fact from his customers.

Warn is another. It hints of impending danger. If you say, "The coach *warned* his players to stand for the national anthem," you suggest that he'll punish them if they don't stand.

Blame implies fault or censure. If you say, "The senator *blamed* the growing number of senior citizens for the Social Security mess," you condemn aging people for the program's deterioration, which they are not responsible for.

Refute is a loaded, often misused, verb. If you say, "The candidate *refuted* his opponents' arguments," you're telling your listeners and viewers the candidate disproved his opponent's arguments. How can you know that without substantial evidence? To be neutral, you should say, "The candidate *disputed* his opponent's arguments."

Choose your words with care. Don't labor over them, but be sure you say what you mean.

CHOOSE WORDS THAT COMMUNICATE

Good writing for radio and television is concise, and we make it concise by choosing the right words. They must generate a sense of action, and they must help our listeners and viewers create or enhance pictures of the events we describe.

Eric Sevareid said, "In radio days, you only had the word. The word had to carry the whole weight. They had to have people with a writer's eye and a sense for words."[6] He didn't think television changed that. "The camera can't take a picture of an idea. I think you're still going to have words."[7]

Watch a television newscast with the sound off, and you'll discover the importance of words. If we choose the right ones, we'll talk to our audiences. If we choose the wrong ones, we'll talk to ourselves.

Exercises

1. Listen to network or local radio or television newscasts. Write down words or phrases you think some listeners and viewers will not understand. Find at least 20. Then write substitute words or phrases you think the audience will understand.

2. Listen to local radio or television newscasts. Write down words and phrases you think attempt to inject emotionalism or editorial points of view into stories. Think mostly of superlative adjectives and adverbs. Find at least 20. Then write substitutes for them such as stronger nouns, more active verbs.

3. Get some wire copy or a local newspaper. Read it and underline wordy phrases and sentences, particularly those that contain redundancies and inactive verbs. Find 20 such examples. Rewrite them to show what you would delete or change to tighten the writing.

4. Read a newspaper story and underline all word combinations that could be contracted conversationally—verb negatives, pronoun-verb and adverb-verb combinations. How many did you find for every 200 words?

5. Some radio and television news departments have people in positions equivalent to newspaper copyeditors. Visit a local radio or television station and ask the news director who is assigned to review news stories before they air. Ask that person what he or she thinks are the most common writing faults. Write a three-page report based on what you find.

Notes

1. Sydney Harris, *Deseret News* (26 April 1973): A9.
2. Richard Powell, "The Magic of Words," in *The Writer's Handbook*, ed. A.S. Burack (Boston: The Writer Inc., 1974), p. 42.

3. B. Drummond Ayres Jr., "Catledge, 80, Says an Editor Isn't Allowed to Retire," *The New York Times* (17 March 1981): Sec. A, p. 14.

4. Walter Cronkite, "CBS Evening News," 7 February 1978.

5. Charles Peters, "Tilting at Windmills," *The Washington Monthly* (July/August 1978): 4.

6. "A Conversation with Eric Sevareid," an interview with Charles Kuralt, CBS-TV, 13 December 1977.

7. Ibid.

6

INTERVIEWING

Self-restraint is a must in television interviewing also. Mike Wallace began as a hard-edged, on-camera prosecutor, but has since developed an effective backhand—a disarming, disbelieving smile when confronted with obviously unpersuasive answers. The thoughtful Edwin Newman is so self-effacing that at times he seems to be turning away from the camera. Barbara Walters often offers a quickstep apology for asking a sharp question, then zeroes right in. Bill Moyers is a moralizer whose imponderable "big" questions sometimes drive his hapless subjects to embarrassingly hasty profundities. But all of these interviewers know that their job is to draw out a person. It is not, as in the quite different "Firing Line" assignment of the agile William F. Buckley Jr., to debate as an equal.

—THOMAS GRIFFITH, "You Have to Be Neutral to Ask the Questions"
Time, September 12, 1976, p. 72

Our listeners and viewers have come to expect us to provide them with news, whether impromptu news occurs or not. If we've scheduled five minutes of news every hour on the hour on radio, we're obliged to provide five minutes of news each hour. If we've scheduled an early evening hour and a late evening half hour for news on television, we must appear at the scheduled hour prepared to deliver news.

Reporters cannot wait for news to come to them. They must look for it. They cannot wait for the National Weather Service to announce a tornado, the police dispatcher to radio a detective to investigate a possible murder, the fire dispatcher to call a third alarm on a fire, the highway patrol to announce a traffic tie-up on an interstate highway, the FBI agent in charge to reveal a bank robbery, the prison warden to reveal a riot—they must *dig* for news.

But even the most observant reporters will find too little news if they rely only on emergency events and scheduled events. They must ask questions, and the journalistic interview is the foundation for most of the news they'll report at newscast time.

Many news directors and editors establish beats in an effort to satisfy the hunger of their media for information. They assign reporters to cover the statehouse, city hall, police station, sheriff's office, courts, legislatures, political parties, and other sources because they know something in the public interest will inevitably happen in each of those public offices.

But few observable events occur, so reporters must ask questions that will generate news. And they discover that, when public offices are closed—in the evenings, on weekends, and on holidays—there's a dearth of news. So news directors establish other beats—education, social services, medicine, science, consumer affairs, urban problems, economics, business and labor, the arts, and others. They need to gather information from every possible source of public interest, and they bank some of it for future use in order to feed their medium's appetite for news.

Most broadcast reporters have too little time to indulge in in-depth or investigative reporting, too little specialized knowledge to speculate about the impacts of events. Their time is spent checking available sources, asking as many questions as possible, recording and digesting the answers, and condensing the substance into stories which, most of the time, will consume less than a minute of air time each.

The ability to ask questions that elicit substantive, interesting answers, and the ability to select the parts of those answers that accurately and colorfully reveal the substance of the news, are talents each reporter must develop to survive on the job.

PLANNING INTERVIEWS

Interviews are seldom spontaneous. Reporters plan them, not only to develop news stories but to generate a discussion of important issues in longer interview programs.

When you listen to Sunday afternoon radio newscasts, watch Sunday evening television newscasts, or read Monday morning newspapers, you become aware that such Sunday morning public affairs programs as "This Week with David Brinkley," "Meet the Press," and "Face the Nation" generate substantial news.

Sunday is a slow news day. Since few spontaneous or scheduled events occur, and most public offices are closed, both broadcast news producers and newspaper editors rely on interview programs to stimulate news.

Other news and public affairs programs also rely heavily on interviews, and their producers know that interesting guests interviewed well can attract audiences. "The MacNeil-Lehrer Newshour" on PBS and Ted Koppel's "Nightline" on ABC are examples of programs that rely on interviews to transmit revealing opinions and attitudes about public issues.

Radio and television talk shows, often comprised of loosely structured and sometimes sketchily prepared interviews, continue to grow in popularity. Telephone call-in programs are abundant.

The interview, in its many forms, is a staple for radio and television. Broadcast reporters conduct interviews with varied objectives in mind: (1) they need to collect facts for narrative news stories, (2) they need a variety of faces and voices on the air to help them keep the attention of their audiences, (3) they need to generate interest and provide balance by staging confrontations between people with opposing viewpoints, and (4) they need to explore the spectrum of ideas that make current issues important.

Because interviewing for broadcast is a specialized form, radio and television reporters need to cultivate techniques that work for them.

PREPARATION FOR INTERVIEWS

Two principles stand out whenever experienced interviewers talk about their techniques: they do their homework and they listen.

Political writer Richard Reeves, who has been interviewed many times and who has interviewed many newsmakers for both print and broadcast, says, "As a veteran guest on talk shows, my own impressions of hosts I have known around the country are that one out of four did not have the vaguest idea who I was, two out of four were confused about why I was in the chair next to theirs, and three out of four did not listen to my answers."[1]

It seems obvious to say an interviewer should be prepared, but some broadcasters fail to listen to that advice. They should, because their listeners and viewers are sophisticated and can see through a shallow interview.

A good broadcast interview will seem spontaneous, sometimes even haphazard, but its spontaneity is probably the result of careful planning and patient execution. Conversely, an interview punctuated by amateurish questions, awkward pauses, inept follow-up, and confusing lack of focus is probably the result of inadequate homework.

In some newsrooms, news directors set up morgues of newspaper clippings or subscribe to computer data banks that provide background information. Other newsrooms may have no more than a stack of recent newspapers, a city directory, an almanac, and an encyclopedia. But no matter how quickly they must prepare for interviews, reporters can always ask news directors, assignment editors, other staff members, and even friends, what they know of the newsmakers about to be interviewed and about the substance the newsmakers are expected to discuss. Reporters must prepare as thoroughly as possible or risk surrendering control of their interview to the newsmakers themselves.

Finding Sources

Most newsmakers willingly submit to interviews. They're flattered to be asked to express their opinions on subjects about which they have ready knowledge.

Whereas such sources are not difficult to interview, some people do find it difficult to answer concisely.

Public officials who are experienced interviewees are adept at answering expansively when they talk to newspaper reporters but succinctly when they talk to broadcast reporters. Others, however, believe some issues are so complex that they cannot be explained in a few words. You can encourage these interviewees to elaborate on the issues to you off-camera, but remind them that your medium demands brevity on-camera.

Some newsmakers, especially those who are solicited often for interviews, tend to withdraw from access to reporters. They may have unlisted home phone numbers and receptionists to screen out reporters. You'll need patience and perseverance to get to such sources.

If the sources are prominent, you may find their names and perhaps their telephone numbers in biographical reference books. City directories available in libraries and in some newsrooms list names, addresses, occupations, and sometimes telephone numbers. City or county clerks keep records of all registered voters, and they may be willing to provide addresses and, perhaps, telephone numbers. Schools and churches frequently publish directories that probably include addresses and telephone numbers of the patrons and members. The morgue file of a local newspaper may include someone's telephone number. If the newsmakers are members of a civic club such as Rotary or Kiwanis, the club office will probably have their names and addresses and may be willing to give them to you.

If you know where the newsmaker works, you may be able to talk his or her receptionist or secretary into helping you make contact. Leave your name and telephone number if the newsmaker is unavailable. If he or she doesn't call within a reasonable period of time, call again and tell the receptionist politely that your deadline is approaching and you'd appreciate an opportunity to talk to the person as soon as possible.

Be straightforward. Identify yourself and your station clearly. Let the receptionist know how important the story is and how important the person's knowledge is to your story. Don't be vague or mysterious. If you give receptionists enough information with a sense of urgency, they'll relay the information, and the newsmaker may return your call.

Sometimes you can create a sense of urgency and importance by saying you have information that may be incomplete, or perhaps inaccurate, and you need to talk to the person before a specified time to verify what you have. Few newsmakers want to risk circulation of information that may harm them.

If the newsmakers are out of the office, ask whether they are near a telephone and when they'll be back in the office. Don't be abrasive, but be earnest. Sound important. You can't waste too much time waiting for your newsmaker, so give him or her a motive to want to call you.

Once you've made direct contact with them, they may decline an interview, but don't give up. If the person is important, try again. And each time, try to find an incentive for them to want to be interviewed.

Preparing Your Source

Try to give your source as much advance notice of the interview as possible. State and local government officials are accustomed to radio reporters who call early in the morning or late in the evening. Many of them will give you spur-of-the-moment answers, but few of them like to be rushed.

Your sources deserve time to think about the substance of the interview so they can answer thoughtfully. A broadcast interviewer who conducts a surprise interview risks inept or fumbling answers that may embarrass the source. An offended news-maker may cut that interviewer off from future interviews.

Considerate reporters give their sources the courtesy of telling them the general substance of the interview—usually not the precise questions but a general overview of the ground the reporter intends to cover.

Occasionally, reporters in a hurry might give their sources a sheet of paper listing three or four concise questions. They want their sources to prepare while they (and their photographer) set up the equipment. Such reporters may save time, but they may also risk sacrificing spontaneity and giving control of the interview to the source.

Whenever it's possible, a reporter should tell the source how long the interview will take so that he or she can set aside adequate time. The reporter should also tell the source how much time will be available for the story so that he or she realizes how concise his or her answers must be.

TELEPHONE INTERVIEWING

Radio reporters interview many newsmakers over the telephone. If they have met the newsmakers face to face, or if they have cultivated telephone relationships over a period of time (as they do with sources on their beats), they have probably already established rapport. But sources may be suspicious and hesitant to talk if they don't know the interviewer. Therefore, radio reporters must develop telephone techniques that prove them to be congenial and reliable.

Learn the federal regulations that govern telephone recording. You have three options, all of which are designed to alert the person you are talking to that the conversation is being recorded.

One, you can install a beep-tone device on the line that's electrically activated every 20 seconds to alert the person that you are recording. Most radio stations have eliminated beep tones because they obliterate the words spoken when the beep tones sound.

Two, you may ask the newsmaker's permission to record the conversation *before* you start the interview. You can protect yourself by recording the newsmaker's voice granting permission and saving the taped permission and interview.

The FCC offers you a third choice. If you think you'll waste time or deter spontaneity by asking for permission to record, you can simply *notify* the newsmaker that you *intend* to record the conversation. If you choose this option, the FCC says your notification must be clear and unambiguous, and you *must* state your intent at the beginning of the conversation and record it as part of the entire taped conversation.

You won't break any law or violate any regulation if you record a conversation merely as a way of backing up your written notes and have no intent to and do not use the recorded voice. But since you're a broadcast reporter, it's safer to establish a habit of asking permission before you record any telephone conversation.

Listen for hints that may tell you how busy your sources are. They may be in a hurry and tell you they are on the way out the door. Interview them quickly, and let them go. You'll often have time to write down three or four basic questions. Keep them in front of you, and if your source seems rushed, get immediately to the heart of the interview.

If your sources are too talkative, interrupt them tactfully. Break into the conversation by repeating something they've said, then use it to build a bridge into your next question.

Listen to your sources. Know what they are saying. It's easy to let your attention wander when you're talking on the telephone and taking notes. If you miss a statement that demands explanation or elaboration, your story will be incomplete.

When you finish the interview, check the tape before you hang up the phone. Tell the newsmaker, "Let me make sure I've got you on tape." Roll it back a few inches and play it. If both you and the newsmaker can hear the playback, you'll both be assured that everything is all right.

And just in case you might need more information, ask your sources where you can reach them later. Most newsmakers want to be sure the story is complete and accurate, so they'll willingly talk to you a second time if you are doubtful about some detail.

Some newsmakers will ask you to call and read the story back to them before you air it. Your news director will probably oppose that practice, because many newsmakers attempt to "edit" stories to show themselves or emphasize their points of view more favorably. Usually, newsmakers drop such requests if you simply tell them, "I'm sorry, but my station's policy is to be fair and balanced with our reporting, so we'll use the interview as it stands." Nevertheless, discuss that possibility with your news director to see if there are exceptions. Sometimes, for example, a newsmaker may refuse an interview unless you allow him or her to review the story. If the newsmaker or his or her information is important enough, your news director may permit such a review.

Before you end a telephone interview, be sure to ask your source how to spell his or her name, how to pronounce it, and what his or her title is. Record that information, too, in addition to writing it in your notes.

Telephone interviews are only substitutes for face-to-face interviews. Telephone transmission, no matter how good your receiving equipment, will lose some quality, and poor quality will often distract your listeners from the substance of the interview. The telephone also eliminates the opportunity to get ambient sound—the natural sounds of the environments surrounding news events—that might enhance your stories. Nonetheless, the telephone saves time: it saves travel time; it saves time when you're seeking out a source; and it saves time when your source is in another city.

A reporter who cultivates an effective telephone technique will be an asset to a news department.

FACE-TO-FACE INTERVIEWS

A radio or television reporter who plans to interview a newsmaker face to face must do more than prepare questions. She must also choose a setting. A newsmaker who is unaccustomed to interviews will probably be most comfortable in his own environment—office, home, classroom, shop. Remove an experienced interviewee from a familiar environment, however; you'll have greater control of the interview.

In either case, choose an environment where sounds or scenes enhance the interview. An economist you interview about how inflation affects business may be more comfortable seated at her office desk. A service station operator you question about how inflation affects gasoline sales may be more comfortable beside his gas pumps.

But if you interview the governor about his proposed state budget, try to use the capitol building as a backdrop. If you interview the shop steward of a striking union, position her where you can see and hear pickets in the background.

Ted Koppel of ABC's Nightline *is adept at interviewing on the air. Here he interviews former presidential candidate Gary Hart.*

Your choice of settings will depend on how fluent you think your sources are. If action settings are likely to distract them, you may decide you'll get better interviews in quiet locations. But if you think your sources can concentrate on the questions and answers, action settings will sustain the attention of your listeners and viewers.

Some memorable interviews are moving interviews—a reporter running beside a jogger, a reporter rappelling with a mountain climber, a reporter catching footballs for a quarterback. But choose the setting that will allow the substance and the mood of the interview to dominate.

Experiment with microphone placement, too. Make sure you have the microphone in a position where your listeners can hear both background sounds and the newsmaker's voice clearly. Documentary producers often use one microphone for voices and another for background sounds, or they record interviews and background sounds separately, then mix them in the editing room. But news reporters don't always have time for complex production, so they try to pick up voices and ambient sound with one mike. Some news directors and producers, however, demand that their photographers capture ambient sound and interviewees separately at the scene of every story they cover, then combine the two in the editing room.

Be aware of unexpected sounds—a helicopter flying over, a cart full of dirty dishes rattling by, a backfire from a passing car. If you hear a distracting sound, repeat your question or acknowledge the sound when you hear it. Focus your listeners' and viewers' attention on the substance of the interview again.

Be aware of the subtle sounds of the environment you're in. Some fluorescent lights emit sounds that won't be obvious until you listen to your tape. Air conditioning systems generate pronounced noise. Outdoors, wind may crackle across the surface of your microphone and overwhelm voices. Try to remember to carry a wind screen at all times, but if you forget, improvise. Shield the microphone against the wind or wrap a handkerchief over the head of the microphone to cut down on background noise.

Remember that the quality of sound on location will differ from the quality of sound in the studio, so if you don't record your narration on location, you'll need ambient sound to bridge between location and studio. Some television reporters who must feed stories from the scenes of events record their narration inside closed vehicles where they can eliminate most of the external sounds. Then their production crews mix the ambient sound with the narration through equipment in their mobile units or editing booths.

SOME DO'S AND DON'TS

Concentrate on Your Interviewee

Your viewers will listen to what's being said if they see you listening. The eyes of most people wander when they're talking or asking questions, but they rarely wander and only infrequently blink when the individual is listening to and is interested in what's being said.

Don't Be Afraid of Pauses

If your source has said something significant, give your listener a brief moment to absorb it. If you think your source has not answered adequately, just wait. You may not need to ask another question; chances are good that she'll start talking again if you simply keep looking at her.

Phrase Your Questions Carefully

Ask questions concisely. A wandering question shows uncertainty. The reporter who asked this question was clearly unsure of himself and probably inadequately prepared: "Can you give us an idea of a particular point of law . . . or a particular law . . . Can you give us an idea of a law that is jeopardized by this decision? Specifically? In specific terms?"

Ask One Question at a Time

If you ask more than one question, your sources may remember only the last one, they may deliberately ignore the first one, or they may choose the one they prefer to answer. The reporter who asked these two questions obviously anticipated the answer to the first one: "Mr. Hunt, it's been said that if you'd put two-thousand dollars on margin last year in buying silver, you'd have something like 120-thousand dollars now. Is that so? And if so, should someone buy silver right now?"

Ask Questions Directly, Then Wait for Answers

If your sources don't understand the question, they'll tell you so. The reporter who asked this question was interviewing a town official who had just won a court order to reopen a manufacturing plant: "There have been some other occasions— I can remember vividly the time the judge shut down the plant. There were some pretty somber faces. That happened over a weekend, and the plant was closed on Sunday morning, and I went to church in town, and I saw some pretty somber-looking people there. Are there now going to be lots of smiling faces on Easter Sunday?" After the reporter completed that meandering journey, the town official answered, "This really is Good Friday." The answer, in five words, contained more meaning than the 66-word question.

Ask Questions That Demand More Than a Yes-or-No Answer

The reporter who asked an angry state legislator this series of questions seemed to be interviewing himself:

> *Were you surprised by the vote?*
> "Yes."
>
> *Did you think you had more support?*
> "Yes, I did."
>
> *Will you try to revive the bill?*
> "No."
>
> *Are you angry?*
> "Yes."
>
> *Is there anything you can do?*
> "Nothing."

The reporter struggled for some meaningful answers but didn't get them. He should have asked some "why" questions to force his source to think about what had happened: "Why did the House reject your bill?" "Why can't you ask the House to reconsider your bill?"

Avoid Leading Questions

Reporters are sometimes tempted to phrase answers for inexperienced interviewees, as this reporter did when she helped a consumer recover an overcharge for an appliance repair:

> *Were you upset when you found out how much the repair shop wanted?*
> "Yes, I was upset."
>
> *Did you want to report the incident to the authorities?*
> "Yes, I wanted to report it."
>
> *But you didn't know who to report it to, did you?*
> "No, I didn't know."

But now that you have satisfaction, does it restore your faith in the system?
"Yes, it restores my faith in the system."

Base Your Questions on Fact, Not Fiction

The reporter who asked a striker this series of questions was creating a story out of rumor and speculation:

> *There have been rumors that the company wants to replace your union with another. Have you heard that rumor, and is there any truth to it?*
> "I haven't heard that rumor, but I guess the company doesn't like the union."
>
> *But why would the company want to get rid of your union?*
> "I don't know. I guess we're asking too much."
>
> *During every strike of your union, there has been violence. Do you think there will be violence this time, too?*
> "Yeah, this time it will be worse."
>
> *Why do you say that?*
> "Because each one has been worse than the last one."

The reporter conducted the interview with an uninformed union member who answered the reporter's speculation rather than providing his own thoughts.

Avoid Loaded Questions

A reporter once asked former United Nations ambassador Andrew Young if he agreed that the government of South Africa was illegitimate. Young paused for a moment and seemed uncertain how to answer. He may have thought that if he answered the question "No," his answer might be interpreted to mean that he approved of everything the South African government was doing. Finally, he answered, "Yes," and the news stories that followed carried the lead, "Ambassador Young says the government of South Africa is illegitimate."

Ask about Motives and Objectives

The reporter who asks, "Why is it important to you?" or "What do you hope to accomplish?" forces his source to think more deeply about his or her plans. Motives may reveal something about the character of your source. Objectives may tell your listeners and viewers whether they should approve or disapprove of the proposal.

Introduce Conflicting Points of View

A reporter who has talked to other sources about an issue can bring opposing viewpoints into the conversation that may force interviewees to expand the logic of their own.

A reporter talked to an attorney who accused a judge of unethical conduct in a murder case. The judge had asked the prosecutor what sentence the convicted man should get. Later, the judge changed his mind and privately told the prosecutor to recommend nothing, but the judge didn't report the conversation to the defense attorney. The defense attorney claimed the judge was guilty of unethical conduct and told the reporter, "It would have been helpful in arguing the sentence if the defendant had known the prosecutor wasn't going to recommend the death penalty."

The reporter then responded, "But the judge's defenders say it's common practice for a judge to ask for a recommendation then decide not to use it." The attorney's voice conveyed his anger when he retorted, "Then I think the bar association should look into this case because the Canons of Judicial Ethics say, and I'm quoting, that a judge 'shall neither initiate nor consider ex parte or other communication concerning a pending or impending proceeding except as authorized by law,' and I know of no authorization for the judge to have this kind of contact with the chief prosecutor in the case."

The reporter's knowledge about the issue helped her draw out a forceful, vivid response, and in her lead-in to the presentation, she explained that ex parte means in the interest of one side only.

Sometimes, You Can Agree Not to Ask Certain Questions

People who are difficult to interview are usually those who have something to hide. If you know what those sensitive areas are, you may have to promise to avoid them. If what the source wants to keep silent about is unnecessary for your story, and the source has something else you need, make an agreement that will help your source relax.

Don't Be Afraid to Keep Quiet

When you sense that the mood of the interview is generating empathy among your listeners and viewers, be quiet. A television reporter interviewed a couple who had just been told that their missing son had been found alive. They were talking

Radio newscasters also make extensive use of the on-air interview. One such interviewer is Susan Stamberg of National Public Radio's All Things Considered.

to the reporter when their telephone rang. The father hesitated in mid-sentence, started to talk again, then excused himself and walked off-screen to answer it when the phone rang again. The photographer zoomed in on the face of the mother and turned up the sound so he could hear the father's voice. The reporter kept quiet. The father was talking to a friend who had heard the news and called to say he was pleased. The relief on the mother's face and the elation in the father's voice combined to charge the moment with emotion.

Probe Gently for Emotions

Never ask the brash question, "How do you feel?" when your source has just endured tragedy or pain. One reporter got what she deserved when she stopped a stretcher being wheeled into the emergency room of a hospital and pushed her microphone toward the face of a man who had just survived an avalanche. Asked, "How do you feel?" he answered, "Like hell. I've got a broken leg, and if you don't mind, I'd like to see a doctor."

Try to elevate such interviews beyond the commonplace. A reporter assigned to interview the family of a man who was missing in a coal-mine fire got some excellent reactions when she told family members, "I won't ask questions, but if you have something you want to say, the camera is rolling." Other reporters have generated successful interviews from suffering family members with such questions as "Where were you when you got the news?" "How did you pass the time while you were waiting for word?" "When did you see him last?"

Remember That You Control the Pace

Most interviewees unconsciously imitate your actions and attitudes. If you ask a question at a rapid pace, your source is likely to answer at a rapid pace. If you visibly relax and ask a leisurely question, your source is likely to relax and give a leisurely answer. An interviewer who lingers over his notes will soon find that his source is straining to see those notes, too.

Don't Tell Your Source When the Interview Will Air

If your sources ask when the story will air, simply tell them you're not sure; the producer will make that decision. You can't be certain what your producer will do, and you'll have to apologize to your source if the interview doesn't appear as promised.

PERFORMING INTERVIEWS

Reporters and photographers have special problems with television interviews. For instance, interviewees frequently react awkwardly to hand-held mikes. They may recoil when you thrust mikes toward them, or they may lean toward them or reach to take them from you. If you use a hand-held mike, position yourself close to the interviewee so you won't have to move the mike too much, or find a position for the mike between you and your interviewee where it will pick up both voices clearly. (*Note:* Two clip mikes or two lavalieres are better than one hand-held mike.)

If you intend to edit the interview, position the mike where it will pick up your interviewee's voice, then edit out your questions. In most cases, television reporters first place the camera behind one of their shoulders, recording the newsmaker almost head-on. Then, when the interview is completed, the photographer positions the camera behind the interviewee's shoulder and shoots the reporters head-on so they can repeat key questions to be edited in later.

Remember to position your sources where the camera can see both of their eyes. Eyes are important. They reveal how newsmakers react to questions and what their emotions are as they answer. If a newsmaker wears glasses, place the camera in a position where the rims or the shadows from rims will not hide his or her eyes. If the newsmaker is outdoors and wearing a hat, suggest that he or she tilt the hat back slightly so it won't shade his or her eyes. When the lighting is good, help your photographer by positioning yourself where your source can look at you directly without straining his or her neck.

The vertical position of the camera is important, too. If the camera lens is looking down on the interviewee's eyes, he or she may look afraid of or inferior to the interviewer. If the camera lens is looking up at the interviewee's eyes, he or she may look domineering. Be sure the tripod is adjusted to place the lens near eye level.

Record the interview in a place that shows the scale of the scene, if scale is important.

- If you're interviewing a seismologist about an earthquake and have decided to shoot the interview near an earth fissure, place the camera where it can capture the size of the fissure in relationship to the height of you and the seismologist.
- If you're interviewing a fire chief about a fire that has gutted a bowling alley, position at least part of the interview near a doorway at the end of the building opposite the camera so you can show your viewers the cavernous size of the building.
- If you're interviewing a sculptor about his newest sculpture, place the sculptor alongside his art work so your viewers can picture its size.

During the course of the interview, avoid movements or gestures that may detract from the newsmaker. Any movement of your head—toward your notes, toward something or someone who moved off-camera, toward something above the newsmaker's head—will divert your viewers' attention and puzzle them about what you're seeing.

Be aware of your posture, too. If you tilt your head away from newsmakers, you may give your viewers the impression that you're skeptical about what they're saying. If you lean back in a chair, you may give your viewers the impression that you're bored. If you sit too straight and stiffly, you may be saying visually to your viewers that you're afraid. If your body position is too static, you may be telling your viewers you're thinking about something else. If you move your head or your shoulders too abruptly, you may give your viewers the impression that you're seeing something they can't see.

Sit or stand so that your body doesn't appear to tilt to one side or the other. If you're sitting, lean slightly foward, and you'll give your viewers a picture of someone who is interested in what is being said. Keep your legs close together, or cross one all the way over the other. Some men tend to cross one leg over the other so that their ankles or shins rest on the opposite knees, but such broad postures call attention to themselves. Adjust your position occasionally, but not too abruptly. Relax your head. Let it move a little. Gesture when you get the impulse, but keep your gestures at chest level, where they're in view of the camera lens. Look at your sources when they're talking. If your eyes suggest that you're listening, your viewers will listen more intently.

At times, you may interview sources who do not want to be identified. If they fear retribution, or have some other valid reason to avoid identification, you can electronically alter their voice or picture them in silhouette or at long range. But your photographer may need you on camera in close-up, too, so that your viewers can see your reactions. They'll sense the significance of what your source says through your eye movements, facial expressions, gestures, and body movements.

Your viewers will react subconsciously in the ways you react, so be aware of the physical messages you deliver to them. Plan your actions to be subtle, because television is an intimate medium, and even small movements will be clear.

Give your interviewees the status they merit in the way you address them. In most cases, avoid calling newsmakers by their first names. You might give your viewers or listeners the impression that you're a close friend who agrees with what the newsmaker says, or you'll give the impression that you consider yourself as much an expert as your source. Instead, when you use their names, address them with courtesy titles and last names—Mr. Smith, Senator Jones, Dr. Brown, Ms. or Mrs. Green. But remember, you'll look foolish if you call a child "Miss Black" or a prison inmate "Mr. Blue."

At the same time, however, you'll seem to be more likeable, and your sources will seem more natural, if you ask them to address you by your first name.

INTERVIEWING STYLE

You'll have to experiment with your interviewing style. Not every reporter can assume the role of a prosecutor, like Mike Wallace, boring in to break down a witness's testimony. "I'm not ashamed of 'confrontation journalism.' If you ask tough questions—and it's for light's sake, and not merely for heat—as far as I'm concerned that's a perfectly sensible way to go about doing our job."[2] But Wallace can also be a gentle interviewer, depending on his target and on the substance he expects to get from an interview.

Barbara Walters has acquired the reputation of being a caustic interviewer. She says she doesn't like that description, but she does say nevertheless, "I have a strong personality. I'm abrasive, aggressive, and ambitious."[3] Her technique of revealing her personal attitudes, then waiting for her source to react to them, stands out in her interviews. She challenges her sources when she suspects they're evading her questions or trying to mislead her, but she smiles and exudes a friendly attitude.

Robert MacNeil and Jim Lehrer handle their subjects gently, for the most part. Reporters have dubbed on-camera confrontation interviews "red meat" journalism, but MacNeil dislikes the term and the approach it symbolizes. He says, " 'Civility' I think is the word—and a very pale word, I'm afraid, in comparison with 'red meat,' but it's a word that I'm not ashamed of."[4]

Lehrer says, "We don't bring people on here to embarrass them or to abuse them. We bring them on because they have some information that fits into our story. . . . What I do not like, and what offends me, is when journalists use strong-arm tactics on people who cannot defend themselves, who do not have the polish and the practice, and all of that."[5]

Choose an interviewing style that is most effective for you, and adapt it to fit your guest and your topic. Learn from expert interviewers, but don't try to imitate them. Study their techniques and experiment with them to see what works for you. Above all, let your own personality emerge in your interviewing style. If you don't, you may seem insincere to your listeners and viewers.

The Newsmaker's Performance

Interviewers should consider the experience of their sources. Interviewing a butcher about the spiraling cost of beef demands a different attitude than interviewing a political candidate who is waffling on important issues. Faced with a camera, a microphone, and a scowling reporter, the butcher may be frightened, afraid to say the wrong things but also afraid not to say anything. The politician may be smiling and confident, certain, perhaps, that he can control the interview.

When meeting either source, begin pleasantly, for although they may suspect your motives or they may be hostile, you can help them relax. Tell them what you expect to cover in the interview. Let them know what to expect from the camera crew. Make small talk.

If you're interviewing them in a studio, help them become accustomed to the setting. Tell them to ignore the cameras and microphones; the technical people will worry about them. Tell them there will be movement and quiet conversation behind the cameras; the crew must communicate to make sure pictures and sound are good. Tell them to talk to you conversationally and not to worry about the audience; viewers are merely eavesdropping on the conversation. Tell them to gesture if they feel like it. Remind them that radio and television are intimate media from which listeners and viewers expect a feeling of informality, or at least an attitude of thoughtfulness.

Some newsmakers, particularly politicians, want to establish eye contact with viewers; they believe they appear to be more direct and sincere when they look at the camera lens. Tell them they can establish such contact if they do so casually instead of abruptly. They can begin an answer looking at you, then let their eyes drift to the camera lens, as if the movement were unplanned.

Once your interview is underway, your source's answers and reactions should help you decide how soft or how hard your questions should be. Watch the interviewee; see what her face and body movements tell you about her emotional attitudes. Watch gestures, postures, facial expressions, and eye movements, and listen to the quality of voices. You'll learn a lot about people.

The best interviewers are those who prepare by writing down their questions and organizing them into logical sequences. Then, they put them aside before the interview begins. If you can free yourself from your notes, you'll be free to watch and listen and control the flow of the interview. The poorest interviews are those during which interviewers spend most of their time wording questions in their minds rather than listening and reacting and following up with questions they hadn't planned.

If you need your notes, keep them in hand, but use them as a prop rather than a crutch. Refer to them when you need to refresh your memory and only when your interviewee seems to be reaching the end of an answer.

NEWS CONFERENCES

News conferences are cumbersome news-gathering tools, but radio and television reporters will be assigned to them often. Adept newsmakers can take control of their news conferences, refusing to relinquish control to reporters. They know what they want to say and usually prepare well. Even when reporters ask hostile questions, they can turn the questions aside and give the answers they prefer. Reporters infrequently get opportunities to ask follow-up questions to keep newsmakers on course.

The more reporters there are present, the more diverse the questioning will be, too. All reporters seem to come to news conferences with their own agendas, and they clamor to be recognized. The sequence of questions is jumbled. Some reporters preface their questions with rambling explanations. Some shout and wave to be recognized. At times, news conferences seem to be chaotic.

Nevertheless, they are useful. They provide convenient formats to allow news-makers to reach many reporters at the same time. And they provide listeners and viewers with opportunities to see how newsmakers react under pressure.

At times, reporters have discussed lines of questioning with each other in advance of news conferences, attempting to focus on narrower areas. But reporters are competitive—they don't like to appear to their listeners and viewers to be colluding on stories—so they most often go to news conferences determined to develop their own stories.

Sometimes, reporters work out agreements with newsmakers so they can ask follow-up questions. That allows them to press for more specific information, but it still prohibits incisive questioning if too many reporters attend.

Small news conferences tend to be more organized and to generate more substance on a narrower range of issues.

Whether the news conference is large or small, call the newsmaker's news secretary or public relations representative or adviser in advance to learn what you can about the subject to be discussed. You can then plan questions and strategies to help you get the story despite the confusion of the setting.

And listen. Avoid the distractions created by other reporters and listen intently for the focus of the story and the nuances that make it vivid. The reporter who learns to hear as much as possible and to organize its essence effectively is the reporter who will produce a story that carries meaning to her listeners and viewers.

Some reporters successfully approach newsmakers after their news conferences end to ask additional questions. At times, they elicit information that the corps of reporters missed. But unless you have a special relationship with the newsmaker, or you happen to be lucky, the technique may fail. Make sure you have sound and pictures from the news conference itself so you don't go back to the newsroom without a story.

You'd be wrong to pass up a news conference simply because all of your competitors will get the same information. After all, other reporters may ask important questions that didn't occur to you.

PANEL INTERVIEWS

Panel interviews are more common than news conferences. "Face the Nation" and "Meet the Press" are staples on networks, and many local stations create similar programs. They rarely draw large audiences, but they are valuable sources of information for listeners and viewers who are interested in public issues.

Usually, two or more reporters question a public official on issues of current concern. One of the reporters acts as a moderator to introduce guests and interviewers, to keep the questioning on target, to keep the pace of the program moving, to watch for time cues, and to close the program. Additionally, the moderator often asks many of the questions.

Another kind of panel interview features one interviewer, who is also the moderator, and two or more guests. This kind of format is useful in exposing varied points of view on controversial issues. The conflict that grows from opposing viewpoints can generate interesting and enlightening radio and television.

Sometimes, producers of such programs also invite telephoned questions from listeners and viewers, but they assign an associate producer to screen the questions. The associate producer tries to choose the best questions while screening prank calls and problem callers. The producer will usually create a "delay" on the telephone line—a five- to eight-second tape loop that allows the associate producer time to listen to the caller before his voice reaches the air. If the caller says something offensive, the associate producer can break the connection before the offending words reach listeners or viewers.

Panel interviews are inexpensive productions, but they often produce news. Program directors often schedule them on days and at times when the news flow is expected to be light. These panel interviews demand thorough preparation, however, because they are difficult to control. Reporters plan lines of questioning before they face the newsmakers they interview, but they may run out of time before they get satisfactory answers. A group of guests can easily stray from the subject unless the moderator is prepared and adept enough to keep them focused on the announced subject.

THE ESSENCE OF BROADCAST INTERVIEWING

Broadcast interviewers can be as dogged as circumstances allow; they should be persistent, but not combative. Whether they're conducting quick interviews for news programs or extended interviews for live programs, they must be alert. They must listen, and they must watch.

On radio, faltering voices, unusual pauses, erratic vocal rhythms, and unexpected enunciation flaws all reveal something about newsmakers.

On television, wandering eyes, quavering facial muscles, nervous fingers, and shifting body postures all reveal something about newsmakers.

Interviewers, listeners, and viewers alike form their perceptions about the truthfulness and expertise of newsmakers from what they hear and see.

Broadcast interviewers need to be alert to both substance and reactions. Their sources' emotional moods and the quality of their answers help interviewers decide how to pursue their questioning. The pictures and sounds of television and radio give dimensions to interviews that print journalists can never hope to achieve. But broadcast interviewers should always keep their viewers and listeners in mind. They need to ask the questions their audiences would ask if they could. They also need to ask questions their audiences may not have thought about in order to reveal information and opinions those listeners and viewers will need to help them make intelligent judgments.

Exercises

1. Develop an idea for a story. Decide what newsmaker would most likely provide useful information for your story. Then develop and organize at least 15 questions you would ask that newsmaker to get the information you need.

2. Think of a business executive, a public official, and a sports figure in your community. Write five questions you would ask each one to elicit information or anecdotes that would reveal their personalities.

3. What is a current controversy in your community? Who are the sources who best represent the major points of view? Prepare questions for at least two of them and interview them by phone. If you have recording facilities available, record your interviews and decide what you would excerpt from them for a radio news story. If you have no recording facilities, take careful notes and decide which direct quotations would have made good sound bites.

4. Choose a newsmaker who is getting current attention for a plan, concept, or project he or she is proposing. Make an appointment for a face-to-face interview

and record the interview on audio tape. Decide what you would excerpt from the tape for use in a broadcast news story.

5. Record an interview with a newsmaker on videotape. Focus the camera on the newsmaker first and tape his or her answers to your questions. Then reverse the position of the camera and focus it on you. Repeat your key questions and tape them. Decide what you would excerpt for use in a story.

Notes

1. Richard Reeves, "I Used to Be Dick Reeves," *TV Guide* (4 October 1975): 18.
2. Christopher Swan, "Mike Wallace: Master of the Tough Question," *Christian Science Monitor* (11 April 1979): B2.
3. Diane K. Shah, "A Million Can't Quell Barbara's Fear That She'll Fail," *The National Observer* (2 October 1976): 16.
4. Swan, B14.
5. Swan, B14.

If investigators found no evidence of murder, how did the prominent person die? Who found him? Was anyone with him when he died? When were police called? Who called them? Why did the caller ask for police officers rather than an ambulance? How long had he been dead? Was he under a doctor's care? Did he have any history of illness? What was his mood when anyone last saw him alive? Had he missed any days of work or any of his habitual activities? Had he complained about any discomfort?

You can think of even more questions. And the answers you get may suggest new questions.

But don't leave the scene without more than answers from officials or family members. Look around. Can you describe the prominent elements of the scene? Is anything distinctive or unusual? Are there any sounds that may contribute to the atmosphere of the scene? What is the environment like?

Think about all of the elements you've learned from sources at the scene and details you've collected through observation. Fit them together into a logical narrative that draws your listeners and viewers onto the scene. If you're confused, talk to your news director, your producer, your photographer, your editor. Have they encountered similar events? How did they handle them?

Give yourself enough time to let the story ferment in your mind. In whatever time you have available, try to fit the story together and fill in the blank spaces. Be sure you're comfortable with and confident in the material you're about to give to your audience. The more mental exercise you demand of yourself in each kind of story you cover, the more confidence you'll have when you pick up the microphone or face the camera to tell a story that demands almost instantaneous reporting.

A Chicago radio reporter ad libbed the following story. We don't need to identify him, but his reporting is too typical of reporters who forget to look for detail, allowing their emotions to dominate. The station put the reporter on the air as soon as he arrived at the scene of an elevated-train accident:

```
    This is a terrible, terrible sight. We don't know
if we're about to describe to you the scene of a
terrible, terrible human tragedy or a miraculous
escape. We just don't know.
    You know the intersection at Lake and Wabash. If
you can imagine the whole intersection filled with
cars from an El train, you'll have an idea of what it
looks like.
    It's a terrible, terrible situation. People could
very easily be trapped in there. It might have fallen
on some who were in the street. We don't know if
anybody got out. It's a terrible, terrible sight --
that's all I can tell you. It must have happened very
quickly.
```

The reporter provided no useful information. He merely talked and, in the process, may have inflamed the emotions of many of his listeners. The emotional quality of the reporter's voice is evident in his choice of words, particularly the repetition of "terrible, terrible."

Contrast that story with Emery King's first report of a Chicago Transit Authority El train crash reported to WBBM Radio. King had no time to ask questions either, but he looked for details that would show his listeners the scene:

> I can see five cars that are derailed. The rest of that train is still up on the tracks. A sixth car still looks like it's derailed up on the track, although it doesn't look like there's too much of a problem there.
>
> As for the other cars that are dangling from the tracks down on Wabash and Lake streets, two of them are just lying flat over on the street like a dead bus.
>
> Firemen now are trying to drill through the top, and some are trying to get through the bottom of those cars, to get inside, to get the people who are trapped inside out.
>
> Ambulances are still coming to the scene. They're trying to clear a pathway for these ambulances to come up Wabash Street, so if you're driving, by all means, please avoid this area because you'll only be hampering those who are trying to save victims from this terrible disaster.
>
> There is one car, particularly, that is up on the tracks, that is dangling precariously from the El tracks down to Wabash Street. Inside I can see the heads of some people, and those heads are moving. So, apparently, if those people are hurt, efforts are being made to get them out. A hook and ladder truck has sent a ladder up to that particular car, and firemen are climbing up that' ladder trying to get inside that car to get those victims out.
>
> You can probably hear in the background firemen and policemen shouting out orders for the spectators who are down here, as well as other people, to clear the scene and get away so all of the ambulances can come down here.[2]

Emery King might have *written* a better story, or, if he had been given time to organize his thoughts, he might have ad libbed a better story, but he had no time.

He was on the air, and he had to verbally draw an instant picture for his listeners to see.

He focused first on the center of the picture, described the scene, then detailed elements and actions within it. He added pieces of atmosphere to help his listeners visualize the story, and he pointed up background sounds to explain what they meant.

Reporter Scott Simon reported the same event to "All Things Considered" on National Public Radio the following day. He had almost 24 hours to gather information and write and produce the story, including actualities (the voices of the newsmakers themselves). He, too, remembered to collect the details that would create pictures for his listeners:

> <u>Simon</u>: It was snowing at Chicago's rush hour home
> last night, and elevated tracks all over the city
> were reported slippery. But on the curve of Lake
> and Wabash streets, one elevated train wasn't able
> to take that corner and turned into another train
> ahead. The cars hurtled off the tracks. Three hung
> from the train platform into the streets, another
> plunged one story down to the sidewalks below, on
> top of people making their way home for the
> weekend.
> <u>Reporter's voice</u>: Can you describe what happened?
> <u>Woman's voice</u>: Well, it happened so fast -- really,
> I -- really, I just heard a bump, and then I
> realized that we was goin' down on the ground, and
> it was dark, and all the glass was broken and
> everyone was screamin' and everything, and I was
> bleedin' everywhere. It was just a nightmare.
> <u>Simon</u>: There were about 300 people suddenly trapped,
> injured or dead inside of and beneath those train
> cars. Those walking out of Loop office buildings
> away from the scene heard a high chilled shriek of
> horns and sirens on emergency vehicles ripping
> past, saw the light several blocks off of police
> globes and arc lamps, heard helicopters overhead
> come close in to hover at the site.
> Stores closing were kept open to care for the
> injured thrown startled from the train into the
> streets.
> Blow torches were suddenly produced from fire
> stations and street crews to cut those trapped out
> from inside of the train cars.
> By the time we came to the scene, the train cars

looked like toys laying out on the floor that a
child had forgotten to put away, except for the
blood, of course, and the artifacts there strewn
around with no apparent sense -- school notebooks,
shopping bags, glasses and single shoes.

Woman's voice: First thing I seen was -- I looked
up, and I saw one guy fall to the ground from --
aah -- one of the windows of the train.

Simon: The mayor of the city came to the scene and
declared a triage -- a city-wide disaster plan that
hadn't been used for years.

Ten hospitals turned their emergency services
over to the care of the injured and dying. We went
to Northwestern Hospital, about six blocks from the
scene, where a downstairs reception area had become
an operating amphitheater, the operating teams
moving quickly between facial cuts from shattered
glass to truncations, wounds, abrasions and
shattered limbs.

"How many are here?" a reporter asked a nurse,
who replied, "I don't know. They're coming in so
quickly we can't count them."

The chief surgeon was asked if this was as bad
as anything he'd ever seen, and he said that it was
a lot like Vietnam, as he remembered it -- nearly
70 trauma cases brought in last night in under an
hour.

Six people died there, too, and their bodies
awaited delivery to the morgue in a pink-tiled room
off of the operating room, perfect white sheets
drawn stiffly from foot to forehead, green paper
tags tied to their toes.

Those patients dismissed were interviewed, first
by doctors and policemen, then, if they chose to
and if they could be found, by reporters.

The air in the corridor stifled quickly in the
press of bodies and the heat of television lights.

Woman's voice: Well, you know, everybody was crying
-- you know, just things like that -- shouting and
crying -- I mean, you know.

Reporter's voice: Oh, all of the dead have been
taken to the morgue, huh? All the dead have been
taken to the morgue?

Another reporter's voice: But you don't know how

many? Someone told me five. We're trying to confirm
it and also get the names and the addresses.

<u>Man's voice</u>: I was just, you know, lookin' out the
window, then the next thing I knew, I was just
holding on for my life.

<u>Reporter's voice</u>: Do you remember falling?

<u>Man's voice</u>: Yes.

<u>Reporter's voice</u>: Do you remember the actual fall?

<u>Man's voice</u>: Yes. It was like in slow motion. I was
holding on, then the next thing I knew, my feet
were on the glass, and I heard the shattering of
glass.

<u>Reporter's voice</u>: What were you thinking as it
happened?

<u>Man's voice</u>: All kinds of things rushed through my
head.

<u>Reporter's voice</u>: Like what? Give us one.

<u>Man's voice</u>: O.K. My life was passing in front of
me.

<u>Simon</u>: Novelist Kurt Vonnegut once wrote about his
days as a reporter in Chicago and remembered
covering the crash of a department store elevator.
He said that's where he began to learn that there's
nothing sensible to be said by anybody about a
disaster.

People who live in very big cities can grow
close to thinking that such things as sidewalks,
elevated structures and subway cars are native to
this planet, that they grow somehow, that the world
to them, no matter how they sometimes complain, is
something to be controlled and affected for our
comfort. And that was what was so unusual about
last night, really -- not an earthquake or a
tornado, but some other disaster to be dismissed as
the work of a higher mind.

But the indistinguishable and routine El car
that bears millions of people daily down to work
and then back home again -- something common among
us and very much of what we've made ourselves.[3]

Scott Simon's details—such elements as "school notebooks, shopping bags,
glasses and single shoes" and "green paper tags tied to their toes"—create vivid
pictures, and they're the kinds of details trained observers remember.

Some broadcast reporters complain that they have too little time to include all of the needed facts and add atmosphere, too. "All Things Considered" gave Scott Simon more than four minutes to tell his story, but most radio stories run barely more than 30 seconds.

Look at what ABC's Tony Sargent accomplished in less than 30 seconds, however. The newscaster's lead-in to the story said former Pennsylvania Congressman Daniel Flood had pleaded guilty to a conspiracy charge, then Tony Sargent picked up the story:

> ```
> Flood always was a showman up on Capitol Hill, using
> a loud, dramatic voice and suitably theatrical
> gestures in most of his speeches to the House of
> Representatives. Most other congressmen looked
> forward to most of it -- it helped them stay awake
> after lunches. But the Flood that was in court, well,
> he was none of that -- just a quiet little man in a
> waxed mustache, admitting he took money from people
> who thought he could help them do business with the
> government.⁴
> ```

The portrait is clear—a congressman who once was dapper and flamboyant contrasted with a man who is aging and repentant. The story is memorable because small details bring it to life.

CONCEIVING THE NEWS

Reporters should begin their stories with some notion of where they're going and what they hope to achieve. On breaking stories, they may not have much time to plan, but if they have been reading local and regional newspapers and news and opinion magazines, they'll probably know where to begin.

You can't walk into a public office and ask, "What's new?" and expect the news to start flowing. Ask that question of almost anyone, and you'll probably get the answer, "Not much" or "Nothing." You must go into a public office with some specific idea in mind.

Perhaps you've read that the tax assessor has been reappraising all of the property in your town—residential, commercial, industrial—and will use the new valuation figures to compute next year's taxes. If you've thought about the issue, you know that taxes will be higher. Unless, by some fluke, the city is providing fewer services and paying less for them, taxes will rise.

Knowing that, you can begin to formulate your story. How much are property valuations going to rise? What will the new higher valuations mean to average homeowners in terms of higher taxes? Has the value of residential property risen more rapidly than the value of commercial and industrial property? Why?

When you formulate such questions, you assume that taxpayers will face the worst—a tax increase. But the information you collect may not verify your assumptions. If not, readjust your approach. If valuations will not increase and taxes will not rise, you have an even better story, because that doesn't happen often.

Just don't lock yourself into trying to prove your assumptions. Keep an open mind, and be flexible.

If you've been assigned to business news, you may have heard that the electric utility located in your community is the target of merger proposals from two big utility companies in other states. You call the public relations officer of the local utility and ask what information she can provide. She says the company's board of directors are talking about two merger proposals they've received, but she won't say whether they're taking the proposals seriously.

You call a local broker who's an expert on utilities; he tells you he expects action soon, but he doesn't know whether the local utility will accept or reject the proposals or which proposal board members favor most. He says the rumors of acquisition have driven the stock prices of the local utility up about two dollars a share.

You know you're onto a story, so you begin to ask yourself questions. How will any merger affect consumer rates? Is one of the out-of-state companies healthier than the other? Does either want the local company because it needs more power for its own customers? Does either have surplus power that could benefit consumers in your region? Does the state public utilities commission have to approve any merger?

One of the state's public utilities commissioners probably has the answers to your questions or can lead you to the answers, so you visit him and ask. Because you pursued the vague suggestion that something might be stirring among utilities and asked some meaningful questions, you'll complete the day with a story that will interest your listeners or viewers, despite the local utility's refusal to provide any more than sketchy information.

Supplement your ability to question and your memory by keeping a file of the stories that you've aired. You may be able to use that information to put related stories into perspective for your audience.

For example, the mayor may have included in his announcement to run for reelection a statement that he intends to install bicycle paths on some of the main traffic routes into the business district. From your memory file, you might recall a similar promise made four years ago. From your story file, you confirm it; the mayor *did* promise bicycle paths when he first ran for office. You check with the city streets department and discover that no bicycle paths have been designated, and you ask the mayor to explain his failure to fulfill his four-year-old campaign promise. Now, your story will give your listeners or viewers a clearer perspective of the mayor's current campaign promise.

Your ability to look, listen, read, and remember could make the difference between ordinary and distinguished stories.

THE NEWS IN ACTION

Television news directors and assignment editors once asked their reporters and photographers a question about proposed stories: Does it move? The question was meant to be only slightly frivolous.

Movement in television pictures is an important criterion. Television thrives on action; movement and change in pictures sustain the interest of viewers. Action draws viewers to live sports (particularly football) telecasts. Action draws viewers to entertainment programs, particularly crime shows. Action within television commercials attracts viewers to the products they advertise.

In television news, utilize either the action inherent in an event or the camera to create action—if the action of the camera isn't too abrupt or too broad. Slow zooms and slow pans are sometimes effective, if you don't overuse them. Short shots of static scenes, when the photographer keeps changing angles or perspectives, can also be effective. But action within the scene is more natural.

The action can be broad, as it is in a football game, or it can be subtle, as it is when people are conversing. But remember that television is an intimate medium, and subtle actions in close-up can be just as vivid as broad actions in wide shots. You'll often see close-ups of nervous hands when newsmakers are talking; they reveal emotional states. An experienced photographer can make a spider web look alive if light reflects from its strands as a breeze sets it to shimmering.

Alert photographers and reporters can sometimes find pictures that communicate what words cannot adequately illustrate. They must train themselves to look for pictures that deliver information, then they'll need fewer words to tell their stories.

But choose pictures that clarify rather than ones that distort. A picture of a legislator sleeping through a debate, or a picture of a legislator reading a newspaper during a debate, may be interesting and off-beat, but such shots will probably mislead viewers about the significance of the issues the legislators are discussing.

If no action within the legislative chamber accurately helps explain a debate over a proposed gasoline tax increase, you may be able to supplement short sound pieces with pictures of traffic and gasoline pumps in action.

If you have nothing more to illustrate a water board's discussion about restricting water use during a drought period than shots of board members sitting around a table, you could make the story more meaningful by including pictures of parched lawns and gardens, low-level storage reservoirs, and dried-up stream beds. Look for pictures that convey facts visually.

NATURAL SOUND

Broadcast reporters have become creative in their use of sound to convey news. Some radio and television reporters use the natural sounds from the scenes of events to enhance most of their stories. They also frequently deliver eyewitness accounts from the scenes of breaking events to give a sense of urgency and importance to their stories. Whereas interviews with knowledgeable sources may still be the heart of the reporting process, broadcast reporters are incorporating sound to bring their listeners and viewers into scenes with them.

The sound of angry residents protesting a school board's decision to close a local high school conveys a vivid sense of the school patrons' emotions, and that sound, as a backdrop to the reporter's narrative explanation, gives the audience a closer kinship to the event. The exultant sound of a channel swimmer's voice shouting, "Sixty miles! I made it!"—mixed with the cheers of onlookers—transmits listeners and viewers vicariously onto the scene.

Sound exists at the scene of almost every story, and broadcast equipment is sensitive and portable enough to record it. Broadcast reporters who are conscious of the sounds around them can use those sounds to reinforce the moods of their stories.

UNDERSTANDING THROUGH EMPATHY

Radio and television audiences absorb more from the sights and sounds of events than they do from words. We absorb best through our senses. We feel the anger, sorrow, fear, and joy of people through what we hear and see. We experience, to an extent, what they experience. Only after we hear and see the event, and talk about it, do we begin to think extensively about it. Much of the information we receive from radio and television is filtered through our emotions. So, broadcast reporters utilize emotion productively.

But that emotion must be inherent in the event; reporters cannot inject it artificially. They can exploit it only when it appears naturally. Broadcast listeners and viewers are perceptive; they can sense deception. And if reporters try to force emotion upon them, they'll resist it or be repelled.

An effective broadcast reporter is sensitive to emotion and transmits just enough of it to stimulate empathic responses from listeners and viewers. Knowing what is enough is a subtle art, one that can be learned but not taught. Five seconds of an anguished cry from a distraught relative of a dead victim of a fire may be enough to convey the feeling of the moment, but seven seconds may be too much for listeners and viewers to tolerate. You can sense the limit only when you listen to and watch the scene. If you cross the threshold of tolerance, your audience will think you are sensationalizing the event.

You can learn to use the emotional content in news if you allow yourself to feel. If you cover the drowning of a child and refuse to feel the anguish of the child's parents, you'll probably fail to transmit the impact of the story. If you cover the rescue of a kidnap victim and insulate yourself from the joy of the victim's relatives, your story will probably lack a feeling for what has happened. Open your senses and allow them to be stimulated and sharpened, then stand back and try to analyze the event rationally.

If you can feel the urgency, the excitement, the pathos, the humor, the sadness, the pain, you can probably transfer that feeling to your listeners and viewers. And the stories that evoke their empathy will be the stories they remember and talk about.

Emotion is abundant in most events that broadcasters cover live. Viewers who watched the shadowy form of Neil Armstrong step down onto the surface of the moon in 1969 felt fear and uncertainty, then exhilaration and relief as he and Buzz Aldrin hopped over the moon's surface as if they were riding slow-motion pogo sticks.

Associated Press Radio correspondent Bob Moon remembers what the explosion of the space shuttle *Challenger* was like for him as a reporter assigned to broadcast that story live on January 28, 1986. He compared it to the memorable broadcast of the similar Hindenburg air disaster of 1937:

> . . . How would I react to a disaster, if it flashed before my eyes during a live broadcast? Would I freeze on the air? Would my mind be able to assemble intelligible thoughts? Would I remain composed?
>
> I never dreamed I would be confronted with such a gut-wrenching task. But the Hindenburg of the Space Age occurred on Jan. 28, 1986. And my colleague Dick Uliano and I watched it unfolding before our eyes, while we were on the air live.
>
> What went through my mind at that instant? It was at once fascinating and horrifying. Things began to move in slow motion. After covering so many successful launches, there was stunned disbelief at first—and a hesitation to actually sound the alarm.
>
> For a broadcaster, that pause seemed to last an eternity. Thankfully, the air check tape shows it was just five seconds. NASA Commentator Steve Nesbitt was still reporting flight data when I interrupted his irrelevant words, blurting out the first thing that came to my mind:
>
> *"Something went wrong here! We've got a problem with, uh, what looks like a second plume of smoke!"*
>
> Uliano was right on my heels, and his homework paid off: *"We do have a problem, Bob. It looks as if one of the solid—it may have lost a solid rocket booster! It's hard to tell."*
>
> By now, only 18 seconds had passed since the air-to-ground radio crackled at the instant of the blast. It was a time to choose our words carefully. Still, the mind wanted to believe that Challenger would somehow emerge attached to one of those pinpoints of flame.
>
> *"There are two separate plumes of smoke, and the shuttle—we can't tell which one the shuttle is now. They've separated."*
>
> Uliano filled in quickly with more astute analysis: *"We should not have had solid rocket booster separation for two-and-a-half minutes after it leaves the pad, and at about a minute-and-a-half . . ."*
>
> The thought was interrupted by commentator Nesbitt, finally noting the disaster after an agonizing 30 seconds of NASA silence: *"Flight controllers here looking very carefully at the situation. Obviously, a major malfunction."*
>
> *"The view from the ground is obscured by this pillar of steam now,"* I explained.
>
> *"We have no downlink now,"* Mission Control reported.

With an eerie, hollow-sounding whine ringing in our ears from NASA's PA system, it was beginning to sink in. Said Uliano, *"Something's gone terribly wrong."*

A lot of us had grown complacent about shuttle launches, but I (along with others in the newsroom) had argued that, despite outward appearances, the technology was still new and the flights were still risky—not routine. We had continued to cover the launches live, even though we knew many stations had stopped clearing the programs. Now it occurred to me that my concerns had, unfortunately, been warranted. Stations which had chosen not to carry the coverage would be hopping on our line.

"If you're just joining us, the space shuttle Challenger has just lifted off the pad, and we've had a problem here—a major problem. We're getting no telemetry— no data back from the shuttle—according to what we're hearing from Mission Control. It appeared that something separated. There may have been an explosion."

Uliano added: *"Bob, we see the long plume of smoke twisted up into the sky and then strings of smoke hanging down below."*

The NASA commentator broke in with the official confirmation: *"We have a report from the Flight Dynamics Officer that the vehicle has exploded. Flight Director confirms that. We are looking at . . . checking with the recovery forces to see what can be done at this point."*

I took a deep breath. It seemed my voice involuntarily dropped three octaves. *"It, uh, would appear that the space shuttle Challenger has EXPLODED, about . . . perhaps a minute . . . a minute-and-a-half into the launch."*

There wasn't much to add. *"There is no radio communication back from the shuttle,"* I said.

My brain was racing with split-second flashes.

Helpless thoughts: I had the urge to scream, "No, no, no!" I managed to restrain myself.

Hopeful thoughts: Surely Challenger was suspended somewhere in that cloud and would re-emerge at any moment to report, in cool "Right Stuff" fashion, "We're coming back home."

Chilling thoughts: Why AREN'T the astronauts talking? Had I just watched seven people die in a sudden, startling flash? And could those out-of-control rockets turn back toward us?

I immediately put that last thought out of my mind. "You're supposed to be a professional," I told myself. "People are relying on YOU to tell them what happened. Get your act together now."

Assistant Managing Editor Brad Kalbfeld was on the feedback line from Washington, acting as executive producer of the broadcast. Up to now, he and others in the control room had been transfixed by the unfolding drama. Occasionally, I could hear them gasping "Geez," in hushed voices.

Suddenly, Kalbfeld snapped into action, barking into my left ear, "I want a description. Tell the listener what you're seeing."

"What we saw as the shuttle was rising into the air was a pillar of steam and smoke that has become so familiar to us on the previous 24 shuttle missions," I said. *"But the shuttle got about midway into the sky, really, and there was a sudden change in what we have come to expect. The smoke divided into two different pillars, and as far as we hear from Mission Control, the ship exploded."*

I handed off to Uliano. *"It looked like we had solid rocket booster separation,"* he continued, *"where the two solid rocket boosters—which carry three-million pounds of thrust—are supposed to separate two-and-a-half minutes after flight. And yet, it looked like they spun off away from the shuttle, and drifted.*

"We had thick, white smoke, and the ship—if it existed at that point—was simply lost behind the cloud of white smoke."

I picked up the story: *"And what we see now in the sky is just what's left of that plume of steam, that pillar of steam. It is starting to dissipate in the clear blue Florida sky now. And coming down from that pillar of steam are some small contrails of what is apparently debris from the shuttle that has dropped back down toward the Atlantic."*

"We're staying with this," I heard Kalbfeld say. *"Just keep talking."*

And we kept talking for five-and-a-half hours, wall-to-wall, with only a half-hour break to feed shuttle actualities and correspondents' reports to our affiliates. David Tirell-Wysocki, on assignment from the AP bureau in Concord, N.H., contributed a heart-rending account from his vantage point in the VIP viewing stands, where Christa McAuliffe's parents and scores of school children had watched the tragic launch.

Back in Washington, the Broadcast News Center was buzzing, providing crucial reports and coordinating remote inserts from around the country.

So, now I know. Neither Dick nor I froze on the air. I hope our descriptions were clear to our listeners. And I was able to remain composed. It wasn't until the marathon programming ended—and the reality of what we had witnessed began to sink in—that some tears began to flow.

Oh, the humanity.[5]

Taped events also carry emotion. When the *Challenger* exploded, taped pictures of the explosions, juxtaposed against pictures of spectators watching the event, carried powerful emotional impressions. The family of schoolteacher Christa McAuliffe, who was the first teacher designated to travel into space, were among the crowd of spectators, along with a group of schoolchildren. Their faces showed tension, then relief as the rocket booster lifted off the launching pad, and, finally, confusion and torment when the cloud of smoke enveloped the rocket and contrails flowered from sections of the rocket careening off in different directions.

A word of caution: Avoid injecting emotion into your narration. Speak seriously, but directly. Let the pictures, sounds, and the voices of newsmakers convey the emotion of the event.

SHOW, DON'T TELL

That advice applies to most of what you do. Show your listeners with sound (and your viewers with sound and picture) people in action, and let them decide what newsmakers and events are like. Reveal the news, as much as possible, in the way people act and react. We all watch people and conclude from our observations what they are like. But we shouldn't try to force our conclusions upon our audiences. Let them decide for themselves.

During the 1980 Summer Olympics in Moscow, Russian police controlled the movements of Western reporters and photographers. They kept them in guarded hotels, followed them when they left their hotels, and tried to prevent them from venturing into areas other than those designated for the Olympics. Whenever Western photographers tried to take pictures of anything other than sports events, Soviet police harassed them.

A CBS cameraman caught one such incident on tape. He focused his camera on CBS photographer Nick Turner, who was holding his camera high overhead, trying to take pictures of Soviet officials leaving Lenin Stadium.

Viewers could see a Russian plainclothesman trying to stare Turner down; then, when Turner ignored him, viewers saw the plainclothesman walk slowly toward Turner, lower his shoulder, and push it into Turner's abdomen, forcing him off balance. Then viewers saw the Russian walk away, pretending to be off balance himself, as if the incident had been accidental. But the recorded action showed that the Russian had been deliberate.

If a reporter had tried to explain that incident without pictures, viewers might have doubted his judgment. But they saw it on tape and knew exactly what happened.

The camera alone in the hands of a sensitive photographer can provide perspective. On radio, the voices of newsmakers and the thoughts they express can provide human perspective without the aid of pictures. And reporters, without the help of newsmakers' voices, can provide that same perspective in well-written straight narration.

On the day before the space shuttle *Challenger* was launched, the engineers who designed the booster rockets met at the headquarters of Morton Thiokol, the Utah company that built the rocket motors. They had been told that temperatures at Cape Canaveral were lower than they had ever been for a launch, and the engineers were afraid the seals that hold the rocket together might fail during liftoff. They recommended, unsuccessfully, that NASA delay the launch.

Three weeks after the explosion of the space shuttle, National Public Radio's Howard Berkes reported from Brigham City, Utah, how one of the engineers was dealing with the aftermath of the tragedy:

> A Morton Thiokol engineer here says he prayed as he watched shuttle Challenger lift off from its launch pad.
>
> We can't tell you his name, his job title or even the color of his hair. His job may depend on this secrecy. But we can tell you something of what he feels, what others may feel, about the right stuff gone awry.
>
> On January 28th, this man prayed for some divine act that would safely guide Challenger into space. He worried that the seals in the solid rocket boosters

would not function properly in the chilly morning
air. He feared disaster.

But as Challenger rose from earth, and as all
seemed well, he began another prayer -- one of
thanks.

But in mid-prayer, the spacecraft exploded. He sat
quietly and cried.

Now, three weeks later, that launch haunts him.
This Thiokol engineer suspected the danger, joined
with his colleagues in trying to reverse the launch
decision and now feels regret that he did not do
more.

This is a space shuttle worker who has had the
utmost respect for NASA, who in the past has been
frustrated by NASA's extraordinary conservatism,
which he says always put safety first.

But as he recalls the decision-making process that
led up to the launch of the Challenger, he grows
silent and wonders aloud why this time was different.

"NASA had a brain spasm," he said. "They forgot
their code of conduct."

He bristles as he quotes NASA's Lawrence Mulloy,
saying, "My God, Thiokol, when do you want me to
launch -- next April?"

And then he turns the anger inward. He said he
should have stood up, answering, "If that's when it's
warm, yes." But he didn't.

Now, he's left wondering what else could have or
should have been done. Depression has set in. And
this proud space program engineer now talks of
meeting with psychiatric specialists he says Morton
Thiokol will provide.

Though he claims NASA managers coerced Thiokol
engineers and managers into approving the launch, he
blames his fellow Thiokol workers and himself for not
arguing more adamantly, for not insisting on a
postponement.

Last night he read in a local newspaper that
vandals scrawled a phrase three feet high across a
railroad overpass. "Morton Thiokol murderers," it
said.

The engineer shakes his head, rises and walks into
another room to watch a television report but turns
away when that haunting image is shown again. "I

should have done more," he said. "I could have done
more."[6]

The reporter cited direct quotations, which radio and television reporters seldom
use in narration, and included enough detail about the actions of the engineer to
paint a clear picture of his remorse.

CHOOSING VIEWPOINTS

Reporting is a process of uncovering the news a fragment at a time. Rarely do
reporters have enough time before their deadlines to collect all of the information
relevant to a story, but they must pursue as many leads as they can to be sure
they present stories that are as complete as possible. They should not accept the
viewpoint of one source and assume he or she knows or is willing to provide all
that is important about the story.

A year-long hostage crisis in Iran was one of the most difficult stories reporters
could be asked to cover.

In November 1979, Iranian militants invaded the American embassy in Tehran
and took control of the building and the 66 Americans in it. They waved their fists
at American television cameras. They demanded that the United States release the
deposed Shah of Iran, who had flown to New York City to ask American doctors
to treat his lymphatic cancer, to them. The militants in Tehran made it clear that
they would not negotiate with the United States for the release of the American
hostages until the Americans released the Shah to them.

Reporters faced the hostile sources in Tehran. Some were militants, trained
perhaps to use methods that attract attention rather than provide information. Some
were officials of the Iranian government, worried more perhaps about their own
political survival and their relationships with Iran's spiritual leader, the Ayatullah
Khomeini, than about negotiations with the United States. Some were American
diplomatic officials, more concerned perhaps about what they should not say than
with what they could say.

Back home, American listeners and viewers wanted information, but reporters
in Iran could provide little more than the sounds and pictures of militants who,
according to some, were in festive moods until the cameras turned toward them.
Then they turned ugly and stayed that way until the photographers stopped shooting.

Reporters were subject to controls over information on both sides. So, in December, when the militants offered ABC, CBS, and NBC an interview with one of
the hostages, Marine Corporal William Gallegos, all three networks were tempted,
but only NBC reached an agreement with the militants on the conditions for the
interview.

The Iranians agreed to let NBC correspondents Fred Francis and George Lewis
conduct the interview without submitting their questions in advance only if an
Iranian camera crew taped the interview. NBC also agreed to allow a militant

At a newsroom story conference decisions are made
about which stories will be run and in what order.

spokesman to make unedited opening and closing statements and to play the interview in its entirety during prime time.

Several newspapers and television broadcasters criticized NBC for relinquishing control of the interview, but the man who was president of NBC News at the time, William Small, defended the agreement, saying that the interview gave insight into the situation in Iran.

NBC News officials knew the risk of allowing the militants time to deliver an anti-American diatribe, but they also hoped to provide information from an American viewpoint, that of the 22-year-old Marine hostage. The Marine told viewers that the hostages he saw were kept clean, fed well, allowed to exercise, read, and sleep, but he also said they were under intense stress and were prohibited from talking to each other.

Reporters rarely have to accept distorted viewpoints as a condition for getting presumably valid viewpoints. But unless you search for verifying or conflicting viewpoints, you could unwittingly distort the news.

That doesn't mean you should deliberately look for someone with information that will dispute what you already have. If you try to establish conflict only for the sake of conflict, you may confuse your audience. For example, if you have a representative who favors consolidation of city and county governments, and she says consolidation will *not* raise the taxes of city residents, you'll serve no purpose in getting a statement from an opponent of consolidation who says it *will* raise the taxes of city residents. You'll be asking your listeners and viewers to decide who is right on the basis of who says it more convincingly or who looks more honest. You'll serve them better if you first try to determine which viewpoint is correct and then substantiate it.

Sometimes, however, conflicting viewpoints can enlighten your listeners. For example, you could have a major industrial plant in your area that manufactures explosives. It's located on the fringe of the county, a mile from any residential area. But builders own the land surrounding the plant, and they have successfully petitioned the planning and zoning commission to allow them to build 150 new houses on the land. They must now ask the county council to approve the plan.

Officials of the explosives plant object. They contend that they're vulnerable to massive damage claims if an accidental explosion should damage nearby houses. They ask the county council to reject residential zoning and protect them with a vacant buffer zone. They threaten to close the plant and move out of the state unless the council grants their request. That would cost the county some three-million dollars a year in property tax revenues the company pays.

The builders argue that they'll lose their large investment in the land unless the county council approves the plan. They say the explosives plant has never had an accident in 30 years at the site, so the risk is minimal. They also argue that if the company closes the plant, the property taxes on new homes would bring the county more revenue than the company now pays.

This is an issue in which your viewers, many of them taxpayers, have a stake, so they should have a chance to hear the arguments on both sides and decide which position they think is the best one. They may want to try to influence the county council's vote.

BALANCING THE NEWS

Broadcast reporters have a more difficult task conveying the news to their listeners and viewers than do print reporters to their readers.

Newspaper readers must want the information from the printed page before they'll read the story. They see headlines that suggest the substance of stories, and if they decide it's something they want to know, they search the columns beneath the headlines. Their minds actively interpret the printed symbols and translate them into meaning.

But radio listeners may be listening only superficially. They may be conscious of the sound but may not hear the substance. Television viewers, too, are passive recipients of information from the screen. The images come to them, they see them, but they may not think about them. Few of us remember everything we read, and even fewer of us remember everything we hear. Therefore, if a broadcast story is complex, we may remember only a fragment or two.

All radio and television reporters can cite instances when their listeners and viewers have complained that they were biased or presented one-sided stories or missed key facts. One television reporter produced an anniversary story five years after a major earthquake had rattled his station's viewing area. He included information about what viewers could do if an earthquake struck again. Five times within the story he reminded them that the information was precautionary only and that no earthquake was expected. But viewers deluged the station with telephone calls asking where and when the predicted earthquake would strike.

A radio commentator assigned to be a media critic criticized his own station and its chief competitor for spending what he called an excessive amount of their air time promoting themselves and their on-the-air personalities. His listeners besieged him with telephone calls and letters accusing him of unfairly using public airwaves to defame a competitor. They hadn't heard, or didn't remember, that he had criticized his own station.

When people read material in printed form, they rarely misinterpret it, because if it confuses them, they can read it again to try to understand its message. But radio listeners and television viewers often think they hear something other than what the broadcaster intended, or they get impressions from ideas or images that lead them to elaborate the meaning in their own minds. And what they think they heard may be very different from what the broadcaster said.

So radio and television reporters have a double-pronged responsibility: They must collect as many facets of information as they can find to round out their stories, and they must write their stories as carefully as they can to make certain each fact gets the attention it deserves.

Too often we may uncover a facet or two of a story and, either because we're pressured or we're lazy, assume our story is complete enough. But contact with one more source, one more check into the files, or one more telephone call may tell us something that will change the story's meaning.

Former professional football coach Hank Stram, who is now a CBS sports broadcaster, talks about one story that fell short. It was based on an interview with a teammate of Lew Alcindor, the former UCLA basketball star who became Los Angeles Laker center Kareem Abdul-Jabbar:

> The story said there was dissention on the team because Alcindor always got orange juice before the game, a steak afterward and got to room alone on the road.
>
> If the reporter had checked with John Wooden, Alcindor's coach, he would have discovered that all players got a steak before the game, but that Alcindor was so keyed up, he wanted only orange juice and asked that he be allowed to eat his steak after the game.
>
> And Alcindor roomed alone simply because he was so tall, the bed had to be especially long, and most hotel rooms could not accommodate two such beds.[7]

The wire services sometimes transmit incomplete stories when their broadcast editors inadvertently omit facts under the pressure of having to rewrite quickly. Here's a hypothetical example:

-- A CIRCUIT JUDGE HAS POSTPONED UNTIL NEXT WEDNESDAY
A PRELIMINARY HEARING FOR A MAN ACCUSED OF CRIMINAL
HOMICIDE AND ARSON IN CONNECTION WITH A FATAL FIRE
EARLIER THIS MONTH IN A LOCAL HOTEL.

JUDGE DAVID EVANS SAID TODAY THE ATTORNEYS NEEDED
ADDITIONAL TIME TO STUDY EXPECTED TESTIMONY AND
EVIDENCE IN THE CASE AGAINST 66-YEAR-OLD GEORGE
LEATHER.

SIX PEOPLE DIED IN THE FIRE AT THE JONES HOTEL
LAST MONTH.

LEATHER IS BEING HELD IN THE CITY JAIL, BUT HIS
ATTORNEY HAS ASKED THAT THE ACCUSED MAN BE PLACED IN
A REST HOME SO HIS HEALTH PROBLEMS CAN BE ATTENDED
TO.

An important fact is missing: Why is George Leather accused of murder and arson? Surely, that fact is available. A reporter who encounters a story like that should call the wire service bureau and ask for more information rather than try to air the incomplete story. In this case, the broadcast editor for the wire service had inadvertently omitted the fact when she rewrote the story from the newspaper wire. Police officers said George Leather had set newspapers afire in the middle of his hotel room because the night was cold. When the reporter's question prodded the wire service editor to look at the story again, she wrote a new version that not only completed the story but added a human dimension to it.

You can achieve balance if you're thorough and if you're inquisitive. Those are qualities that will help you develop into a successful reporter.

Exercises

1. Choose the lead stories from any three television or radio newscasts and analyze them according to the criteria for deciding what's news—impact, magnitude, prominence, proximity, conflict, unusualness, timeliness, and empathy. Do the same with the closing stories in any three newscasts. Which criteria made them news?

2. Observe an event—a sports event, a concert, a speech, a public meeting, or any other newsworthy event you encounter. Look for details that will make the story vivid. Write them down and explain why you think it's important to include each observed element.

3. Develop an idea for a news story, then develop a plan to cover the story. Write down what you expect to find, and name the sources you intend to contact. Write the questions you want to ask to reveal the story. Ask your instructor to approve your plan, then develop the story.

4. Develop another story idea and a plan to cover it. As you work on the story, look for actions that will explain what the people in the story are like and how they are reacting. When you write the story, show the newsmakers in action and utilize either sound bites or direct quotations that reveal their character.

5. Read through broadcast wire copy until you find a story that is incomplete. Call the wire service bureau, and ask the writer to give you more details. Or, ask for a copy of the same story from the newspaper wire. Rewrite the story to give your listeners or viewers a complete version.

Notes

1. "Exclusive Interview with Richard Salant," *The Editorialist,* VI, no. 2 (Spring 1980): 7–8.

2. Emery King, WBBM-AM, 4 February 1977.

3. Scott Simon, "All Things Considered," National Public Radio, 5 February 1977.

4. Tony Sargent, ABC Information Network, 26 February 1980.

5. Bob Moon, "Something Went Wrong Here!" *Network News,* 5, no. 2 (March/April 1986): 1–2.

6. Howard Berkes, "Morning Edition," National Public Radio, 20 February 1986.

7. Bill Worth, "A Game Plan for Sports Reporting," *APME News* (December 1979): 9.

assigned to beats will have more time to develop such sources, but all reporters need to befriend people who can help them find news.

A friend who keeps in touch with politicians can point you to potential candidates who are being wooed by party regulars. A friend who talks to business professionals may hear about urban revitalization plans. A friend who works in a hospital may hear about new medical research. A friend who goes regularly to ball games may hear about pending player trades and salary disputes.

You need to maintain contact with such friends and listen appreciatively to what they can tell you. Not every tip blossoms into a story, but your willingness to listen to your friendly sources and to call them occasionally to find out what they know will pay off with many stories.

You also need to befriend secretaries, file clerks, foot patrolmen, garbage collectors, receptionists, and all kinds of lower-echelon workers. You'll probably never interview them on microphone or on-camera, but they'll often lead you to information they hear hints about. Successful reporters probably could never sit down at their typewriter and list all of the people who help them, but they can probably address all of their sources by their first names when they encounter them.

In *The New Muckrakers*, Leonard Downie Jr. wrote a revealing summary about how Pulitzer-Prize-winning reporter Bob Woodward convinced a *Washington Post* editor that he should be hired and how he developed front-page stories after he was hired. It includes a picture of Woodward working to cultivate sources:

> Woodward was as Ivy League and starch-shirted as any of them, but he made himself an unusually bright success on the night police beat by reverting to the behavior that had helped him cope with the pressure of rank and regimentation in the Navy. With wide-eyed earnestness, almost obsequious deference, and quiet persistence, he ingratiated himself with the middle-level officers who ran the night shift. He tried to befriend individual policemen by taking them out for drinks or dinner or sharing a snack with them at headquarters and listening intently as they talked about themselves and the unappreciated drudgery of their work, something few reporters bothered to do. In return, Woodward got fast, accurate information about what was happening. In time he was also let in on the gossip about politics and scandal inside the police force that helped him produce some of his first investigative stories for the *Post* on police corruption. . . .
>
> Overlooked city government offices seemed a good source of stories, too. "I sat down with a D.C. government directory," Woodward said, "and went through it department by department to see what they were doing." When a telephone call produced an interesting lead, he went out to see the bureaucrats and go through their records himself, often on his own time. In the department that manages city property, he found that much of the D.C. government's vacant downtown land was being used for commercial parking lots for little or no rent to the city. Both the bureaucrats and the parking firm's executives said they were not making money on the lots, so they were not paying the city much. "I went out and counted the cars on the lots for three days in a row," Woodward said, "and found that the company was making plenty of money at the city's expense."

Woodward frequently found bureaucrats "who had never seen a reporter before, except when they were being questioned about some problem." They were anxious to tell him what they had been accomplishing for the taxpayers with little or no public credit. The city's health inspectors said few people realized how many well-known, expensive Washington restaurants fail inspections. Woodward took down and published the names of the restaurants and their health deficiencies in a story that attracted considerable attention and prompted *Post* editors to make it a regular practice. Woodward's new friends in the city's health inspection office also tipped him to grocery stores selling illegally fatty meat and pharmacies selling defective, outdated, and mislabeled prescription drugs—providing Woodward with more front-page stories.

"Whenever I visited a city agency," Woodward said, "I'd start by asking what were the good things they were doing. Then I'd get around to asking them if they had any problems. In the Bureau of Condemnation, for instance, they told me they had trouble getting the buildings they condemned torn down because of legal red tape. Meantime, they said, people were still living in some of the buildings. I checked and found hundreds of condemned buildings standing all over the city, with people living in at least 10 percent of them. It made a great story."[1]

Bob Woodward's style may not fit your personality, but his ability to listen to his sources is worth remembering. A reporter who listens earns friends—and stories.

Bob Woodward (right) and Carl Bernstein. Their investigative reporting of the Watergate break-in and subsequent coverup eventually contributed to the resignation of then President Richard Nixon.

Yet while you befriend your sources, don't get too close to them. You may find them part of the news someday, and you may be obligated to cover their misdeeds. Or you may discover that they have deceived you into withholding information in which they had selfish interests.

A reporter who works the science beat may spend months developing sources. It's a difficult beat to cover because scientists and researchers experiment with theories that sometimes succeed and sometimes fail, and they don't want to publicize their failures.

One reporter patiently cultivated sources at a medical center where he knew doctors were trying to find a way to separate twins who had been born conjoined at the tops of their heads. The doctors and other personnel gradually warmed to the reporter and occasionally talked about their work, but they cautioned him against telling his audience about the project. The doctor in charge of the medical team told the reporter he'd be the first to get the story when they decided to operate.

But on the day the surgeons successfully separated the twins, the chief surgeon called a news conference and gave the story to everyone simultaneously. The reporter who had worked so patiently to develop his sources, and held the story because doctors asked him to, found himself just one of the crowd at the news conference.

Keep a barrier of skepticism between you and your sources. Your obligation is to your listeners and viewers, and your job is to find everything you can to keep them informed.

Evaluating Sources

One of the most difficult tasks for reporters is deciding whether or not their sources are telling them the truth. Sources sometimes lie. They may have hidden motives for misleading you. They may want to trick you into pursuing a hoax so they can divert your attention from something else. They may be trying to float trial balloons to get public reaction.

Generally, you can rely on sources who have consistently given you valid information, but even dependable sources may sometimes mislead you due to a self-interest in trying to manipulate you or your listeners and viewers. Try to determine your source's motives for giving you information, uncover contradictions in that information, or find other reliable sources who can validate or discredit what you've been told.

One reporter received several valuable tips from a city government employee. One tip led to a city purchasing agent who had been buying road-building equipment from his brother-in-law. Another led to a police detective who was demanding protection money to keep quiet about prostitution. Another led to a parking meter repairman who had been stealing money from meters.

One day, a week before a city election, the tipster brought the reporter a copy of a cancelled check written by a prominent land developer, payable to a city council member who was running for reelection. The tipster also brought a copy of city council minutes, which included an entry detailing the transfer of some city land to that same developer. The implication of the documents was clear—the check seemed to be a payoff for the city council member's influence in the land transfer.

But the reporter hesitated. He knew that publication of the information would sway voters, and he didn't have time to check the records thoroughly to confirm the story before the election, so he told his tipster he'd wait until after the election to follow up the tip.

The tipster was angry. He said he'd take the information to a local newspaper. He did, but the newspaper held off publication, too, until it could investigate and confirm the story. It published the story about a month after the election, and the city council member was eventually tried, but the jury acquitted him. The jury said it found no evidence that he had unduly influenced the land sale. As a matter of fact, during the trial, the defense attorney subpoenaed the land developer, who testified that he and the city council member had been long-time friends, and he had contributed to his friend's campaign.

The television reporter later learned that the tipster had been working on the campaign of the city council member's opponent.

Although they're often difficult to discover, find the motives of your sources if you can. Think about possible motives and weigh them before you accept the word of your sources.

You can also question your sources in ways designed to subtly elicit contradictions in what they tell you. You may not want to offend sources by challenging them to prove what they've told you, but you must try to determine if they're telling the truth.

If you know something about the agency, the institution, the issue, or the plan that your source is talking about, ask questions to which you already know the answers. Then if your source answers incorrectly, you'll know he or she is lying.

A source told a reporter that the biggest hotel in the city was about to be sold to a major hotel chain. The reporter asked how the source learned about it. The source said he knew the hotel manager. The reporter knew the hotel manager, too—Henry Sillar—so he asked his source, "Does Hank Sillar know?" The source replied, "Who?" The deception was thus unveiled.

Ask simple questions. Ask innocent questions. Sources tend to open up more readily to reporters who genuinely seem to want to know.

Ask for details, too. If sources really know something important, they'll probably know quite a bit about it. A source who is interested enough to call you and tell you that six members of a National Guard unit have been hospitalized with a mysterious ailment probably knows what unit they belong to, where they were working, what kind of work they were doing, what hospital they were taken to, who their commanding officer is, and many other details that will help you evaluate the importance of the story and lead you to other sources who can fill in the blanks. In many instances, a second source can help you confirm or deny the truth of a story. If you ask two people who saw the same event from similar perspectives, and their stories differ, one of them is probably misleading you.

A rumor once swept the western part of the United States. It said pornographic film makers were kidnapping children from Disneyland in Anaheim, California, and transporting them to Mexico to film what they called "kiddie porn movies." The more the rumor spread, the more local it became. Soon the rumor said kidnappers were taking children from nearby amusement parks, even from neighborhood shopping malls. An enterprising reporter merely had to call the Anaheim, California, police department to learn that officers there had no records of any kidnappings, and the rumors were quashed.

Perhaps you'll be unable to unveil motives, discover contradictions, or find second sources you can trust. Then you're left with your own intuition. Ask yourself: Am I comfortable or uncomfortable with the information? Is there anyone I could hurt if I go ahead with this story and it turns out to be false? Is there anything in the expressions or actions of my source that makes me suspicious? If you're not satisfied, either look for more information to substantiate the story or abandon it.

Check and Recheck

Sources often complain that reporters, particularly broadcast ones, transmit erroneous information. Because radio and television reporters are assigned more often to a wider spectrum of events than are newspaper reporters, broadcast reporters have less time to become experts at particular kinds of news.

You'll often hear complaints like this one from an executive of a taxpayers' lobby group:

> I have to educate radio and television reporters whenever they come to my office because they don't understand the tax system in this state. They ask questions that are irrelevant, and they ask questions that demand expansive answers. So whenever a radio or television reporter asks for information, I tell them not to turn on their recorders or cameras until I give them some background.[2]

That kind of attitude can be helpful to you if you know too little about the story you're assigned to cover. Spend whatever time you have available learning from such people about issues and concepts. Then you'll be adequately prepared when you're ready to write and edit your story.

Sometimes, reporters omit essential facts because their sources are too busy to provide them. In most such cases, you can find a second source who will be helpful.

Assume, for example, that you have covered an industrial accident. A forklift operator at a chemical plant accidentally rammed a support under a huge storage bin. The bin collapsed and poured 30 tons of aragonite over the operator. Other workers dug him out, and an ambulance took him to a nearby hospital with unknown injuries.

You ask officials of the company for his name. They refuse to tell you because they want time to collect more information about the accident for their insurance reports. You ask the nursing supervisor at the hospital. She says the young man is in surgery with two severely broken legs, and she hasn't yet had time to get his name. You try to call the police officer who has been assigned to investigate the accident, but he's somewhere between the chemical plant and the police station. The name, age, and address of the injured man are essential to your story, but it looks as if you've reached a dead end, and your newscast is ten minutes away.

Then you remember! In most such cases, police call private ambulance services to take injured people to hospitals, and they record names and addresses because they'll bill the victim later for transportation. Sure enough, the ambulance service has his name, address, age, and information about the extent of his injuries because the ambulance crew gave him first aid.

If you had given up the search after any one of your failures, you'd have given your audience an incomplete story. But because you looked for other sources, you gave your audience the whole story. No matter how many roadblocks stop you, you can frequently find one more source who will give you access.

Sometimes, we erroneously assume our stories are complete and abandon our search for facts simply because a story sounds good as it is. In the late summer of 1979, former President Jimmy Carter went fishing on a lake in Georgia. He told reporters later that a vicious rabbit swam at his canoe, and he had to beat it off with a paddle. An official White House photographer happened to be along on the trip, and he snapped a picture of the moment. He enlarged it to show that it was a rabbit, but reporters refused to believe it. They chuckled and wrote humorous stories about the "killer rabbit." Some called it the "banzai bunny." None of the rabbits they had read about ventured into water, much less attacked human beings, so President Carter's claim that a predator must have startled the rabbit and it mistook the canoe for an enemy trying to block its escape prodded reporters into more laughter.

But *Sports Illustrated* checked one more source, a zoologist who told the magazine that two species—the swamp rabbit and the marsh rabbit—do swim, and they live only in the southeastern part of the United States, particularly in Georgia.

Reporters should have suspected, if they didn't know, that not all hares are jackrabbits or cottontails.

One more suggestion about sources—never trust another medium to be accurate. Every reporter makes mistakes, and if you adopt information you get from another medium, you may be reinforcing an error.

A newspaper published a story that said the U.S. Forest Service would close a mountain motorbike trail because too many vehicles were leaving the trail and scarring surrounding terrain. The story reported that the Forest Service had issued

422 citations in a single year to offenders whom rangers had caught off the trail. The newspaper editorialized against abusive motorbikers. The wire services picked up the story, and broadcast stations picked it up from the wire services. Soon most of them were saying 422 motorbikers had been cited in one year.

A radio reporter looking for a new angle to the story called a Forest Service supervisor to ask about the extent of the damage on the mountainside. He asked, "Is this right—you cited 422 bikers in one year?" The Forest Service official said, "No. We cited 422 off-road vehicles—motorbikes, four-wheel-drive vehicles, dune buggies, even a few pickup trucks." But the radio reporter's story was too late to soften the undeserved blame other news agencies had heaped on motorbikers because reporters kept repeating the error.

While you're searching for new angles on stories you pick up from other media, try to confirm the information in the original story, too.

Laying the Background

Reporters immerse themselves in news. At times, they seem to live in the stories they report—observing, listening, questioning, reading, absorbing. They rarely write or tell all they know about any story because they have too little time. Sometimes they become saturated with information if a story continually gets time in newscasts day after day, and sometimes they tire of a story when it drags on.

They tend to forget, periodically, that their audiences expose themselves lightly to the news most of the time, and they retain little of what they hear. So, when reporters forget to include background information, assuming that their listeners and viewers remember it, they cheat their audiences of a complete understanding of events.

Much of the time, the needed background can be written in a single concise sentence:

        Circuit Judge David Evans has postponed a preliminary
        hearing for a local man accused of murder and arson.
        The man was accused in connection with a fatal fire
        early this month at a hotel that housed derelicts.
            Judge Evans says the attorneys need more time to
        study testimony and evidence in the case against
        George Leather.
            Six people died in the fire at the Junes Hotel.
        Police say Leather set fire to a stack of newspapers
        to warm his cold room.

You need the last two sentences of background to refresh your audience's memory about the event that led to the charge against the man.

Look at this hypothetical story, too:

> The new basketball coach at Arcadia University says
> he hopes the N-C-double-A doesn't make an example of
> his school because of a sports scandal that shattered
> its athletic program.
>   Coach Willy Carlson says he doesn't know how the
> N-C-double-A will punish the university when
> investigators complete their report.
>   State prosecutors say they found evidence last
> month that some of the credits of three basketball
> players were counterfeit.

Again, you need the last sentence in that story to revive your listeners' and viewers' memories about an earlier event from which the current news has grown.

Join the present elements of the story with its past elements to complete the story's meaning. A story that says the Pope has given Vatican employees a 50 percent wage increase means little unless you tell your audience that Vatican employees had been threatening to organize a union and strike.

A story that says the president will spend a holiday at Camp David will be shallow unless you add that he planned to spend it in Maine, but he decided to stay close to Washington because of rising tensions in the Middle East.

The news often develops in fragments, and when it does, you'll need to give your listeners and viewers enough background information to help them understand why today's story is important.

IMPACT OF NEWS

Routine news sometimes seems to be monotonous, but we don't always have a steady flow of exciting news—scandals, disasters, narrow escapes—to spice our newscasts. Most of the news is routine, but under the surface we can find an abundance of information that will attract listeners and viewers and show them how events are affecting their lives. With a little work, we can explain complex issues in vivid ways. We must look for their impacts on the people in our audiences.

Here's a devised example of a factual, but uninteresting, story:

> The National Research Council says the earth's ozone
> layer is eroding rapidly. The study says
> fluorocarbons are eating away at the ozone layer
> despite the fact that aerosol spray cans have been
> banned. More fluorocarbons are being emitted from
> automobile air conditioners, garment cleaning
> processes, sterilizing medical supplies and fast-
> freezing food.

We need to find a reason for our audience to listen to that information because it's impersonal and unimportant as it stands. It contains an unspoken effect on humans, and we need to write *that* into the lead:

```
     We're in greater danger of getting skin cancer,
according to the National Research Council. The
council says fluorocarbons are eating away the
earth's ozone layer, the layer that filters out
ultraviolet rays -- rays that are potentially harmful
to us.
     The council conducted a study that shows we cut
the number of fluorocarbons when we banned aerosol
spray cans, but now more fluorocarbons are being
emitted from autombile air conditioners, garment-
cleaning processes, sterilization of medical
supplies, and fast-freezing food.
```

The second version takes a little more time to read, but it should have a greater impact on our audience because we have shown the potential effect of the information it contains.

Here are two invented related stories that belong together in a newscast. Their impact is a little more obvious:

```
     The Labor Department has confirmed it -- the price of
gasoline has gone up. Department economists say
gasoline prices increased, on the average, a little
more than a cent a gallon from last month.
     The price of jet fuel is also rising, and at the
same time, some airlines have announced they're
raising fares next month.
```

People who drive or fly may understand the effects of those stories, but we can help them by emphasizing the stories' impact:

```
     We may be walking more and staying in our home towns
more in the next few months. The price of gasoline
and the price of jet fuel are both going up, and
airlines say they'll raise fares, too.
     The Labor Department says gasoline prices have
risen more than a penny a gallon since last month,
and airlines say they'll have to charge higher fares
to pay for jet fuel.
```

Most stories that are newsworthy contain some human element that will draw your listeners and viewers in. Look for that human angle and emphasize it.

Sociologist Herbert Gans says journalists also need to add a "bottom-up" view of the news. Currently, reporters spend most of their time covering institutions, particularly governments and corporations, reporting on their policies, then collecting and transmitting reactions from other high officials. Gans says we should also be collecting reactions from "citizens in various walks of life who would be affected by those policies . . . [and] reporting on the activities and opinions of ordinary Americans from all population sectors and roles."[3]

In some ways, radio and television reporting is moving in the direction Gans proposes. We see more government announcements of welfare cuts balanced by reactions from welfare recipients. We see more urban revitalization proposals balanced by reactions from poor tenants who will be displaced. We see more announcements of government agriculture policy balanced by reactions from farmers whose production will be affected.

Broadcast reporters need to look for more of the impacts of institutional policies and programs all along the spectrum of people who are affected. They'll need more time to search for facts and opinions, but if they take that time, they'll be contributing vital information and exposure to the people who need it.

Stimulation versus Provocation

News, to be effective, must stimulate listeners and viewers. But radio and television reporters must be sensitive to the difference between stimulation and provocation.

You stimulate people when you elicit reactions or emotions. You provoke them when you incite or rouse them, usually to resentment or anger. The two are separated by an almost invisible line, and broadcast reporters must cultivate a sensitivity that warns them when they approach that line.

Your listeners and viewers enjoy news that stimulates them; they usually react negatively when they sense you are trying to incite them. They feel safe when you keep an objective distance; they feel threatened when they believe you're trying to invade their space.

You can incite listeners and viewers through vocal nuances, exaggerated words, rumors, and, sometimes on television, through visual appearances. You've heard some newscasters or reporters emphasize the character of an event by abruptly changing the tone of their voices or injecting exaggerated pauses or emphases into their narration. You've heard some who seem to deliberately inject editorial points of view through the way they speak or visually react to opinions.

One reporter told about a man who died from a heart attack that an ambulance crewman apparently failed to treat. The reporter emphasized the fact that ambulance crew members are trained to administer "cardiopulmonary resuscitation," then added dramatically, "But Mrs. Smith—the mother of 12 children—says she can't forget that early morning—when her husband died—sitting in the green chair—in their living room." The reporter lingered on the last syllable of each phrase, then waited for the sound to fade before he started the next phrase. Listeners sensed that he wanted them to be angry at the ambulance attendant.

Another reporter told a story about a plane crash that killed several residents of his city. He said, "Here's an update on that *terrible* plane crash that killed *scores* of people." Besides emphasizing terrible and scores, he added this sentence: "There was only one survivor, and there were 31 aboard." A simple mathematical calculation tells you he was exaggerating the scope of the tragedy. It was serious, but not catastrophic.

Sometimes a reporter will jump to the conclusion that events will follow patterns set by similar events that occurred earlier. One who will be nameless did just that when he announced the beginning of a strike:

```
    Picketers anticipate the strike will be a long one.
We remember the strike eight years ago. It lasted
eight long, long months. And then four years ago --
another strike lasted seven months.
    None of the pickets will say how long they think
this strike will last.
    Maybe you're asking: Why are we nere in the first
place? Why are we covering this strike with such
intensity? Well, we're here because almost two-
thousand people are out of work. They were out of
work at one minute past midnight because they went on
strike.
    Of course, they chose that path, but they're
without jobs and without income. And they will be for
a long time.
```

The story is charged with provocative thoughts, contradictions, and speculations. In reality, the reporter has created a rumor and used it to justify broadcasting live from the scene.

Listeners and viewers who hear such stories are likely to become irritated and resentful. They recognize overstatement, and they resist being drawn into a story as emotional participants.

Listeners and viewers who are stimulated, instead of provoked, however, enjoy the sense of witnessing the news, because they can listen and watch from an emotional distance.

RUSHING TO DEADLINES

All of us get caught up in the chase for stories, especially when we find something beyond the routine of meetings, speeches, and interviews. Sometimes, we allow ourselves, under the pressure of wanting to be first, to push ourselves into making wrong decisions.

Former CBS anchor Walter Cronkite felt that pressure despite his experience:

> We all know so well the need for accuracy, and we need not dwell on that. But let me ask you a question I frequently ask myself: Do we always live by the old precept, "Get it first, but first get it right?"
>
> I know I'm guilty of letting uncertain statements slip by because I have run out of time to check them out. Every time I do, I kick myself, even when the statement proves right. And I wonder, What was all the rush anyway? Where really is the advantage in being first? Haven't we let old newspaper problems of replating, extra editions, transport complexities and street sales dictate a rather meaningless tradition?
>
> Of course, it is better to get the story on tonight's six o'clock news rather than wait until the eleven, or tomorrow's six o'clock. But it isn't worth the chink in our reliability it may cost.[4]

Every reporter makes mistakes:

- Reporting a plane crash, based on a telephone call from an anonymous source who sounded reliable, only to find it was a hoax.
- Predicting a legislative action, based on a leak from a state senator who had provided dependable information in the past, only to learn that the legislator wanted to prod public reaction against the bill.
- Reporting the death of a prominent resident who had the same first and last name as 14 others listed in the telephone book, only to find that you had the wrong middle initial.

Those kinds of mistakes force you to be more cautious the next time.

But you could make a more serious mistake by letting the pressure of competition force you into an ill-considered decision. At times, you'll come up with a story you haven't been able to confirm, and you may be aware that your competitors have it, too. You'll need to resist the temptation to air an incomplete story simply because you're afraid your competitors will beat you.

The following story is factual, but the names have been changed to protect the people who were involved:

> The key figure in the Simon case is an 18–year–old resident named Harold Doubty. We first became aware of him last July when he approached us offering to provide information about Councilman Samuel Simon.
>
> On the afternoon of July 27th, we videotaped these scenes of Doubty with a concealed camera. At that time, Doubty was 17 years old and claimed to have had a homosexual relationship with the councilman. He

also claimed to have provided drugs for the councilman on one occasion.

Doubty told us he had a falling out with Simon and was willing to do anything to damage Simon's reputation.

While we were trying to establish whether Doubty's story was true, he tried to get money from us in return for the details of his allegations. We refused, and that was the last we heard from him for several months.

About four weeks ago, according to law enforcement sources, Doubty devised another scheme to make money at the expense of Councilman Simon. He allegedly approached the operators of several massage parlors with tape recordings and information that would be damaging to the reputation of the councilman. According to investigators, Doubty thought the massage parlor owners could use the information to blackmail Simon so he would support their requests when they came before the city council.

Sources say the massage parlors reported Doubty's offer to police. The county sheriff assigned an undercover agent to a meeting attended by Doubty and a massage parlor operator. Police sources say Doubty was taken into custody before any blackmail deal could be consummated.

Sheriff's investigators say they considered filing an extortion charge against Doubty, but so far they've filed nothing.

Because of Doubty's activities, investigators became aware of the claims he was making about Councilman Simon's private life. Sources say Simon may be charged with contributing to the delinquency of a minor, among other possible charges.

One top law enforcement official says the potential for other blackmail attempts is the main reason for concern. On the city council, Simon makes many decisions involving hundreds of thousands of dollars. Investigators say that if Simon does not resign, his position on the city council could be seriously compromised.

We've made repeated attempts to get answers from Simon on this story, but he's been unavailable. However, in the last several days, he has issued

> denials of any improprieties through his office
> staff.
>   Doubty, by the way, has not given up on his
> effort to make money. Yesterday, he tried once again
> to get money from us in return for more detailed
> accusations. We have not paid him anything.
>   Doubty also hinted that he has asked other news
> organizations for money, apparently without success
> so far.

The story has all the elements of a major political exposé. But if you read it carefully, you can see the hazard of airing it without confirming the young man's accusations. The reporter has revealed no evidence, only the accusations of a youth who clearly has a motive for wanting publicity.

The last sentence of the story suggests the competitive pressure that prodded the station into airing the story—"he has asked other news organizations for money."

The council member was later charged on the basis of the young man's accusations, but a jury acquitted him. Meanwhile, because of the negative publicity, the council member lost the election.

The precept Walter Cronkite cited is worth thinking about: "Get it first, but first get it right."

Exercises

1. See a government attorney in your area—city, county, state. Ask for a copy of the law that regulates public records. Also ask the attorney to cite several examples of public records that are open to reporters and several that are closed to reporters.

2. Call or write the attorney general in your state. Ask if a committee or board exists to classify government information as public or private. Ask for the name, address, and telephone number of the head of that body, if it exists. Then call or write that person for a copy of the information practices law in your state and an explanation of how it works.

3. Talk to at least two radio, television, or newspaper reporters in your area who cover governmental agencies. Ask them to tell you about successes and failures they have encountered in attempting to use public records.

4. Decide on a beat you would like to cover if you should be employed by a radio or television station in your area. List some of the potential sources on that beat by name. Develop a story idea, write some potential questions, then make appointments with at least two of the sources on your list. Try to determine how useful they will be as regular sources on that beat.

5. Look for a controversial issue under discussion in your area. Read as much background as you can on the issue, then make appointments with two opponents on the issue. Prepare questions for each and design them to check the validity of the position each opponent takes on the issue.

6. Read wire service copy to find stories that fail to call attention to the impact of the information on your listeners or viewers. Research further at least one of the stories by calling the sources named by the wire or talking with others who are likely to know more about the story. Decide what the impact of the story is and rewrite the story to include it.

Notes

1. Leonard Downie Jr., *The New Muckrakers* (Washington, DC: The New Republic Book Co., 1976): 25–27.

2. Jack Olsen, Interview, 12 May 1988.

3. Herbert J. Gans, *Deciding What's News* (New York: Pantheon Books, 1979): 313–14.

4. Walter Cronkite, speech delivered to the Radio-Television News Directors Association, Denver, Colorado, 25 September 1970.

9

THE SOUND OF NEWS

I have a crazy theory that television is an audio medium and that radio is a visual medium. I obviously don't mean that quite literally, but what I mean by that is that good radio, which depends on words, requires of the listener a whole range of visual images in his mind in order to be part of that radio broadcast. Television, with its pictures, is almost useless without good words to go with it. So I tend to want to emphasize the words on television and the images created on radio.

—WILLIAM LEONARD,
"TV News of the Future —As Seen by Network Chiefs,"
U.S. News & World Report, November 20, 1978, p. 53.

Broadcast historians have dubbed the 1930s and 1940s "The Golden Age of Radio." It was an era when radio reporters and commentators like H.V. Kaltenborn, Elmer Davis, Gabriel Heatter, and Edward R. Murrow dominated the airwaves. It was also an era when newscasters conveyed the essence of the news, and commentators explained the meaning of the news, by the spoken word alone. To hold their audiences, they adopted dramatic reading styles and sometimes stentorian voices because voice was their only medium of communication.

Early television newscasters like Douglas Edwards and John Cameron Swayze carried that style over into the new visual medium. They were good readers with animated voices who could catch the attention of their audiences and hold them for 15 minutes of news.

As television producers began to illustrate their news with pictures, radio reporters began to illustrate their news with sounds. At first, the sounds of radio news were the recorded voices of newsmakers and the voices of other reporters. Gradually, radio reporters introduced ambient sounds. Now, without those sounds to supplement spoken words, radio news seems lifeless. Sounds stimulate mental images of the scenes that surround events.

Television producers, too, have adopted audio environments for their stories, but viewers can understand few television stories without supplementary words to fill in the blank spaces between the information provided by audio and video.

On December 20, 1980, NBC Sports' producers telecast an experiment—live football coverage without commentators. They broadcast a game between the Miami Dolphins and the New York Jets without the voices of announcers. They placed microphones in the stadium to pick up crowd sounds, the public address system, and the voices of referees and players, and they frequently superimposed printed information on the screen.

But most of their viewers were dissatisfied. Some were confused. They needed the voices of announcers to explain the elements of the game that they either missed or didn't understand. One television critic said the telecast without voices "was not unlike seeing a foreign film in which the subtitles are running a little late."[1]

Both radio and television news need the words of narrators to transmit the total picture, and both need supplementary voices and natural sounds to enhance interest and create images in the minds of listeners and viewers.

VOICERS AND STAND-UPS

Voicers—stories read or ad libbed by radio field reporters—and stand-ups—stories delivered on camera by television field reporters—are still staples in broadcast news. Reporters tell many such stories themselves, either because they must report them quickly to meet deadlines or because they have no voice or natural sounds or no pictures to supplement or illustrate their stories.

Changes in voices and faces help reinforce the attention of listeners and viewers. So, we frequently hear and see broadcast reporters relating stories from the scenes of events because their voices and faces give newscasts pace and variety.

Some radio news directors prefer the striking change in vocal quality they get with telephone voicers, as long as the quality of the telephone line is clear. Others prefer sound quality from the scene that almost matches studio quality.

Many television news directors like to show their reporters at the scenes of the events because reporters on location give a greater sense of urgency and reality to their stories.

Most news directors prefer short voicers and stand-ups, too. Some limit such reports to 40 seconds or less because the drone of the human voice or the static nature of one visual shot tends to grow monotonous and bogs down the pace of a newscast. Therefore, field reporters must find concise and colorful ways to present their information.

Sometimes, the story itself is so unusual that it will sustain interest as a straight narrative. Reporter Jake Jacobs of KNX Radio in Los Angeles reported a story to

CBS about a Beverly Hills doctor who had been convicted of "slumlord" activities, then sentenced to serve time in his own tenement building:

```
Doctor Milton Avol (AY-vall) was sentenced on July
13th to 30 days in the cockroach- and rat-infested
building.
     He was also equipped with an electronic device
around his ankle to monitor his movement. If he
wandered more than 150 feet from his room, the device
would sound an alarm.
     Avol was given the unusual sentence for repeatedly
ignoring court orders to bring the building up to
health and fire standards.
     When the sentence was completed, Avol refused to
leave the building, saying he would remain in his
room until about a dozen reporters and television
camera crews camped outside the building left.
     But reporters remained all day, monitoring all
exits without even a glimpse of the Beverly Hills
neurosurgeon.
     And by nightfall, it was not known if Avol had
eluded reporters via a secret escape route or was
still in his room.
     It was the first time a slumlord had been
sentenced to time in his own building, and Avol
became the first prisoner in Los Angeles County to be
equipped with an electronic leash to monitor his
movement.[2]
```

The story is just 180 words long, and Jacobs read it in just 54 seconds, but it's complete. He gave listeners a clear view of the day's happenings, along with the background of the story and an understanding of the uncommon nature of the sentence, all without wasting words.

Newscasters and field reporters often share elements of stories to give their delivery a conversational tone. They use the technique particularly when field reporters are on the scene.

On a late summer evening in 1987, a Northwest Airlines flight took off from Detroit bound for Phoenix, Arizona, and Orange County, California. Within seconds after takeoff, the plane lost power, wobbled, struck a freeway overpass, crashed, and burned near a car-rental agency. Only one person of the 150 aboard survived. She was a four-year-old girl whose father, mother, and six-year-old brother died in the crash. Authorities couldn't identify her until more than 24 hours after the crash. Then NBC Radio newscaster Gary Nunn and correspondent Alan Walden combined to report on the youngster's condition:

> Gary Nunn: Four-year-old Cecilia Cichan (SHEE-uhn)
>   clings to life now as the only person aboard
>   Northwest flight 255 to survive the Sunday night
>   crash, found in the arms of her dead mother.
>   Correspondent Alan Walden is with us live from
>   Detroit now where Cecilia is listed in critical
>   condition this morning.
> Alan Walden: Gary, I talked to the hospital a few
>   minutes ago. She is expected to make it.
>   Cecilia is suffering from third-degree burns
>   over about 30 percent of her body. She has a broken
>   leg and a broken collar bone.
>   The interesting thing was the identification
>   made by her grandfather. He said he told the
>   hospital officials she had a chipped tooth and
>   purple fingernail polish. And the little girl they
>   had at the hospital had both of those.
>   Gary . . .
> Gary Nunn: Precise numbers of how many people died
>   are impossible to determine. During the night,
>   several bodies were pulled from vehicles destroyed
>   in the crash, either when the plane hit them or
>   showered them with flaming fuel and debris.
>   The "New York Times," quoting officials close to
>   the inquiry, reports the pilots had no indication
>   of trouble until a computer voice declared, "Stall,
>   stall," indicating flight 255 was not flying fast
>   enough.[3]

Correspondent Alan Walden avoided the formal story structure. Instead, newscaster Gary Nunn read the lead, filled in the background, and identified the correspondent. Then Walden informally provided information on the girl's condition and the method of identification. He blended his voicer with the newscaster's narration by using the first name of the newscaster at the beginning and the end of his report. Radio and television reporters often utilize such techniques to insert voicers and stand-ups, especially when they're reporting live.

Television reporters infrequently report stories entirely as stand-ups; they're more likely to utilize them as introductions or tags or both, to stories. They'll tell the rest of their stories, voicing the narration over the video and inserting sound bites from newsmakers. Sometimes, they'll use stand-ups as a bridge between elements of stories when they have no other video to draw the elements together.

ACTUALITIES AND TALKING HEADS

Radio and television have an advantage over print media because they can give their listeners the *feeling* of the news in addition to its substance. Actualities—the voices of newsmakers on radio—and talking heads—the faces of newsmakers talking on television—give listeners and viewers a sense of receiving news directly from the sources.

Most actualities and talking heads originate with interviews, speeches, and news conferences. They can be effective in transmitting news, especially if the newsmakers are colorful and concise.

During a period of intense anti-American terrorism in the Middle East, American journalist Charles Glass, a former ABC News correspondent, was kidnapped in Lebanon. Two months after the kidnapping, Glass escaped from his captors, and Syrian soldiers took him to Damascus. NBC Radio reported the development in a voicer from Syria and actuality reactions from Glass's wife in London:

> Gary Nunn: American journalist Charles Glass, after
>   two months in the hands of kidnappers, escaped
>   before dawn in Beirut. Correspondent Tom Aspa
>   reports that Glass is waiting now to fly to London.
> Tom Aspa: Gary, American hostage Charlie Glass is
>   here in Damascus, a free man.
>   He was transported overland from the Lebanese
>   capital Beirut early this morning by Syrian
>   security men, and he's now at the home of the
>   American charge d'affaires in the Syrian capital.
>   He looked extremely fit and well. He says the
>   worst part of the ordeal was the suffering his wife
>   and family must have gone through.
> Gary Nunn: Charles Glass' wife Fiona has been
>   waiting in London, and our correspondent Fred
>   Kennedy talked with her.
> Mrs. Glass: I'm just amazed and very thrilled.
> Fred Kennedy: An overjoyed Mrs. Glass after hearing
>   her husband is free. Their ordeal is finally over.
> Mrs. Glass: It's been awful -- once somebody's a
>   hostage and then the acceptance of outrage it's
>   taken, given the state of play between Iran and the
>   States right now.

> <u>Fred Kennedy</u>: Charlie Glass telephoned, saying he's heading home.
> <u>Mrs. Glass</u>: He just said that he was fine, that he loves me and he should be home tonight.
> <u>Fred Kennedy</u>: For the first time in 62 days, Charlie's wearing a smile, and it's as big and as bright as a piano keyboard.[4]

The newscaster read the lead to set up the story and introduce the reporter in Damascus. The reporter's voicer told us the victim's location and condition. The newscaster bridged to the correspondent in London. Then the correspondent utilized three quick actuality bites to give us an empathic sense of how the victim's wife reacted.

Your objective in selecting actualities should be to catch the atmosphere and meaning of the event. Choose concise actuality bites that state clear thoughts to help listeners and viewers focus on the main idea of the story. Short, punchy statements will attract your audience, and they'll remember them. Long, rambling statements may only discourage them. In general, think of a good sound bite as one that runs no more than 10 to 15 seconds. Only if newsmakers compel attention through what they say, or how they say it, should you allow the actuality to run longer.

Be governed by the degree of interest you think the actuality will generate. Former NBC News President Reuven Frank says you risk boredom if you choose actualities indiscriminately:

> Most people are dull. That is, they communicate ineptly. If they are dull, their description of interesting events will be dull. Sometimes they are interesting, but for the wrong reasons. They suffer from speech defects, tic, or strabismus, and what may make them interesting is precisely what interferes with their contribution to information. Those who communicate aptly—politicians, actors, and the like—tend to be self-serving.[5]

Your own impressions when you listen to taped voices of newsmakers should guide you. If you think the actuality will hold the attention of your listeners and viewers, use it. If not, discard it. You have no reason to use an actuality simply because you've recorded one. It must contribute something to your audience's interest and understanding of the story.

Often, you can raise the interest level of an actuality if you incorporate the ambient sound that exists at many events. Experiment with microphone placement and camera position to take advantage of audience reactions to a speech, for example. A second microphone placed where it can pick up vocal reactions from the crowd, or even a second recorder onto which you tape crowd sounds only, may help, if you can balance the sound accurately or if you can mix crowd sounds with voice sounds in the studio. The sound will draw your listeners into the scene.

A camera placed where it can capture part of the audience, or cutaway shots photographed when the camera is not shooting the speaker, will give your viewers an idea of how the crowd accepted the speaker.

The best actualities are usually the spontaneous voices of participants in an event when they react to what they are experiencing. Consumer reporter David Horowitz and a television crew found themselves in the center of the story when an angry consumer burst into their studio. CBS Radio's Bill Whitney reported:

> Bill Whitney: In Los Angeles late today, a man with
> a gun invaded the studios of KNBC-TV and confronted
> consumer reporter David Horowitz during a live
> newscast. Here's what happened:
> Horowitz: Well, one of the nicest things about
> shopping by mail order . . . (noise) . . . Pardon
> me . . . (off-camera voices) . . . What is this?
> Off-camera voice: He has a gun.
>
> (More voices, indistinguishable.)
>
> Horowitz: All right. (Noise) All right. Well, let me
> read this. Folks, we have . . . we have someone on
> the set who's standing here and would like me to
> read . . . uhmm . . . to read this . . . aah . . .
> this copy which he's just handed me. You want to
> tell me your name . . . or not? (Voice mumbles)
> . . . What is it?
> Voice: Terry . . .
> Horowitz: And, Terry, where are you from?
> Bill Whitney: At that point the screen went black.
> Horowitz read the man's statement, which is
> described as rambling and nonsensical.
>   Then security people moved in, the man was
> disarmed, and no one was hurt.
>   The weapon turned out to be a plastic replica of
> a 45-caliber gun.
>   But Horowitz, whose motto as a consumer reporter
> is "Fight back," says it looked very real to him.[6]

Listeners couldn't understand most of the off-camera conversation, but Horowitz's explanation helped them grasp what was happening, and the off-camera voices gave listeners a feel for the tension of the moment.

Vary the way you utilize actualities. Sometimes, you can draw listeners and viewers into the story if you begin with an actuality. NBC Radio's Jay Barbaree used a tape from the files to introduce a story about space exploration. Newscaster Ann Taylor set up Barbaree's story:

Ann Taylor: Take a space ride in the future and you
    may end up on the moon. That's what some U.S. space
    officials are now recommending. And as
    correspondent Jay Barbaree reports, this could be a
    stepping stone to Mars:
Voice of Neil Armstrong: Tranquility Base here. The
    "Eagle" has landed.

(Sound of Armstrong's conversation with Mission
    Control continues under narration . . .)

Jay Barbaree: If Sally Ride's recommendations are
    followed, America could have astronauts living on a
    moon base by the turn of the century.
        Only Americans have walked on the moon, and
    Ride, the first American woman to go into space,
    told NASA officials the moon base could be used as
    an outpost to begin a manned mission to the planet
    Mars.
        Astronaut Ride headed a task force appointed by
    NASA to determine what America's future space goals
    should be.[7]

The file tape of Neil Armstrong's voice was recorded on July 20, 1969, when
he and Edwin Aldrin became the first men to land on the surface of the moon. It
was a familiar sound that aptly fit the context of Barbaree's story.
    If the actuality you use to open the story is not understood, you should follow
up immediately with an explanation. ABC Radio's Ian Hunter opened a story about
minority children in schools with the sound of a chant, then followed with an
identification of the voices:

(Voice shouting) I am . . .

(Crowd of children echoing) I am . . .

(Voice shouting) Somebody!

(Crowd echoing) Somebody!

(Voice shouting) I am . . .

(Crowd echoing) I am . . .

(Voice shouting) Somebody!

(Crowd echoing) Somebody!

(Ian Hunter) Black activist Jesse Jackson and his rallying cry that many black Chicago school children have chanted.[8]

That opening consumed just eleven seconds, including the identification of Jesse Jackson and the children, and it drew listeners in to hear the substance of the story that followed.

Sounds recorded on the scene add dimensions to radio and television stories that might fall flat without them. But choose sounds that contribute to the meaning of the story, not sound merely to have sound. Listeners and viewers react positively to sound that is genuine; it adds to their understanding of the event.

Radio and television reporters sometimes step away from stories to let the participants in events tell the story themselves. Although they need to patiently practice such a technique, their finished stories will often be more effective than stories with narration only. Gene Hering, a news photographer for KGW-TV in Portland, Oregon, demonstrated that skill when he covered a teachers' strike:

"The strike had been going on for quite a while, and in that kind of a situation, people begin to get hostile," says Jerry J. Schneider, head of news photography for the NBC television affiliate owned by King Broadcasting Company.

"He could have covered the picketing by the book. You've seen it a thousand times," says Schneider. "An angry spokesperson in the foreground talks to a reporter with picketers in the rear. But Gene has a good instinct for finding the pictures and natural sound that tell the story without a lot of dialogue."

In this situation, he let the crowd get used to his presence, so it didn't play to the camera. "There was just this guy with a film camera, and he didn't attract a lot of attention."

Then came the opportunity: a teacher walking to work, through the picket line. The outrage was there on the faces and in the voices of the picketers.

"Why are you doing this?" one pleaded.

The teacher going in stared straight ahead, expressionless, moving slowly through the crowd.

Hering was right there recording the action and sounds. It was the next best thing to the viewing audience being on the line seeing it happen.

> possibility. I think access routes--a variety of
> things -- but there are going to be actions that
> can be taken in courtroom facilities in existing
> buildings.
>
> <u>Ted Robbins</u>: Vickrey did say extra precautions were
> taken today because of Gardner's history of
> violence and escape. He praised the work of
> officers.[10]

Without the reporter's narration, this story would have been rambling and confusing. Robbins summarized the important details concisely and used the actualities to highlight them.

EYEWITNESS REPORTS

Radio and television reporters often act as eyewitnesses for their listeners and viewers, giving them an impression of being present at the scenes of events.

Radio is a more active medium than television in the sense that it demands more listener involvement. Listeners must create their own pictures from the words and sounds they hear.

Former CBS commentator Eric Sevareid remembers listening to radio reports about the assassination of President John Kennedy: "It was far more dramatic and engrossing than television. Just those voices, and your mind paints those pictures."[11]

Radio reporters are becoming skilled at delivering eyewitness reports—detailed descriptions of events as reporters see them—often delivering them live or recording them on location, where they can take advantage of the sound surrounding the event. Reporter Alex Sullivan walked through a burning residential suburb of Los Angeles as he narrated this story for KNX Radio:

> As we walk along down this main road in the Riviera
> section that overlooks the Pacific Ocean, we can see
> other burned-out houses, homeowners shaking their
> heads, looking down at what had been perhaps a living
> room or a bedroom.
>
> The sun is peeking through the smoke. Up above,
> you can see a borate bomber, a helicopter, dropping
> water.
>
> But the damage has essentially been done -- 250
> homes, many of them destroyed, homes that had been
> built with loving care years ago.
>
> Walking through memories, as we look over -- and
> there's another house right there. There's a station

wagon completely burned out. A very large home,
obviously, and that apparently had a tile roof on it.
     As you walk through the brush here, the fire is
still going. There's a gas main, obviously, in the
middle of that house, and it is going briskly. It has
to be a gas main with that kind of flame coming out
of it. And the heat is very intense. We'd better move
back. This house probably went up a couple of hours
ago, and the heat is still very strong.
     Throughout the day today, firemen will be keeping
the pressure on, hoping the wind doesn't shift. It
was the wind last night that was the most devastating
as the fickle finger of fire came down and selected
at random various houses, and they popped up like
tinder -- fire engines unable to reach them in time.
     And now, it's assessing the damage which will be
in the millions-of-dollars range.[12]

Sullivan narrated the story in present tense and used the personal pronoun "we"
in a familiar tone that helped his listeners absorb the detail and recreate the scene
in their minds.

Eyewitness reports can be effective in continuing stories when a newscaster
interviews a reporter live, on the scene, as Keeve Berman did with Tom Schell on
ABC's Contemporary Network, when authorities found a bomb in a Nevada casino:

<u>Keeve Berman</u>: Authorities at Stateline, Nevada, are
     about to hold a news conference, and it's
     speculated a decision has been made to evacuate
     some neighboring hotels and casinos while a bomb
     squad tries to either defuse or detonate a large
     explosive device sitting inside Harvey's Wagon
     Wheel Casino and Hotel. Live on the phone with me
     is ABC's Tom Schell. Tom, can you confirm these
     reports?
<u>Tom Schell</u>: Keeve, I can only tell you that there
     will be a briefing here within a half an hour, but
     I am in the hotel, Harrah's, right across the
     street from Harvey's. We have not been told that we
     will have to evacuate, and as far as we know, no
     evacuation plans have been revealed.
<u>Keeve Berman</u>: And what's the scene like right now at
     Harvey's Wagon Wheel?
<u>Tom Schell</u>: The Wagon Wheel is closed. The casino
     has been shut down since early yesterday morning.

> The hotel has been evacuated. The street, the road,
> and the main highway, 50, that runs in front, is
> blocked off for blocks on either side to keep cars
> and pedestrians from moving, just in case this bomb
> should accidentally detonate. It is a large bomb.
> If it did go off, the authorities say it could
> cause damage in a wide area.
>
> Keeve Berman: That's ABC's Tom Schell, live, in
> Stateline, Nevada. Now, whoever set that device
> claimed in a letter it contains a blast—yield
> equivalent to about eleven—hundred pounds of T–N–T.
> The letter demands what sources say was three—
> million dollars and a helicopter in exchange for
> defusing instructions. Nevada Governor Bob List
> appealed today for more information, but nothing
> has been received yet. And to reiterate something
> that Tom Schell just said, a law enforcement source
> says that even though that bomb is surrounded by
> sandbags, if it goes off, it could demolish the
> first four floors of that eleven—story hotel, cause
> some heavy damage up to the seventh floor and blow
> out U–S Highway 50 in front of the hotel on that
> California—Nevada border. [13]

Both the newscaster and the reporter were ad libbing from notes and observations, and their narration carried a natural conversational flavor.

NATURAL AND WILD-TRACK SOUND

Sound is a vital dimension for radio and television reporting. The sound of construction equipment at the site of a dam being built, the sound of a crowd at a
football game, the sound of cattle at a roundup, the sound of cars and trucks during
a traffic jam, the sound of voices at a public hearing—all of these contribute to
your listeners' and viewers' feeling for the story.

Most news photographers record the natural sound of events as they photograph
them, then they play those sounds underneath the narration of their reporters. For
this reason, radio reporters frequently record their stories in locations where they
can hear sounds in the background. A helicopter flying over a burning forest, rescue
workers digging through the debris of a building shattered by an earthquake, aircraft
and gunfire during a fighter attack—these are the sounds that are natural to their
environments and give viewers and listeners a sense of reality for what they see
and hear. Silent pictures and stories narrated from silent rooms no longer match

the impact of pictures and narration fleshed out with the atmosphere of sound. Natural sounds fill the void in spaces where narration is pointless or unnecessary.

Sometimes you can use wild-track, or generic, sound—sound typical of but not recorded at the event—to generate an atmosphere for your listeners or viewers. If the sound need not coincide precisely with the narration, wild-track sound may create an atmosphere that is typical of the moment. You can use such sounds as those made by trains, cars, motorcycles, aircraft, machinery, and crowds if they contribute to the realistic atmosphere and do not distort the factual nature of the event.

For example, the sound of applause may either underemphasize or overemphasize a crowd's reaction to an action. The sound of vigorous applause, accompanied by pictures of an impassive crowd, would tell your viewers that the scene is unrealistic. Silence, accompanied by pictures of vigorous demonstrators, would tell your viewers that the scene is a distortion of reality.

A word of caution, however: Many producers disapprove of wild-track sound under any circumstances because it could damage the credibility of the station if listeners and viewers discover the sound is artificial.

Occasionally, you can find an effective use for recorded music to enhance a news story. One reporter juxtaposed pictures of litter along a highway against the music of "America the Beautiful" to tell his viewers a story without narration.

LEADING TO SOUND

You can find many ways to integrate sound into a newscast; you're limited only by your ingenuity. In most cases, you can blend newscaster and reporter, newscaster and newsmaker, or newscaster and natural sound so well that stories would seem incomplete without any of these elements.

In many stories, the newscaster delivers the lead, a field reporter or correspondent elaborates the specifics of the story, and then the newscaster adds a fact or two to tie the story into a package. In the following story, CBS Radio newscaster Bill Lynch integrated a story from reporter Barry Peterson into his newscast:

> <u>Bill Lynch</u>: Hours after government officials
>   appealed for restraint, new street battles erupted
>   today in two South Korean cities, pitting striking
>   workers against riot police.
>   Even so, Barry Peterson tells us from Seoul
>   officials still hope for labor peace.
> <u>Barry Peterson</u>: The government says it believes the
>   strike situation across the country is settling
>   down, that more strikes now are being settled than
>   new ones are breaking out.
>   But the real problem is focused in the small

seaport town where a striking shipyard worker was
killed over the weekend. The government has rushed
in extra riot police, and there is concern about
tension in the area — concern that will grow as
the funeral approaches Wednesday for the dead
striker.

    The government hopes it will be peaceful. In
fact, labor leaders are saying they want it to be
peaceful, as well.

<u>Bill Lynch</u>: Union leaders say a cemetery has refused
to accept the body of that slain striker.[14]

If the voices of the newscaster and the reporter are distinct, as they were in
this case, the reporter need not sign off his story in the traditional way, and the
two can blend the facts into a complete package, almost as if the reporter had
been reacting to the newscaster as a newsmaker would.

Newscasters and reporters can blend the voices of newsmakers into their stories
in the same flowing style. ABC Radio's Kate Doordan read the lead, filled in the
background, and introduced the newsmaker in this story:

<u>Kate Doordan</u>: Ricky, Robert and Randy Ray went to
school today in Arcadia, Florida. The youngsters,
aged ten, nine and eight, went with a court order
and a police escort, their parents leading the way.

    The boys, who all are hemophiliacs, have tested
positive for AIDS, meaning that it is certain that
they have been exposed to the virus, and the whole
town of Arcadia knows it.

    Some people threatened the Ray family, and many
people threatened to keep their kids out of school.

    Principal Donald Knoche (kih–NAW–kee) says the
campaign did have an effect.

<u>Donald Knoche</u>: Attendance today was down about 45
percent, but we expect — you know, a lot of
parents kept their children home, I feel, because
of the concern over the activities and everything
— the press that would be here — and they wanted
their children to have a good first day. So I think
things will improve as the week progresses.

<u>Kate Doordan</u>: The Ray brothers have been out of
school since last fall.

    After the year–long court battle, their parents
say the youngsters are very excited about returning
to the classroom today.[15]

The story moves from one element to the next as a continuous narrative, and the newsmaker's voice adds substance and credibility.

You can blend natural sounds into the flow of your stories, too, if they help create an atmosphere characteristic of the event. CBS Radio's Douglas Edwards generated some subtle suspense to set up his listeners for sound:

> Douglas Edwards: An hour from now, Mayor Dianne
>   Feinstein will cut a three-foot-wide ribbon, and
>   after an absence of nearly two years, a familiar
>   sound returns to the streets of San Francisco.
>
>   (Sound of bells clanging, up for eight seconds,
>   then under)
>
> Douglas Edwards: Cable cars gearing up for full
>   service after a 60-million-dollar renovation. It
>   will be a lavish welcome back, complete with
>   balloons, bands, cable cars made of salami, sour
>   dough and chocolate, and at nightfall, fireworks at
>   Fisherman's Wharf featuring pyrotechnical cable
>   cars displays. [16]

The story consists of facts that create a festive picture, and the bells of the cable car make it more vivid. But, to avoid potential confusion, Edwards identified the source of the bells after he utilized the sound to reinforce our attention.

Wraparounds

Radio and television reporters produce many stories as wraparounds, or packages—they wrap their narratives around the statements of newsmakers. Reporters introduce the stories, summarize the background, introduce the voices and faces that appear in one or more sound bites, and then summarize the stories.

On ABC, Kathleen Sullivan produced for radio a wraparound about women who have chosen professional careers in the armed forces:

> Kathleen Sullivan: Women are earning their stripes
>   in the spit-and-polish atmosphere of the U-S
>   military academies.
>   In May of this year, Christine Holdereid was the
>   first woman to graduate at the top of her class at
>   the U-S Naval Academy.
> Christine Holdereid: Women are accepted at the
>   academy right now because they're there, and it's

obvious they're going to stay there. There's still
some diehard resistance, but it's not a big factor.

Kathleen Sullivan: Navy Ensign Holdereid is now
pulling her first duty assignment with the Sixth
Fleet in Rota, Spain.

Meanwhile, this term at West Point, Senior Cadet
Karen Short is the first woman regimental commander
to bark out the orders.

Woman's voice, shouting: Battalion commander . . .
(Voice fades under for narration.)

Kathleen Sullivan: Cadet Short says it's not just
the military which is starting to get into step by
putting women into leadership roles.

Karen Short: I think that it's the time for women in
society — that women are being looked upon and
being given the opportunity to demonstrate their
ability.

Kathleen Sullivan: Women have been attending service
academies since 1976. Two–hundred–ninety–four have
graduated from Annapolis, 335 from West Point and
490 from the Air Force Academy.[17]

Kathleen Sullivan condensed the essence of the story into her own narrative, complemented by the sound bites of the ensign and the cadet characterizing the opinions of women about their places in military professions and the natural sound of the woman cadet officer. All added interest to the story.

The wraparound is much like a concise newspaper story that utilizes the voices of newsmakers rather than direct quotations, but it has the added advantage of natural sound to recreate atmosphere.

Television reporters employ the technique, too, but they have pictures to clarify the atmosphere of the event. WTVF-TV of Nashville, Tennessee, used pictures and sound at Graceland Mansion to cover the tenth anniversary of Elvis Presley's death:

Video	Audio
(Graceland Mansion and crowd of tourists)	(REPORTER) For the thousands of fans making their pilgrimage this week to Memphis, Graceland is a
(Elvis' grave)	mecca, a place to share the spirit of a man they call "The King."

(Dan Marquez, fan)	(MARQUEZ) I think he just had such an impact during a period of time when we were looking for heroes in this country, and I think he just represented so much of what we call Middle America.
(Roxanne Sirabo, fan)	(SIRABO) People who give a lot of themselves, express themselves in music and other ways . . .
(Grave)	and just spread it across the world . . .
(Woman holding rose)	I mean, I just think they're so beautiful.
(Guide)	(GUIDE) Graceland is a southern colonial-style mansion . . .
(People at mansion)	(REPORTER) This anniversary of Presley's death has brought some 50-thousand new faces to Memphis,
(Picture of Elvis) (Another picture)	many of them here to tour Graceland to get a glimpse of a life that was cut short, a life that brought
(People putting roses on the grave)	joy to millions, both here and abroad.
(Pam Cross, fan)	(CROSS, in British dialect) It still hurts . . . but it's good that he's still remembered, I think, anyway.
(Elvis poster)	(REPORTER) While Elvis became a legend in the U-S,
(Wide shot crowd)	his legacy lives on in countries around the world,
(Medium shot crowd) (Male fan talking to crowd)	attracting national media, as well as other celebrities who knew Elvis as their friend.

(Actress Barbara Eden)	(EDEN) He was a joy, just a joy to know –– a very genuine, direct, kind man, and a very talented one.
(Author Carl Perkins, "Blue Suede Shoes")	(PERKINS) He wanted people to have fun, and that's what this place was, and it's –– there's a sweet kind of sadness that creeps up on you here now.
(People at grave)	(REPORTER) In his day, Elvis had a reputation for getting people "all shook up."
(Woman with rose)	Ten years after his death, his fans are still shaking with grief.
(Kathy Louviere, fan)	(LOUVIERE) This is my seventh time, and it hurts. This is my . . . (She begins to weep . . . pause) I miss him. I wish I could have known him, got to see him. But . . . (Off–camera voice) But you didn't have to meet him or know him. (Louviere) Nope . . . still love him.[18]

The reporter blended a variety of personal impressions of Elvis Presley with his narration to create a mood and a feeling for the emotion evoked by the rock singer's death.

In the radio wraparound, the reporter identified the voices by name and title as she led into each sound bite. In the television package, the producer super-imposed names and titles over the lower third of the screen so the reporter didn't have to identify them in the narrative copy.

When you need to identify people in radio stories, drop their names and titles into the narrative copy as close as you can to the sound bite so your listeners will understand immediately who's talking. When you identify them in television stories, superimpose names and titles as soon as possible after they appear on screen in the sound bite.

Sometimes in a television story, you can juxtapose the opposing opinions of two newsmakers against each other without a narrative bridge between the two sound bites. The change of faces on the screen, supplemented by superimposed names and titles to identify the newsmakers soon after their faces appear, gives your viewers enough visual information to keep identities clear.

If you try to juxtapose voices in a radio story, however, you risk confusing your listeners, unless you identify both clearly just before you roll the tape or unless the sound bites are short and the voices distinctly different. On radio, listeners find it more difficult to separate voices.

Indirect Lead-ins

To introduce sound, radio and television reporters and newscasters utilize indirect lead-ins more often than any other kind. Indirect lead-ins are written as complete sentences and do not suggest to listeners or viewers that any other voice (either a reporter's or newsmaker's) will follow. For example, Beryl Britt of Associated Press's Network News led into a reaction from a public official this way:

> <u>Beryl Britt</u>: The saga of the Mobro Four-thousand is
> over. The infamous Islip garbage barge has a home.
> It pulled into a dock here at a Brooklyn, New York,
> incinerator after five months adrift, six-thousand
> miles travel and rejection by five states and three
> countries.
>
>   Its arrival was rather unceremonious, with T-V
> cameras running and a handful of public officials
> watching, like New York City Sanitation
> Commissioner Brendan Sexton, who agrees the barge
> has taught the nation a lesson about garbage
> disposal.
> <u>Commissioner Sexton</u>: We really, as a society, the
> public, everybody has to pitch in. This is all of
> our problem.
> <u>Beryl Britt</u>: The trash will be off-loaded slowly,
> inspected and burned, with the ash going back to
> Islip, New York, where most of the refuse
> originated.[19]

The story would have seemed complete without the sound bite. The sentence preceding the sound bite is a complete sentence, so Britt closed the thought vocally with a downward inflection. But he also wrote the lead-in to introduce the sanitation commissioner and summarize the essence of his comment without repeating his exact words. So, Britt didn't detract from the comment when it appeared.

Rob Armstrong introduced only the organization the newsmaker represented when he led into the sound bite, then he named her at the end of the bite. The technique is especially useful if the name of the newsmaker is unfamiliar. In this case, her organization's name alone gave credence to her statement. But her name at the end reinforced the organization's credibility.

Surprise lead-ins are probably more effective in radio news than they are in television, where superimposed names and titles establish identity while news-makers' faces are on the screen.

Split-Sentence Lead-Ins

Once in a while, you can split a sentence between your lead-in narration and your newsmaker's statement to blend one idea between both voices. This effective, but sometimes difficult, technique is useful when you have a newsmaker's statement that is too long or too rambling, and you have trouble finding a concise, meaningful segment. You can summarize part of the statement concisely in your own words, then let the newsmaker complete it.

You'll find it easier to blend ideas if you find a natural break between independent clauses, then lead into your newsmaker with a conjunction. That's what UPI Radio's Pye Chamberlayne did when he reported that a group of congressmen had failed to defeat a missile program:

> Pye Chamberlayne: The opponents say the more you
> think and talk about the M—X, the worse it looks.
> They say their uphill battles are worth fighting.
> Democrat Levin of Michigan, for example, said he
> knew perfectly well that his group could not kill
> the missile this year, but . . .
> Levin: . . . we have a better chance of winning next
> year, and if we lose next year, we'll have a little
> better chance of winning the year after because
> we're making a fight now. It's a fight which is so
> critical that it literally could mean the
> difference between the survival of the species.
> Pye Chamberlayne: Supporters of the missile say it
> is needed to show Russia we have the will to defend
> ourselves and thus will encourage the Soviets to
> negotiate arms control agreements. Support is less
> than fervent for the M—X —— even the Republican
> Senate has cut the president's M—X production
> program in half.[24]

The split-sentence technique is also useful for getting out of a sound bite comfortably when the newsmaker tends to ramble and speak in open-ended sentences— sentences that end with inconclusive upward vocal inflections. Without a pause, add another of the newsmaker's thoughts in your own narration. Begin it with a conjunction, and it will appear you are helping newsmakers complete their idea rather than interrupting them.

Lead-ins to Natural Sound

Often, you'll cover events where natural sounds contribute atmosphere to your stories, and sometimes, you'll want to use such natural sounds to attract the attention of listeners and viewers at the beginnings of stories.

In television, your viewers will probably be able to see the source of the sound, but in radio, you'll need to identify the sound to avoid confusing your listeners. Usually, the identification can be subtle and indirect, as it was when ABC Radio's Kate Doordan told about an aborted space shuttle mission:

> Kate Doordan: If you're a rocket ship, you don't get
>   much closer than this:
> Mission Control voice: Seven, six, five . . . We
>   have main engine start . . . We have a cutoff . . .
>   We have an abort by the on—board computers of the
>   orbiter "Discovery."
> Kate Doordan: And so we had a launch pad shutdown
>   for the space shuttle mission —— four seconds
>   before liftoff. A computer saw that something was
>   wrong in an engine.
>   NASA has no idea yet when it can reschedule the
>   launch.
>   Officials say the crew was never in danger.[25]

Kate Doordan didn't need to identify the voice or even say it was from Mission Control. She merely had to reiterate the fact that computers had sensed trouble and canceled the launch, and we understood what the Mission Control voice had told us.

Lead-in Traps

Avoid repetition and exaggeration in lead-ins. Try not to diminish the impact of your newsmaker's statement, and try not to make it seem more important than it is.

If you duplicate newsmakers' words in your lead-in, you'll detract from what they say. Here's an example of such redundancy:

> Reporter: Heavy, wet snow accumulated at area ski resorts overnight, but it may not help skiers. The Forest Service has issued an extreme avalanche alert.
> Forest Service representative: We've issued an extreme avalanche alert.

Such a lead-in makes the newsmaker's statement unnecessary. Rewrite the lead-in to set up what the newsmaker says without repeating it. You could simply remove the reporter's second sentence:

> Reporter: Heavy, wet snow accumulated at area ski resorts overnight, but it may not help skiers.
> Forest Service representative: We've issued an extreme avalanche alert.

Now, identify the newsmaker, and the lead-in will blend with the actuality, and both will be essential elements of the story.

Don't try to spice your lead-in with exaggerated words or phrases. Let the tone of the actuality be the tone of your lead-in:

> Reporter: The strike of city firemen continues this morning, and many local businessmen criticize the strikers. Grocer Harry Brand calls the strike an abomination.
> Grocer: It's a sad situation. I think it's sad for a businessman who's been paying taxes all his life to find nobody's around when he needs fire protection.

Nothing in the grocer's language suggested a word as strong as "abomination." If he used it, the reporter should have included it in the sound bite or should have identified it clearly as the grocer's word in his lead-in. In this instance, the reporter was trying to attract listeners or viewers rather than provide them with factual information. Some of his audience may interpret his lead-in to mean he's editorially opposed to the strike.

The lead-in would have been more natural if the reporter had merely suggested the grocer's attitude, then allowed the grocer to express himself in his own way:

> Reporter: The strike of the city's firemen continues this morning, and many local businessmen criticize the strikers. Grocer Harry Brand is unsympathetic.

> Grocer: It's a sad situation. I think it's sad for a
> businessman who's been paying taxes all his life to
> find nobody's around when he needs fire protection.

The word unsympathetic is closer to the tone of the grocer's complaint; it establishes the mood of the actuality without distorting it.

THE SOUND DIMENSION

Sound is the complimentary dimension in radio and television news that completes the scene and brings a sense of realism to your listeners and viewers. Whereas words alone can relate facts, the human voice enhances those words with subtle emotion, and pictures accentuate the facts and the mood. Sound helps your audience feel the presence of the news.

The measured enunciation of a reporter telling a story from the Middle East gives us a sense of distance. The strident voice of a politician gives us a sense of the size of his crowd. Such background sounds as martial music, cheers, gunfire, cows lowing, demonstrators chanting, children laughing, or sirens wailing give us a sense of location and story substance.

When television news was young, producers imitated motion picture newsreels and played recorded mood music under a reader's narration, amplifying it when the reader had nothing to say, fading down when he started to read again. Today, such background music would sound amateurish, because listeners and viewers have come to expect realism in radio and television news.

Exercises

1. Write a voicer or standup script for a story you have covered. Time it to run approximately 40 seconds, oral reading time. Read the story to an audio tape recorder or video camera, trying to make your delivery as conversational and natural as you can. Play back the tape and analyze your story. Was it clear for your listeners or viewers? Was your delivery conversational? Were there any phrases or clauses that were difficult to read? Why? What do you need to do to improve your next voicer or stand-up?

2. Organize in your mind the essential facts from a story you've covered. Write some concise notes on a small card or piece of paper. Deliver the story extemporaneously (i.e., ad lib) to an audio tape recorder or video camera, referring to your notes as infrequently as possible. Play back the tape and analyze your story. Was it complete? Were the main ideas clear? Did your delivery sound conversational? What do you need to do to improve your next story?

3. Develop a story idea. Interview one or more newsmakers on audio tape or videotape. Choose at least two concise sound bites that you think add most to your story, and write a wraparound, or package script. Record your narrative and edit in the sound bites. Analyze the story. Was it complete? Did it flow smoothly from voicer to actuality to voicer? Ask someone else to listen to or watch your tape. Was the story clear to your listener or viewer? What could you do to improve the story?

4. Look for a scheduled event where you expect news to be made—a meeting, a speech, a news conference, a public hearing, a demonstration, a sports event. Before the event occurs, find someone who can give you background information and some idea of what is expected to happen. Attend the event and observe it until you have a sense of what's taking place. Position yourself unobtrusively but in a location where your microphone can pick up background sounds or your camera can picture the scene behind you. Record an eyewitness report that explains what's happening and describes some of the details and action at the scene. Play back the tape and analyze your reporting technique.

5. Look for an event where natural sounds will be prominent—a locker room where a winning team is expected to react to its victory, a speech where an audience might applaud or respond vocally, a meeting or public hearing where the voices of participants can be heard prominently, a fire where you can hear the sound of pumper trucks, a school playground while children are in recess. Record the sounds without narration. Then, in the studio, record your narrative story and mix the natural sounds with the story in a way that enhances it. Ask someone else to watch or listen to your complete tape. Analyze their reactions.

6. Produce a story with at least one actuality included in it. Write the story with three different kinds of lead-ins—indirect, direct, suspended, question, surprise, or split-sentence. Record each of the three versions and analyze them. Which kind of lead-in worked best? Which least effectively? Why?

Notes

1. Richard F. Shepard, "TV Without Voice: A Neophyte's Report," *The New York Times* (21 December 1980): 65.
2. Jake Jacobs, CBS Radio News, 12 August 1987.
3. Gary Nunn and Alan Walden, NBC Radio News, 18 August 1987.
4. Gary Nunn, Tom Aspa, and Fred Kennedy, NBC Radio News, 18 August 1987.
5. Reuven Frank, a memo to the staff of NBC News, reprinted by A. William Bluem, *Documentary in American Television* (New York: Hastings House, 1965): 270.
6. Bill Whitney and David Horowitz, CBS News, 19 August 1987.
7. Ann Taylor and Jay Barbaree, NBC News, 17 August 1987.
8. Ian Hunter, ABC Entertainment Network, 19 August 1980.

9. "Photography Station of the Year," *Telek,* 3, no. 2 (1980): 12.

10. Ted Robbins, KALL-AM, 2 April 1985.

11. "Eric Sevareid: He Was There," *Broadcasting* (12 September 1977): 38.

12. Alex Sullivan, KNX-AM, 1977.

13. Keeve Berman and Tom Schell, ABC Contemporary Network, 17 August 1980.

14. Bill Lynch and Barry Peterson, CBS News, 24 August 1987.

15. Kate Doordon, ABC Information Network, 24 August 1987.

16. Douglas Edwards, CBS News, 21 June 1984.

17. Kathleen Sullivan, ABC Information Network, 19 September 1984.

18. WTVF-TV, Conus News Exchange, 14 August 1987.

19. Beryl Britt, Associated Press Network News, 24 August 1987.

20. Harold Dow, CBS News, 25 August 1987.

21. Alan Walden, NBC News, 19 September 1984.

22. Douglas Edwards, CBS News, 14 September 1984.

23. Rob Armstrong, CBS News, 26 August 1987.

24. Pye Chamberlayne, UPI News, 15 June 1984.

25. Kate Doordan, ABC Information Network, 16 June 1984.

10

A VIEW OF THE NEWS

This instrument can teach, it can illuminate; yes, it can even inspire. But it can do so only to the extent that humans are determined to use it to those ends. Otherwise, it is merely wires and lights in a box. There is a great and perhaps decisive battle to be fought against ignorance, intolerance, and indifference. This weapon of television could be useful.
— EDWARD R. MURROW, "A Broadcaster Talks to His Colleagues,"
The Reporter (13 November 1958): 36.

Television techniques have changed in striking ways since the pioneering Edward R. Murrow telecasts of the early 1950s. You could look now at a kinescope recording of his "See It Now" or "Person to Person" and consider the technique unsophisticated. Radio skills, too, have been finely honed since his "This Is London" broadcasts of the late 1930s and early 1940s, during the Battle of Britain. You might think Murrow's language beautiful, but his voice ponderous.

But Murrow released the shackles that restrained radio and television as journalistic media, and he searched continually for better ways to report the news. Biographer Alexander Kendrick said,

> Murrow's independent, imaginative and incisive reporting helped radio and television to become important journalistic media, instead of only channels of entertainment or advertising. After his radio war reporting and that of his staff had made him internationally known, his "See It Now" television documentaries set the standard for all networks. Against the pressures of the commercial environment, which sought to keep news and public affairs as conformist and "noncontroversial" as the rest of television, these programs shook up America by questioning, arousing and stimulating, the true fulfillment of the medium's potential. . . .
>
> Murrow always regarded himself as a reporter rather than an analyst, but he was more. He was a disturber of the peace and a collector of injustices. Radio and television are by their very nature ephemeral. He endowed them with a sense of permanent substance by giving them a purpose.[1]

TELEVISION TECHNOLOGY

Television's technical equipment has improved in striking ways since Murrow's time. Equipment that was once ponderous is now light and portable: cameras are small and compact, transmitting equipment is simplified and mobile. Photographers can shoot and edit videotape in the field. Satellite ground stations are portable, and set-up time is minimal. Technicians can generate graphics with computers.

Until the 1970s, film limited the flexibility and speed of television news. Technicians had to process film before they could project its images. They had to painstakingly cut and splice film before they could utilize it to tell their stories. They had to transport it to established transmission facilities before they could air it. They needed from two hours to five days to get a film story from the scene of an event to the television station's projection room.

When they wanted to transmit live, they had to carry hundreds of pounds of equipment to the scene of an event, find a location where they could transmit in a line of sight from one microwave unit to another, and assure themselves of adequate power to transmit pictures and sounds over distances—the greater the distance the more the power.

They had to draw and paint graphics manually and either mount them on cards in front of camera lenses or transfer them to 35-millimeter slides and project them into camera lenses. They produced names and other printed information to superimpose on the screen in the same laborious ways.

But electronic news-gathering equipment, relatively inexpensive satellite transmission equipment, and computerized character generators changed the nature of television news. Now television crews can transmit from the scenes of events almost as soon as they arrive.

But the principles of producing visual information are essentially the same. The speed of modern television demands that its technicians be more adept and its reporters more knowledgeable, and both must have the ability to make immediate decisions. They have less time to think, so they are more prone to err. They must, therefore, learn their craft more intimately.

VIEWER PARTICIPATION

Television has the ability to draw its viewers into its scenes as vicarious participants in events. Pictures give scenes the image of reality, sounds enhance that reality, and together they give viewers the power to make their own judgments about what they see.

Pictures transmit information without words. The information is raw. Viewers don't have to decode it as they do words on a printed page. They see what people look like—how tall they are, how stocky or slim, what color their hair and eyes are, the shade of their complexion, the nature of their dress. They interpret people through their speech—the volume, force, timber, tone, and pace—and their actions—gestures, facial expressions, movements, and postures.

Pictures also transmit information through emotions. Viewers react empathically to the people they watch on television; they understand newsmakers' feelings and reactions because they vicariously feel and react with them. Television's unique quality is its ability to transmit understanding through emotion.

But television reporters must utilize emotion that manifests itself naturally; they must not try to inject emotion artificially, or their viewers may resist them and turn away. Viewers like to participate when feelings subtly infiltrate their senses; they withdraw and may grow angry if they sense that someone is trying to force them to participate.

During the Iran-Iraq war, U.S. ships patrolled the Persian Gulf adjacent to the two countries, trying to keep oil shipments moving through the Strait of Hormuz into the Gulf of Oman. An Iraqi Mirage jet unexpectedly fired two missiles at one of the American frigates, the U.S.S. *Stark*. They struck the ship, igniting fires and killing 37 crewmen.

Two and a half months later, the *Stark* returned to Jacksonville, Florida, with its surviving crew. WBTV of Charlotte, North Carolina, sent a camera and reporter there to record the return of a Charlotte seaman. The juxtaposition of the scenes and the sounds mixed the joy of the surviving sailors and their families with the sorrow of those sailors for their dead shipmates:

Video	Audio
(CU*, mother and son embrace in midst of a crowd)	(NATS** -- band music, up and under) (REPORTER CHRIS CLACKUM) Bobby Kummrow came home today to a mother who, two months ago, had her doubts she would ever see him again.
(CU, hand one person holding little finger of another)	
(CU, Mrs. Kummrow)	(JACKI KUMMROW, sailor's mother) Right now, it's just one big wagonload of relief. What else can you say? That's the most beautiful sight I ever saw.

*CU = Close-up
**NATS = Natural sound

Video	Audio
(LS,* balloons float up over the ship)	(Applause, crowd noise.)
(MS,** sailors lined on deck)	(CHRIS CLACKUM) But Kummrow's arrival here on the U–S–S "Stark" was a bittersweet reunion. He was here.
(LS, sailors on deck)	Thirty–seven of his colleagues were not.
(CU, Bobby Kummrow)	(BOBBY KUMMROW) They'll be truly missed. We lost a lot of good ones. They'll be truly missed in the service . . . and in the country.
(MS, sailors on deck, ship moving through frame)	(CHRIS CLACKUM) The "Stark's" arrival back to the Mayport Naval Station at Jacksonville was supposed to be a joyous occasion.
(Ms, woman and sailor embrace) (MS, another couple embraces) (Wide shot, crowd on dock, ship background)	It was more a reunion of relief for the sailors and their families. The Navy docked the ship with its good side turned to the crowd.
(MS, sailors on deck)	No need to show the damaged other side —— a grim reminder of just what happened to the "Stark" on
(LS, sailors on deck)	the night of May 17th when it was hit by a missile from an Iraqi war plane.

*LS = Long shot
**MS = Medium shot

Video	Audio
(MS, floral wreath, tilt down to sailors disembarking under it)	Kummrow, the 24-year-old Charlotte native, says he did a lot of growing up that night.
(CU, shoulder patch, "U.S.S. Stark")	He has a year and a-half left in the Navy.
(CU, Bobby Kummrow)	(CHRIS CLACKUM) Is what happened to the "Stark" going to have any sway in what you decide as to whether or not you're going to stay in the Navy?
	(BOBBY KUMMROW) It might. I'll just have to wait until the time comes near. I'll decide then.
	(CHRIS CLACKUM) Do you have any feelings about it now?
(Kummrow looks down, purses lips)	(BOBBY KUMMROW) (five-second pause) It was a terrible thing to happen, but -- ah -- sometimes that's the things, the stuff you have to take.
(Wide shot, crowd on dock)	(CHRIS CLACKUM) Kummrow and the other crew members of the "Stark" get some leave time now.
(LS, U.S.S. "Stark")	As for the ship -- it'll stay here for three months, then off to a shipyard in Mississippi for repairs.[2]

The story allowed viewers to participate because the emotions were subtle. Most of the people in the pictures were obviously exhilarated by the reunion, but the narration reminded us that they had had a brush with a tragic event. Pictures, sounds, and words combined to allow viewers to quietly relive the event.

Viewers prefer to watch from a distance as emotions develop naturally and penetrate only the periphery of their senses. Reporters and photographers must remember that they cannot force emotion or let it linger too long. Pictures and natural sounds reveal emotions. Reporters should not try to elicit them by asking inciting questions, and they should not try to emphasize them by injecting emotions into their own vocal or written narratives.

Some of the natural sounds of people affected by emotion may be too strong for viewers to accept, however. The wail of a distraught mother whose child is trapped in a burning house may continue for several minutes, but viewers may be able to tolerate no more than a few seconds of the sound. Television journalists need to develop intuitive senses that tell them when emotions enhance stories and when they distract. Their own sensory reactions should guide them.

CONTINUITY

Because pictures should tell as much of a story as they can without words, you need to lead your viewers logically from scene to scene.

First, place your viewers in the scene; give them a view of the environment in which the event occurred. Photographers do this most often with an establishing shot—a wide shot that presents as much of the location as possible with the newsmakers within the frame.

Then, introduce your viewers to the newsmakers in the event; show them in juxtaposition to their surroundings. Photographers most often introduce participants in stories with medium shots. Show your viewers the relationships between newsmakers; let them see the newsmakers' physical relationships and their reactions to each other. Photographers usually show relationships with wide shots.

Finally, let the video footage tell the story. Let it unfold in a logical sequence so that you carry your viewers smoothly from one shot to the next as if they were moving through the story's environment with the camera.

In Detroit, WXYZ told the story of an unusual advertising campaign designed to attract young men to the Catholic priesthood. The photographer led viewers on a consistent path through the story, from opening to closing, from establishing shot to concluding standup shot:

Video	Audio
(Wide shot, interior cathedral, choir in background)	(Choral music, up five seconds, then under)
(MS, male choir in shirtsleeves)	(REPORTER GORDON GRAHAM) They are members of a small, elite group of men.

Video	Audio
(CU, profile of two singers)	They are men of unusually strong faith,
(CU, organist, over left shoulder)	dedicated to the service of mankind.
(ECU,* candle, pan to young man listening)	At Sacred Heart Seminary, they are preparing for a life of total self-denial.
(CU, single singer)	It takes a rare kind of personality.
(CU, priest)	(PRIEST) . . . that God is present among his people and that he is calling some to the priesthood. So we're looking for people who are called by God.
(File video from commercial -- woman at desk, priest walks in) (File, CU priest, he winks)	(GORDAN GRAHAM) Because of an impending shortage of priests, an unprecedented advertising campaign was launched last April,
(File, MS, priest walks away, down hallway)	aimed primarily at those young men on the fence.
(CU, first priest)	(PRIEST) We are working with a good number of people right now as a direct result of the campaign -- who have called us.
(Cutaway, MCU,* reporter over priest's shoulder) (CU, priest)	They've been meeting with us a number of times. And I'm sure some of them will be entering in January, next fall, as a direct result of the campaign.

*ECU = Extreme close-up
*MCU = Medium close-up

Video	Audio
(MS, seminarian over shoulder of reporter)	(GORDON GRAHAM) For those considering the call to service,
(CU, reporter)	some advice from seminarians.
(MS, seminarian)	(SEMINARIAN) If they have a sincerity in following the will of God,
(Zoom slowly in to CU)	you know, through prayer and through speaking with peers and with others who have gone before them, they've discerned that this is God's will for them, then to follow it. But if it isn't, be honest with themselves also.
(Wide shot, billboard, "The Work is hard, but the rewards are infinite.")	(GORDON GRAHAM) So the few good men the archdiocese has been looking for
(Tilt down to reporter standing in front of billboard, MCU)	have responded to the unorthodox advertising campaign. And for those who have heard the call and have not responded, the offer still stands.[3]

Read the video column alone and you'll see how the photographer carried his viewers step by step through the scene. First, they saw the cathedral with the choir in the background in the lower third of the screen. Then they moved into a medium shot to see the choir members in relationship to each other. Then they saw selected members and elements of the scene in close-up—two singers, the organist, a candle, a single singer.

Now, with the scene and the characters established, the photographer and reporter showed viewers one of the priests who was part of the project and let him explain motivations and accomplishments. They showed viewers a little of a commercial used in the advertising campaign, let them see and hear how one young seminarian reacted to it, and, finally, took viewers outdoors to see a campaign billboard and hear the reporter's conclusion. The action flowed from scene to scene in a logical sequence.

Early, experimental television equipment was ponderous and unreliable.

The editor compressed the story into a small package that conserved viewers' time but didn't sacrifice understanding. The transition at the end from the young seminarian in the cathedral to the outdoor billboard carried the reporter easily and reasonably from one location to another. And the billboard helped the reporter and photographer put an exclamation point on the story.

Photographers sometimes utilize another kind of shot to introduce a story. They call it a *discovery* shot. Producers have used it often to open telecasts of football games: they show viewers a wide overall shot of the city, then zoom back to show the football stadium in the foreground. Viewers "discover" where they are.

ABC's director for program development, Av Westin, says he learned the technique from CBS correspondent Bill Stout, who worked in the network's Los Angeles bureau:

> Taxi fares had rocketed, and one of the cab companies had been accused of tampering with its meters in order to bilk riders. Because of our budgetary restrictions, there was no camera crew available to film a fully illustrated story for the "Morning News." For his "stand-upper," Stout added the missing ingredient that made the difference. He equipped himself with a hand prop: the tiny gear that clicked the meter's numbers into place when the taxi was running. One tooth of the gear had been filed away so that the clicking occurred more rapidly than it should. Stout began with an extreme close-up of the doctored part; as he explained what the missing tooth meant and how it affected the fare, he helped the report along with the tip of his finger, pointing out the file marks. The picture then widened to show him standing in front of a cab as he completed his explanation of the

scam. By using a very rudimentary production device, Stout had presented an illustrated, informative and interesting report. Every cab rider in the country who saw the effort would know how a taxi meter worked and how one might better protect oneself from an unscrupulous operator.

Stout's technique impressed me so much that years later, in a memo to ABC News correspondents, I suggested they begin all their stories by concentrating on the smallest entity in them before widening back to the broader aspect.[4]

The discovery technique is similar to a broadcast newswriter's technique of structuring a story. It focuses first on the specific aspect of the story you want your viewers to remember, then expands to include the supporting elements. But it still follows logical continuity; it expands the overall scene instead of narrowing it.

No matter which technique you adopt for a story, be continually aware that you must lead your viewers as if they were walking with you through the scene.

COMPOSITION

Good picture composition will focus television viewers' eyes on the important elements of the scenes you shoot. It will eliminate distractions and accentuate movements that bring the story to life.

Photographers know that viewers focus their attention somewhere away from the center of the screen—to the left or the right, above or below. Photographers believe that most viewers focus their attention a third of the way from the top of the screen, or a third of the way from either side of the screen, so they call their shooting guideline "the rule of thirds."

If you set up an interview and choose to shoot the interviewee in close-up, head and shoulders, consider his or her position. If he's looking slightly to the right of the lens, frame him in the picture slightly to the left of center. If she's looking slightly to the left, frame her to the right of center. Leave a little space on the side toward which the interviewee is looking. Photographers call this "looking room."

Frame the interviewee's head slightly above center so that her shoulders are apparent, but not so that you cut off the top of her head. Leave a little screen space above the top of her head, but remember that too much space there calls attention to the space and detracts from the person.

Be aware of elements in the background that might distract viewers. The line of a wall seam that appears to penetrate the interviewee's head or body vertically, or the line of wainscot that appears to penetrate the interviewee's head horizontally, will only call attention to the abnormality in the scene and divert attention from the newsmaker. If there are lines or objects that create distractions, move the camera so they are toward the edges of the screen. Let them frame the person who is the center of attention.

Be aware of lighting and colors in the background. If you place the interviewee in front of a window, the camera will absorb more light from the window than it

to the right of the camera, zoom in on the face of the person on the right. Then move to the other side of the axis, focus on the face of the other person, and zoom out to show both again. The technique will carry your viewers across the axis with you, and they'll understand the change in screen direction as the two people pass you. This maneuver works best if the two people are looking at each other.

Reaction shots—shots of one or more people watching the central action—can help you change screen direction. Visualize a squad of soldiers changing the guard, watched by an elderly man on a bench. Shoot the soldiers marching toward you, shoot the elderly man turning his head to watch them pass, then shoot the soldiers from the other side of the axis as if they had passed the onlooker.

Reaction shots not only help you change screen direction, they also help you compress the time of an action. They serve as transitions between two parts of an action. For example, shoot a picture of a taxicab coming toward you, perhaps a block away, then shoot a picture of a woman standing on the curb, hailing the cab. Finally, shoot the cab as it pulls alongside the curb to pick up the rider. You will have saved several seconds of real time, but your viewers won't think they've been cheated.

You can also use reaction shots—sometimes called cutaways—to bridge two sections of an interview. That's why television photographers shoot reversals of interviewers. They not only shoot medium and close-up shots of reporters asking their questions a second time, they also record their reporters simply listening to newsmakers talk. Then, if the editor deletes the material between a newsmaker's second and fifth answers, for example, a few seconds of video footage can be dropped into the space between the two answers to mask the fact that they were not consecutive. The editor thus saves viewers time by not forcing them to listen to answers that did not bear directly on the main point of the interview.

Reaction shots also mask jump cuts. If you were to join two separate answers from the newsmaker without a reaction shot between them, your viewers would notice an obvious change in her position. That's a jump cut; the figure jumps, even if the change in position is subtle. The closer the shot, the more obvious the jump. The reaction shot, edited between the two shots of the newsmaker, masks the change.

HUMANIZING VIDEO COVERAGE

Many news stories focus on ideas—concepts, plans, technical developments, research achievements, and the like. If you fail to show the human impact of such ideas, you may lose your audience. Your listeners and viewers need to know how they will be affected or how they relate to others who are affected.

Economic news need not be dull. Inflation affects the earning and buying power of everyone. Reporters and photographers must show us how. Perhaps a young married couple with two children is buying less food. Perhaps an industrialist is laying off workers. Perhaps state welfare agencies are serving fewer clients.

Education news is more than buildings, books, taxes, and teacher salaries. When a school district closes one of its high schools, it must reassign all of its students to other schools, perhaps readjusting the boundaries of other school regions and relocating some of their students. If the state legislature cuts public school budgets, some students may face larger classes, double sessions, shortages of textbooks and other classroom materials, cancellations or cuts in programs, or year-round attendance.

Science news should go beyond theories, experiments, and discoveries. Nuclear energy is both beneficial and threatening to human beings. Orbiting satellites contribute to communication and knowledge. Artificial organs improve health and prolong life. Reporters and photographers who can find ways to show the impacts of such seemingly impersonal technology on individual lives will help all of their listeners and viewers understand how abstract concepts can change their lifestyles.

In most cases, you can focus your story on an individual or group affected by concepts; through that person or group, let your listeners and viewers see how common such experiences are to all of us. Often, that means watching the affected people close-up so we can see their faces, watch their expressions, sense their reactions.

Reporter Christopher Gaul of WBAL-TV, Baltimore, showed the impact of an inherited eye disease called retinitis pigmentosa by finding one of its victims and letting her explain how her peripheral vision had gradually deterioriated:

Video	Audio
(ECU, woman's face)	(WOMAN) Do you know what it's like to look up in the sky and see three stars? I do. So does everyone else with R-P. I don't know what
(Woman looks upward)	a thousand stars look like.
	(CHRISTOPHER GAUL) Thirty-seven-year-old Evelyn Schweiker is describing what it's like to have the degenerative eye disease, retinitis
(Same woman, wearing dark glasses and carrying white cane, walks down house steps and across lawn to mail box -- camera zooms out slowly to include box.)	pigmentosa -- R-P -- a condition shared by a hundred-thousand other Americans. In the daytime, she can see only what is directly in front of her.

Video	Audio
(CU, mail box. Woman moves into scene, opens box, removes mail.)	At night, she is blind. Soon, she won't be able to see during the day.[5]

Gaul then told his viewers that researchers at Johns Hopkins University had isolated photoreceptor cells and opened the way for a possible cure.

But first he gave his viewers a clear impression of a victim's insecurity and let them empathetically feel her plight. Her facial expressions and her voice conveyed a vivid sense of her fear of total blindness, and her apprehension gave viewers a foundation for understanding the scientific facets of the story.

WRITING FOR TELEVISION

Three elements contribute to successful television news stories: the information, the illustration, and the writing. All three need to blend; if they clash, stories may fail. The information must be complete and logically organized. The videotape must enhance the information; it must not only illustrate the facts, it must add to them. And the writing must fill in the blank spaces the visuals cannot explain.

Some video footage can tell most of the story by itself. Pictures of a mentally handicapped young man competing in a springboard diving event during a Special Olympics competition illustrate one such incident.

The photographer showed the young man climbing onto the diving board and edging toward the end. He moved awkwardly and hesitantly. He leaned down toward the board and extended his arms diagonally for balance. He kept his head steady, but moved his eyes right and left toward the water. He lifted his left hand and brushed his hair back from his forehead. He seemed to be talking to himself. Halfway out, he hesitated, then he began to move again. At the end of the board, he sat down gingerly and began to lean forward.

Just as he seemed about to fall into the water, a gray-haired woman appeared behind him, talking to him. He turned to look at her, listened for a moment, then turned to look at the water again. After a moment, he climbed to his feet, balancing himself with his hands. Once upright, he abruptly leaned forward and fell from the board, head first.

The photographer followed the action in one continuous medium close-up. And the reporter needed to explain only that this was a participant in competition for handicapped youngsters, and when and where the event occurred. The videotape gave viewers a clear picture of the young man's struggle to succeed and a feeling for his sense of achievement when he reached his goal. It told the story.

Most video coverage will be less complete, however. You'll need to explain many of the details that are not apparent. Pictures of a severe windstorm will give your viewers impressions of its severity. You can videotape clouds of blowing dust, uprooted trees, upended billboards, overturned semitrailers, stripped roofs, broken utility poles, and pedestrians leaning into the wind. But you'll need to tell them what caused the storm, who was affected and how, where it inflicted its worst damage, how widespread it was, when it started, how long it lasted, what hazards it left in its wake, and anything else that you decide your viewers will need to know. The video footage will leave vivid impressions but not enough detail to be fully understood.

WJLA-TV in Washington, D.C., utilized file videotapes to help tell the story of a young man acquitted on charges of supplying cocaine to an All-American basketball player who died of an overdose.

University of Maryland basketball star Len Bias had been drafted by the Boston Celtics on June 19, 1986. The following day, he died of what a medical examiner called cocaine suffocation.

Police charged Brian Lee Tribble, a friend who had been with Bias the night of his death, with trafficking cocaine and conspiracy. They said he had supplied the drug that killed Bias.

Almost a year later, a jury acquitted Tribble, and WJLA-TV persuaded him to submit to his first interview since the death of Bias. The station took video footage from its previous year's files to remind its viewers of the story's background:

Video	Audio
(File video, MCU, pallbearers carrying casket)	(REPORTER DAVID PAULSON) On the day Len Bias died, people started looking for answers to questions no one bothered asking before.
(File video, basketball game action featuring Len Bias)	The microscope focused on the University of Maryland and college athletics in general.
(File, CU, basketball coach Lefty Driesell) (File, CU, athletic director Dick Dull) (File, MS, Len Bias playing) (File, WS,* basketball game)	Many took the fall for what was the tragic celebration of a rising star and a few good friends who used cocaine. Investigators went looking for the man responsible.

*WS = Wide shot

Video	Audio
(File, MS, Tribble and officer walk through gate past cameras)	(POLICE OFFICIAL) Mr. Tribble, after an extensive manhunt and negotiations with his attorney, was surrendered this morning to the sheriff's department by Mr. Tom C. Morrow, his attorney, at 10:05 a.m.
(File, CU, police official)	
(File, MS, Tribble and attorneys walk behind bush toward building)	(DAVID PAULSON) Brian Tribble had his day in court, and a jury said he did not possess cocaine, that he did not supply the cocaine that killed Len Bias, that he was not a mid-level cocaine dealer.
(CU, Tribble)	(DAVID PAULSON) Did Brian Tribble bring the cocaine in that killed Len Bias?
	(TRIBBLE) No.
	(DAVID PAULSON) Did Brian Tribble use cocaine that night?
	(TRIBBLE) (Pause) I'm going to ask my attorney to step in right now.
(CU, Morrow)	(DAVID PAULSON) It was the first time Brian Tribble had been asked that question, and it threw him off-guard. His lawyer, Tom Morrow, who sat in on the interview, advised his client to lay

Video	Audio
(MS, Tribble, attorney, Paulson)	it all on the table.

(CU, Tribble)	(DAVID PAULSON)
	    Did Brian Tribble use cocaine that night with Len Bias?
	
	(TRIBBLE)
	    Yes.
	
	(DAVID PAULSON)
	    It's a mistake you readily admit?
	
	(TRIBBLE)
	    Yes, it's a mistake I readily admit, and I admit it, you know, truthfully, and now, right here on camera, whatever. And I'd like to say recreational-type usage was, was going on. There wasn't no abuse or no habit-type thing.

(File, MCU, men carrying casket)	(DAVID PAULSON) What will remain unanswered is the origin of the cocaine that killed Len Bias. Tribble refuses to shirk responsibility by placing that load on the shoulders of the dead man.
(File, MS, Tribble in shorts, walking through gate and past cameras and reporters)	After watching a close friend die and then scrambling to sidestep the camera's glare and a prison term, finding the words to put all that's happened into perspective is difficult.
(CU, Tribble)	(TRIBBLE) I'm still trying, and I'm still, you know,

Video	Audio
	getting myself back together, and my thoughts are it was a very frightening experience, it was a tragic experience, and I feel that now, that I've learned a great deal from it.
(File, MS, Tribble and attorneys walk past cameras into building)	(DAVID PAULSON) After his acquittal, Tribble pleaded guilty to an unrelated traffic charge and fleeing a police officer, offering to tell his story to troubled youngsters as a community service in lieu of stiffer penalties.
(MS, Tribble over Paulson's shoulder)	His message is obvious but a little more complicated than just saying "no" to drugs.
(CU, Tribble)	(TRIBBLE) I want to tell them also that you don't have to be an abuser or a long—time user . . . just recreational use can definitely turn your whole life around and get you in more trouble than you can ever imagine, or put you to more pain and put your family to more pain than you can ever imagine.[6]

WJLA-TV's file videotape gave viewers a sense of the events that led to the interview with Brian Tribble. It reminded them of the prominence and talent of Len Bias. It refreshed their memories about how Tribble had evaded reporters and photographers for almost a full year. And it gave them a feeling for the significance of the event.

Words Reinforce Pictures

In most stories, you'll try to match words to pictures to reinforce what your viewers see on the screen. If words conflict with pictures, they may distract viewers from your message. Pictures have more power than words, and they'll dominate your viewers' attention. A sportscaster who includes pictures of game action as a background over which to superimpose names of teams and scores may fail to reach his viewers. They'll want to wipe away the names and numbers so they can see the action clearly. If he stops the action and uses a still frame as a background, however, his viewers can concentrate on the names and numbers.

Let your narration work harmoniously with your pictures, but don't let the words repeat what is apparent in the video footage. If you use a close-up picture of the governor talking to a legislative session, don't say, "This is the governor talking to legislators." Instead, refer to him indirectly when he appears. For example, "The governor told legislators. . . ." That way, you subtly identify the face on the screen and his location.

Oklahoma City's KWTV produced a feature story about an elderly couple moving 300 miles through the midwest, carrying their belongings in a shopping cart. The photographer pictured the couple on Interstate 35 near Guthrie, Oklahoma.

Video	Audio
(WS, road embankment foreground, guard rail above. Couple with shopping cart walk into frame from right, move through frame in silhouette and out left. Vehicles speed by in opposite direction.)	(REPORTER GAN MATTHEWS) (Sound, shopping cart rolling on pavement, up two seconds, then under narration.) It's not your customary way of making a move, but it's George and Charleyne Poole's way. Two weeks ago, the couple left Fort Worth. No work there, they say. And in another week, they plan to reach Wichita. They hope to find work there.
(MS, from rear, ground level shot of couple pushing cart away. Car speeds by.) (CU, from rear, ground level shot of feet walking) (MCU, from front, woman pulling rope, man pushing cart)	In the meantime, they average about 18 miles a day on foot. The Pooles are hauling all their belongings in this converted shopping

Video	Audio
	cart. The load is heavy. The weather is hot.
(MCU, shadow of cart and man moving by)	But the Pooles say they're doing just fine, thank you.
(ECU, George Poole)	(GEORGE POOLE) I am 68 years old. My wife is 55 years old. We feel like we're real young children anymore. We like to show the young people what an old person can still do.
(MS, fence post and barbed wire in foreground, guard rail in background. Couple with cart walks into frame from right.)	(GAN MATTHEWS) The Pooles start walking before sunrise. They quit when they get tired. They sleep under the stars. They say they like it.
(CU, man's face from below)	Some people might say the idea is crazy.
(ECU, Mrs. Poole)	(CHARLEYNE POOLE) I don't think it's crazy. I think some old people will do it. Get out and get a little exercise, and you live longer.
(MS, woman and man with cart walk into frame from screen right)	(GAN MATTHEWS) The Pooles say no one has bothered them on their trek.
(CU, faces of man and woman)	Motorists sometimes stop, wish them well, leave them a few dollars.
(CU, man's feet from ground level)	They seem genuinely happy to be on the road . . .
(CU, cart wheels, ground level, from behind) (CU, woman's hand, pulling rope)	and optimistic they'll find a better life . . . at their journey's end.

Video	Audio
(MS, man pushing cart)	(GEORGE POOLE) You can take the strap loose now. We're going downhill.

(Pan left to woman placing rope on top of cart)
(MS, cart, man and woman walking toward camera. Truck speeds by in opposite direction)
	(CHARLEYNE POOLE)
	    O-K.
	(Traffic sounds up for five seconds and under for narrator.)
	(GAN MATTHEWS)
	    Gan Matthews reporting from Oklahoma City.
	(Traffic sounds up for three seconds and out.)[7]

The story is a model. An imaginative photographer created the feeling of the event in the video footage. The reporter added the missing information in his narration, and only once did he refer directly to what we could see in the pictures—when he said "this converted shopping cart."

Sometimes, you can contrast words and pictures in a form of harmonious counterpoint to reinforce your message. For example, you could juxtapose pictures of street crews sweeping up debris after a parade against the sounds of a marching band to show how careless festive crowds can be. You could juxtapose pictures of a mass of tax protesters demonstrating on the steps of the state capitol against the sounds of calm legislative debate to show how little the lawmakers were affected. Be honest with such contrasts. Be sure the pictures and the sounds reflect reality.

You'll need to practice writing for television. You can't write more than you can read aloud to accompany any videotaped scene, or the videotape will race ahead of the story. If you lose the synchrony of ideas and pictures, you'll confuse your viewers. They'll puzzle over the pictures and lose the sense of the story.

You can always write less narration than you need, however, to cover any videotaped scene. Natural sound helps you fill the blank spaces in a narration. But even if you have no natural sound on your videotape, short pauses in narration give your viewers more time to absorb ideas from both the script and the video footage.

WORKING WITH YOUR CREW

At most television stations, reporters act as field producers. They are in charge of the crew and responsible for the success of the story.

If you have been assigned to a story, your assignment editor expects you to suggest shots or scenes to your photographer. Whether you work with a photographer alone or have a sound technician in the crew, your producer also hopes you will suggest sounds to enhance the story. If you have a lighting technician, you may need to suggest placement or intensities of lighting. Your producer expects you to work with the tape editor to create as much of the story from visuals as you can.

A successful reporter relies on the creativity of each specialist in his or her crew. You can suggest approaches to the story, but you should not preempt their enthusiasm for helping to structure it.

Good photographers have intuitive senses for composition and perspective. Good sound technicians know when the ambience of the environment adds to or detracts from the message. Good lighting technicians can see when they have highlighted the prominent elements of the scene and subdued the surroundings. Good editors have a talent for telling stories with pictures.

You need to tell fellow crew members what you expect from the story. Then, let them help you achieve it. Whereas you need to know the technology your crew utilizes, remember that they know it best. A domineering reporter eventually fails to get results from his or her crew. A diplomatic reporter produces stories that consistently convey useful and entertaining information to his or her viewers.

Unlike radio reporters, television reporters cannot work alone. They need help, and to succeed, they need to convey a feeling of shared success to their crew members.

Exercises

1. Make an appointment with a television reporter to accompany him or her on a story. Ask how she envisions the story and how she plans to approach it. Follow the reporter and her crew through the shooting, editing, writing, and production of the story. Analyze the finished story. How closely does it resemble what the reporter planned? How much of the videotape they shot did they discard? How well did the video footage alone tell the story? How much did the reporter have to add in her script to supply information the visuals failed to contain?

2. Call a local television news director. Make an appointment to visit the newsroom and spend at least four hours before and during a newscast. Talk to assignment editors, producers, tape editors, reporters, photographers, anchors, and others who directly participate in the production of news stories. What problems do they encounter? What strengths do they praise in the work of their colleagues? What weaknesses do they complain about? What would they like to change to improve the quality of completed stories?

3. Tape a local television newscast, but do not watch it. Listen to the tape. Choose three stories from the newscast and analyze them. How much of each story

can you understand without seeing the pictures? What seems to be missing? What would you have done to illustrate each story?

4. Watch a television newscast with the sound off. Record it on videotape if you can. Choose three stories from the newscast and watch them a second time. How well did you understand the stories? What seemed to be missing in the video coverage? What questions do you want to ask to complete your understanding of each story?

5. Watch a television newscast and choose one story you think has the greatest impact on you and the rest of the television audience. Analyze it in terms of the emotions it produced in you. Did those emotions come from the pictures, the sound, or the narration? Or did they arise from a combination of elements? Did the emotions arise naturally, or did the producer, writer, or narrator manipulate story elements to generate emotional reactions? What would you have done differently to make the story more natural?

6. Record a newscast onto videotape and choose one story you can study for editing technique. Does the videotape tell a complete story alone? Is the continuity logical and clear? Are the transitions effective? Does the script supplement the video footage or detract from it? What elements of the script could the reporter have eliminated without diminishing your understanding? Did any parts of the script call unnecessary attention to the video coverage?

Notes

1. Alexander Kendrick, *Prime Time* (Boston: Little, Brown and Co., 1969): 3–4.
2. Chris Clackum, WBTV, 5 August 1987.
3. Gordon Graham, WXYZ, 3 September 1987.
4. Av Westin, *Newswatch: How TV Decides the News* (New York: Simon and Schuster, 1982): 43–44.
5. Christopher Gaul, WBAL-TV, 2 October 1987.
6. David Paulson, WJLA-TV, 21 July 1987.
7. Gan Matthews, KWTV, 30 July 1987.

11

NEWS ON THE AIR

Working in television news is like swimming in a goldfish bowl. The entire country—including the government—watch every move of the television journalist. When he makes a mistake, especially during a live special event, it is there for 10 to 30 million viewers to see. It all hangs out.
　　　　—ELMER LOWER, "A Quarter Century of Television News: From Talking Heads
　　　　　　　to Live Moon Landings," *Television/Radio Age* (28 August 1978): 220.

Your first appearance on live microphone or live camera will be an unnerving one. You may see visions of thousands of pairs of ears and eyes listening for every nuance, watching for every expression. It will be intimidating.

Under such pressure, some neophyte broadcast reporters freeze. They can't speak without stumbling. They can't think in logical patterns. Even experienced broadcast reporters who have been away from microphones and cameras for several weeks return with trepidation. And when the microphone switch goes on, or the camera's tally lights turn red, they shake.

Broadcast reporting is not a trade for timid people. It demands the stage presence of an actor who has played the role a hundred times, the eye contact of a lover, the voice control of a priest, the body control of a dancer.

AN INTIMATE STYLE

Radio and television are intimate media; don't think of delivering your messages to an audience of thousands but to an audience of one—that one individual who is listening to you because he or she thinks you have something to say that he or she needs to hear. He or she may listen because your voice is warm or because you are direct, credible, knowledgeable, and calm.

David Brinkley remembers how he and Chet Huntley visualized their audience in 1956, the year they began their successful tenure as co-anchors on NBC News:

> It was a style of doing the news that nobody had even seen before. I thought, Huntley thought, Reuven Frank thought—he was our producer—that if you're going to be on television every night you should simply try to be natural. The basic fact of television is that you're talking to 25 million people in groups of one, two and three. So you talk as if you're talking to somebody in the same room. That had not been done before.[1]

Huntley and Brinkley changed the style of news delivery and set the tone for modern newscasters. The bombastic reading styles of radio in the '40s and television in the early '50s began to disappear. Reporters and newscasters today read in direct, conversational styles. They avoid projecting their voices because they know they'll risk sounding like orators instead of storytellers. They avoid injecting their voices with emotion because they know they'll risk sounding artificial. They know their audience wants to feel comfortable with them, and they will, as long as they are approached naturally and unpretentiously. Once listeners and viewers sense pomposity or pretense, they grow uncomfortable and turn away.

Few stage actors make good news readers because they've trained their voices to reach auditorium audiences and to assume the affectations of dramatic characters. Newscasters and field reporters must nevertheless, in their own ways, become actors, but subtle ones who understand the small nuances of voice, facial expressions, and bodily movements and gestures. They learn how to adapt them quietly and unobtrusively into their performance skills.

A REPORTER'S PERSONALITY

As you begin to sharpen your performance skills, you might help yourself by watching or listening to a newscaster you like. Analyze his or her techniques. Listen to variations in her vocal expression—volume, pace, pitch, pauses, phrasing, emphasis, breath control. Few will match the declamatory style of Paul Harvey or the satiric style of David Brinkley or the incisive style of Susan Spencer or the paternal style of Walter Cronkite. But each successful newscaster will be distinctive and original.

Each of us is unique, and our reading styles are characteristic of our personalities. So, the techniques we adopt must fit our personalities. If we imitate rather than originate, our listeners and viewers will reject us. They want to be comfortable with us as reporters, not as impersonators.

Study yourself. Listen to your voice on audio tape. Study your face, body, and gestures on videotape. What pleases you? What makes you uncomfortable?

Ask someone else to listen to and watch you critically. What qualities can they sense that will add to your effectiveness? Which of your mannerisms might distract your audience from your message?

Expose yourself to constructive criticism. Develop a self-critical attitude. Only when you become honestly aware of yourself will you begin to develop and build on the skills you have and the skills you'll need to communicate orally and visually.

Try some of the devices that successful newscasters employ, but record and critique your performance. Decide if they work for you or if they make you feel, sound, or look uncomfortable. If a particular technique works, if it fits your personality, practice it and sharpen your skill. If it is uncomfortable, abandon it and try something else.

Above all, be yourself. Find ways to project your unique qualities, to vocally and visually enhance your voice, expressions, and movements.

In radio and television, the substance of your stories is still the most important element of the messages you transmit to your audiences. Words, sentences, and story structures are vital to their understanding.

But your listeners and viewers can hear and see you, too, and they'll judge your performance as much, perhaps even more, than they'll judge the substance of your stories. Your audience hears you read and watches your actions. They'll judge you first as a person, a personality, and second as a reporter or writer. Most listeners and viewers seem to be drawn to the personality of a newscaster or reporter. Only a minority will, at first, see beyond that personality to the quality or competence of reporting.

But you'll need both skills to succeed. Performance will attract audiences; journalistic ability will keep them.

MAKING CONTACT WITH AUDIENCES

Newscasters and field reporters must first be believable. Believability, in itself, is an abstract concept, and no one can accurately evaluate why audiences trust one reporter and distrust another. But each of us can cultivate skills to enhance our innate believability.

Radio and television technology is already working to help us earn the trust of our audiences. If we've been alert at the events we've covered, we'll have recorded sounds and pictures that will draw our listeners and viewers into the scenes with us, where events will unfold for them as if they were there.

If we're covering an event live, and we've placed ourselves where the ambient sounds of the environment are clear but not distracting, or where the action of the event substantiates what we say, then we've invited our listeners and viewers to participate in the event with us. They hear and see it for themselves and, therefore, believe it.

But we strain believability if we ourselves fit awkwardly into the sound or picture environment. If we talk too loudly, too rapidly, too erratically, or too intensely, we'll appear to be manufacturing the mood around us. Look for the people who are the focus of the event and let their mood infect you. Be sensitive to the sound of your voice and the expression on your face. Adapt your delivery and actions to the mood of the moment. If our voices or our movements clash with the environment, we may seem to be trying to entertain rather than to inform our audiences.

CBS News storyteller Charles Kuralt has talked to journalism students about how he and his producer perceive such clashes:

> We have adopted what we call the "tricycle principle." We watch a lot of local television; everywhere we go we see the local news. Izzy and I were in his motel room someplace watching the local news when a story came on about a children's tricycle race, little kids trying to ride their tricycles fast. Pretty cute story. And Izzy said, "You know what? Before the story is over that reporter is going to ride a tricycle." And I said, "No, he wouldn't, because that would ruin it." Sure enough, he signed off—"Joe Doakes, Eyewitness News," and the camera pulled back to watch him pedaling down the sidewalk on a tricycle. Then and there we adopted the tricycle principle, which is very simple: "Don't ride the tricycle." Try to keep yourself out of the story if you can. Don't appear on camera at all if you can avoid it. People are not interested in the reporter, or shouldn't be, and if the reporter does his work well, people will be interested in the story he is telling. If they end up thinking about him instead of the story, he has succeeded as a celebrity but failed as a storyteller.[2]

You can visualize the discord in the picture—an adult "reporter" pretending to be a child in the hope of drawing a chuckle. The clash between the pretense and the environment of the story may entertain viewers, but it also damages credibility. Feature reporters who adopt such techniques regularly may be accepted. But straight reporters who step out of character to entertain rather than to inform may lose the trust of their audiences.

VOICE IS THE FOUNDATION

On radio, your listeners' only contact with your message is your voice, so let it reflect what is happening. But avoid heavy emotionalism. Be calm and straightforward. If you inject more than a hint of emotion into your voice, you'll suggest to your listeners that you're trying to impress or incite them, and they'll resist. Excess emotion makes listeners uncomfortable, and they're likely to respond by ridiculing you.

Edward R. Murrow possessed a sense of the drama in news, but he visualized his listeners as reasonable, restrained, mature people who could interpret emotion sensitively. He said, "I have reason to know, as do many of you, that when the evidence on a controversial subject is fairly and calmly presented, the public recognizes it for what it is—an effort to illuminate rather than to agitate."[3]

You can subtly acknowledge the mood of an event without absorbing it. You can adjust the pace of your speech to the mood without allowing overt emotion to creep in. You can adjust the volume of your voice to the mood of the event and still seem calm. You can utilize brief pauses to emphasize ideas that highlight the mood, thus sounding analytical rather than rhetorical.

Radio reporters make contact with their listeners only through their voices, so they talk a little more rapidly than normal, with a little more force than normal, with a touch more exaggeration than normal conversation allows. Yet, they still seem to be talking to friends about exciting events they have witnessed rather than declaiming.

The voices of play-by-play announcers at football games erupt into shouts when spectacular plays occur because their vocal moods help us *see* the plays. But even in such an atmosphere of excitement, their words must be enunciated clearly enough to allow us to hear what they say.

TELEVISION'S VISUAL IMPRESSIONS

The voices of television reporters are more natural than those of radio reporters because we can see them and absorb their facial expressions, their eye movements, their postures, and their gestures. As in conversation, we absorb much of the meaning of what they say through their body language.

Your eyes are most important. Although you look only at a piece of glass—the lens of the camera—or at the rolling words on the teleprompter, you must appear to be looking your viewers in the eye. You must concentrate not only on the words you speak but on an image of a viewer you imagine you're talking to. Do not allow your eyes to stray, or you'll destroy your viewers' concentration, too.

Sometimes, reporters move their eyes deliberately away from the lens to objects or persons or groups or scenes they want to emphasize. When they do, they stimulate their viewers to follow and absorb what the reporters themselves see or seem to see. Similarly, weathercasters who look at their maps and charts of highs and lows and fronts direct their viewers' eyes toward those same maps and charts and away from themselves.

AD LIBBING

Radio and television reporters today are more frequently required to appear without scripts, on-mike or on-camera, to ad lib intelligent accounts of events they have witnessed, statements they have heard, or stories that are just unfolding. Live coverage of events is becoming commonplace. Modern technology makes instant news not only possible but expected.

Broadcasters have always been prepared for live coverage of scheduled events— political conventions, rocket launches, and such internationally important occasions as coronations, papal tours, and summit meetings. But nowadays, reporters often find themselves eyewitnesses to such unexpected events as terrorist attacks, assassinations and attempted assassinations, volcanic eruptions, floods, and avalanches.

A CBS radio announcer in the field at the Democratic
national convention in Atlanta in 1988.

Network and station executives expect their anchors to be ready for major
breaking events, and those are the times that test the reporters' skills. NBC's John
Chancellor says moments of crisis are a measure of the anchor's experience. Most
of the time, he says, anchoring is "a little like being a clergyman. Most of the
week you conduct standard religious services, but the importance is when something
goes wrong. Right now somebody could come to that door and say, 'A candidate
has been shot, go on the air.' I'd walk in, draw on a lot of experience in this field
and ad lib for five hours."[4]

Certainly, experience is the mark of successful ad libbers, but knowledge ranks
alongside it. Reporters who understand instantaneously what they see and hear
need fountains of knowledge to draw from. They must be well read, with a finely
developed ability to recall what they have read, seen, and heard. Unless they can
relate what is happening now to what has already happened, they will fail to deliver
the news to their listeners understandably. Ad libbing is more than talking; it is
talking intelligently.

Ad libbers with experience and knowledge will be able to analyze events based
on what they know from observation and memory, to discard whatever is irrelevant,
and to talk about facets of information that will mean something to their listeners.
They will know their communities, geographically and culturally. Good ad libbers

can immediately organize the information they have winnowed so their listeners will understand it.

To ad lib effectively, you must think in ideas rather than mere words. Ideas carry the sense of stories. Organize the three or four ideas that carry the sense of your story, then talk about them. The words will fall into place in your own natural style. They won't create memorable prose, but you should be able to convey the essence of the story clearly.

Your skill at writing will enhance your ad libbing skill, however. When you continually work to improve your skill at putting words on paper concisely and precisely, you will organize your mind to think quickly and concisely when you must speak extemporaneously.

Some reporters prepare ad lib reports by scrawling abbreviated notes on scraps of paper. The written notes refresh their memories and ensure the logical progression of ideas. Other reporters mumble their ideas half-audibly to implant the sounds in their minds, thereby vocally reinforcing their memories. Still others plan deliberate movements or gestures to accompany specific ideas. Their actions motivate or elicit ideas. Some reporters tape record their stories, then pretend to ad lib on television, although they're really listening to their own voices through hidden earphones to prompt their narration.

No one can tell you which technique will work best for you. Practice all of them. Decide how you can translate thoughts into words most effectively, then work to refine that technique.

REPORTERS ON THE SCENE

Sophisticated portable radio and television equipment enables reporters to broadcast live more often, but the new technology demands more of them. They must cultivate the talent to collect facts quickly, organize them meaningfully, and ad lib them narratively, as storytellers would.

Additionally, they must develop the skills to be their own directors and producers. When they report live from the scenes of events, they rely only on themselves to be accurate and credible. They don't have the luxury of making decisions over their computers or editing equipment. They must make decisions on impulse— as aware as they can be of the environment and the facts but also trusting their own instincts and knowledge.

Anchors sit at the focus of newscasts. They motivate diverse field reports and provide the framework upon which to build the disparate elements of programs. They provide the continuity to draw fragments of news into a semblance of unity.

But field reporters provide the substance. In a sense, they are characters in the stories, catalysts who make things happen. Field reporters are highly visible players in the drama of the news.

These qualifications may seem excessive, but to a degree, field reporters need the probing mind of a scientist, the organizational instincts of a corporate executive, the technical imagination of an inventor, the compositional awareness of an artist, the word sensitivity of a poet, the camera presence of a film star, the audience awareness of a revivalist, and the preoccupation of a professor. At the least, field reporters must be prepared to accept and evaluate stimuli from diverse sources. Eventually, some of their work will become habitual or instinctive, but each new story and setting will demand imagination and adaptation.

Reporters need to develop the ability to concentrate. Standing in the midst of city council hearings, relating information about the council's actions, they must blot out any awareness of eyes watching them, focusing their own eyes on the camera's lens and their minds on the thoughts that make their stories. Sounds and pictures of the setting give the event credibility, but reporters cannot allow those sounds and pictures to distract them from what they have to say. At the same time, they must be sensitive to the volume and energy of their voices; they must match their delivery to the character of the event. They must also react to unexpected changes in the visual and sound environment and to unexpected movements within camera range.

Reporters must know when the camera's angle is wide, medium, or close-up and adjust their physical and vocal attitudes to the degree of the camera's intimacy. They must also feel the emotion of the event and let it subtly influence their presentation. Reporters train their minds to receive and evaluate all kinds of sensations, rejecting those that do not apply to the moment and balancing the rest into the context of the narrative.

Field reporters must plan as thoroughly as possible before their microphones and cameras go live. If they know what their photographers are seeing, what their microphones are hearing, and what emphasis the lighting gives to the scene, they can plan their narratives to elaborate on what their listeners and viewers see and hear. If they're confident that their technical crews are working toward similar effects, they can concentrate on delivering the substance of their stories and still be alert to unpredictable shifts in the action.

Projecting Emotion

Reporters who deliver news vocally can never remove emotion from their voices. They'd be foolish to try. Radio listeners and, to an intensified degree, television viewers absorb much of what they hear and see through their emotions rather than through their intellect. News stories that contain low levels of emotional content and high levels of intellectual content are less likely to attract and hold an audience. Stories that contain poignant emotions are more likely to be absorbed and remembered.

Help your listeners and viewers feel whatever sensations exist in the events you report. Edward R. Murrow was a reporter who could convey to his listeners his involvement in stories. His producer, Fred Friendly, said, ''What made Ed Murrow the man we remember was his intensity of conscience. You could feel his emotions when he covered the Battle of Britain."[5]

Even now, listening to recordings of Murrow's stories from Europe, you find yourself drawn into events, feeling what he was feeling. But Murrow didn't deliberately strain for emotion. Emotion existed in his verbal pictures, and he was enough of an actor to let it subtly rise to the surface.

An atmosphere, a mood, exists in every event. Sensitive reporters feel it, and they transmit it quietly so their listeners and viewers can feel it vicariously. Good broadcast reporters have learned how to utilize empathy without forcing it upon their audiences.

Webster defines empathy as imaginative projection of one's own consciousness into another being. Note the emphasis in the definition—not conscious projection of imagination but imaginative projection of consciousness. The emotion must be real. You must feel it before you can project it. If you try to manufacture emotion or pretend you can feel it, you will probably distort the mood, and you'll make your listeners and viewers uncomfortable. They will sense the falseness of the mood and suspect you of trying to sensationalize the event. But if you feel the mood, you can subtly amplify it to enhance your audience's understanding of it.

Your interest in the story is the key. If the story bores you, look a little deeper. Try to find some facet of interest within it. If you try to deliver a story in which you lack interest, you'll transmit only a sense of boredom. And if you try to pretend to create a mood, you'll transmit only insincerity.

If you come across a serious auto-pedestrian accident at a downtown intersection, look for the facts, of course. Who is the victim? Who is the driver? How serious are the victim's injuries? How did the accident happen? Is there anything unusual about this intersection? Simultaneously, try to absorb the mood of the crowd at the scene. Listen to what people are saying. The investigating officers and ambulance crew have been through this kind of experience. If they feel anything, they probably don't show it. They're all business.

But one bystander may tell another the car barely missed her. She was lucky. Another bystander stares silently at the unmoving victim. Another tries to joke about how this is a method of population control, but nobody laughs. Another looks away from the victim but stands still, listening. Each reacts in a different way. Some may remember themselves in similar incidents. Most of them feel some pain, fear, and compassion. Some have mentally substituted themselves for the victim or the driver or the emergency technicians, and they feel the sense of urgency surrounding the scene.

Perhaps you'll hear pieces of conversation, or you can describe small actions, that will help recreate the mood. If you can relate some details that pull your listeners and viewers into the scene, you can make the story more vivid for them. At the least, if you've allowed yourself to absorb the atmosphere, it will quietly infect your delivery, and your audience will vicariously feel it, too.

Restrain your emotions, but be sensitive to them. Allow yourself to feel the mood, but don't permit your feelings to overpower your narrative.

Movement and Gestures

Television newscasters are confined to their settings. They usually sit behind desks under lighting that confines them to narrow areas. They hold scripts in their hands and rest their hands or forearms on their desks. Their movements are restricted: perhaps they move their heads and shoulders a little, perhaps they make small gestures with their hands. But the close-up, intimate quality of the picture demands that they restrain their movements to casual, abbreviated, subtle ones. Broad or abrupt movements make them seem unnatural.

But field reporters having working space. They can take advantage of wider camera perspectives in which broader movements and gestures seem natural. Newscasters might point out some detail with a hand or finger movement, but field reporters can extend their arms or move toward an object to point it out.

Picture yourself in a quiet conversation with a friend across a restaurant table. You move little, and gesture unobtrusively. You talk quietly.

Picture yourself in a classroom talking to a group of 30. You walk a little, shift your weight frequently from one foot to the other, and punctuate your thoughts with hand and arm gestures. You speak with a full voice. You enunciate your words carefully.

Picture yourself on a stage in front of an audience of five thousand. If your microphone is cordless, you cover the breadth of the stage, trying to reach each segment of your audience. You often extend your arms to their full length to gesture, and sometimes you move them vigorously to make a point. You speak in a loud voice, almost shouting at times. You speak more slowly, pushing each phrase out to the audience in the back row, allowing brief pauses for phrases to settle before you attack the next ones.

Field reporters will adapt themselves at times to that full range of physical and vocal attitudes as they conform to the settings and camera perspectives that help them tell their stories. They would look foolish declaiming loudly and gesturing broadly in a calm legislative hearing, and they would look equally foolish talking quietly and gesturing narrowly in the midst of a noisy stadium crowd. They have to adapt to the settings and nature of events.

They must also qualify each movement and gesture. The words they speak must corroborate their movements and gestures, or their viewers will sense and be distracted by the clash between words and movements.

Learn to put yourself at ease in front of the camera. Draw in a few deep breaths, stretch your arms over your head and out to the sides, slump your shoulders and drop your head. Now, concentrate on the ideas you are ready to transmit, and let gestures and movements grow naturally out of your thoughts.

Watch your performance on tape as often as you can. Look for movements or gestures that seem unnatural or repetitive. Remember them, and the next time you appear on-camera, consciously avoid them. Plan many of your movements and gestures. For example, if you're at the airport waiting for the president to arrive, plan to begin your stand-up as Air Force One reaches the apron and begins to taxi toward you. Then as you say, "The president has just arrived," you can turn your head and your body toward the jetliner to focus your viewers' attention on it.

Remember that body movements begin with the eyes, then progress to the head, the shoulders and trunk, and finally, the feet. Practice moving in that sequence. The movements follow in sequence so quickly that they may appear to be simultaneous, but if you practice the movements slowly in sequence, you'll look more natural when you move on camera. Avoid abrupt movements. They'll startle your viewers. Relax, and let your viewers see by your eyes that you're about to move.

Maybe you have a line in a story that says the favorite came within a neck of losing the Kentucky Derby. If you're on the news set in a shot that includes only your head and shoulders, you can gesture simply with your thumb and forefinger just an inch apart. But if you're on the scene, ad libbing a report in a camera shot that includes your full figure, you can hold both hands out, 18 inches apart, to get the same effect. (Note: Make sure your hands are up around chest or shoulder height, or your gesture may seem meaningless. Gestures at waist level seem weak and indefinite; those above shoulder level seem exaggerated.)

If you have a guest you intend to interview, plan movements or gestures that will draw her into the scene naturally. If you are on the news set, isolated on-camera for the introduction, simply turn your head toward your guest at the moment you want her included. The movement signals your camera operator to zoom back to a two-shot or signals your director to cut to the guest on a second camera. It also tells your viewers they can shift their attention from you to your guest.

If you're on location to do a stand-up interview, isolated in a medium shot for your introduction, turn your head and shoulders toward the guest and extend your arm toward him. That will signal your guest to move toward you, and as your viewers shift their attention to him, you can move your body and your feet to face him.

The number and variety of movements and gestures possible is limited only by the incentives your ideas provide. As long as you plan movements and gestures to supplement and emphasize ideas, they will contribute meaning to your stories. Just remember that your body works with your mind to communicate your thoughts.

A REPORTER'S VOICE

The days are gone when everyone in broadcasting must have a deep, resonant voice. Broadcast reporters who have low-pitched voices probably have an advantage, because listeners seem more comfortable with them. Low-pitched voices also seem to carry greater authority and lend greater credibility to stories. But modern listeners and viewers accept a wider range of vocal qualities, as long as the voices are giving them what they perceive to be valuable substance.

Attitudes about voices have changed slowly. Until the 1970s, listeners seemed to accept women's voices only if women reporters sounded masculine. Now they allow women to be themselves. Until the 1970s, listeners seemed to accept medium-

and high-pitched voices only for humorous or off-beat stories. Now they'll listen to voices that seem to be scraping over sandpaper or singing mezzo arias—as long as they're delivering quality information.

Nowadays, excess resonance sounds pretentious. Listeners and viewers are accustomed to the natural sounds they hear every day.

Nevertheless, you can train your voice to assume more fullness and tone. Too many fledgling reporters who have learned how to report and to write, but not how to use their voices, talk through their nasal passages. They may need to find voice teachers who can diagnose their voices and suggest remedies, but they can also work on their own to improve their vocal performance.

First, put yourself at ease. Relax. Some simple exercises may help you.

Stand up. Spread your arms and hands out horizontally. Extend them until your muscles strain a little.

Spread your legs apart, as far as you can without straining.

Breathe naturally. Don't try to force your breath into any rhythm.

Hold the position for a few seconds, then bring your feet together, extend your hands and arms high above your head, and hold that position until your arms and shoulders begin to tire.

Now lower your arms, bend forward, and stretch your hands toward your feet. Hold that position for a few seconds, then stand in your natural posture again.

Repeat the routine five or six times, but not so much that you begin to breathe harder.

Then sit down and read your script aloud.

Kneel down. Cross your arms over your chest and place each hand on the opposite shoulder. Bend forward. Think of touching your forehead to the floor, though you probably won't be able to stretch that far without straining. Hold the position for a few seconds, then return to an upright position and drop your arms to your sides. Relax for a moment. Then repeat the routine five or six times.

Go back to your script and read it aloud again.

You can invent similar exercises, but don't pressure yourself. Move broadly, stretch your muscles, particularly your abdominal ones. Breathe naturally, and pause for several seconds after each series of movements.

Don't strain. You're trying to relax, not to amplify your tension.

You'll probably feel uncomfortable performing such exercises where others can see you, so do them privately. When you're on set or on location, waiting for your cue, you can at least stretch your arms outward and upward slowly. You can walk around, taking full, slow steps, letting your arms swing broadly. Inhale and exhale deeply and slowly several times.

Tension constricts your muscles; it may stimulate muscle spasms and even force your vocal pitch higher. So, do whatever you can to put yourself at ease. When your body relaxes, your voice relaxes, your words flow easily, and your voice seems a little deeper and clearer.

Now, you need to learn how to generate breath from inside your body, not from your voice box. You must learn to push your breath upward from your diaphragm—that group of muscles which separate your chest cavity from your abdomen.

Put your fingers on your stomach, about four inches above your navel. Talk with a moderate degree of volume. If you can feel pronounced movement in the muscles above your abdomen, you're breathing from your diaphragm. If you can't feel that movement, you're probably working your vocal chords excessively, i.e., they're helping to force the sound out. And if that's true, your vocal quality is probably thin and nasal. If you read aloud for any length of time, your voice probably grows tired and sometimes hoarse.

You can develop vocal fullness and deeper pitch if you'll learn to use your diaphragm. Take a couple of your scripts to some remote place where no one can hear you no matter how much noise you make. Read your scripts in a shouting voice. Read slowly enough to be sure the words are clear, but keep forcing the words out with all the air you can inhale. Shout a short phrase, then inhale deeply and shout another. Keep at it until you begin to tire, then rest.

Next, talk through your script forcefully. Speak loudly, but don't shout. Be sure you're forcing air up from your diaphragm. If you're not, resume shouting until you can feel your diaphragm expand and contract.

Try counting vigorously by inhaling deeply and forcing the sound out sharply. Attack the beginning of each sound, then let the end of the sound linger until your breath supply is exhausted. ONENNNNNN. Inhale. TWOOOOOO. Inhale. THREEEEEEEE. Inhale.

Practice your exercises often. Roll your car windows up when you're driving on the freeway, and shout whatever comes to mind. Get into the crowd spirit at a football game. Shout encouragement to your favorites, and, if you like, shout abuse at the referees.

Talk above the sound of the television set when you're watching it alone.

Go into the broadcast booth or studio. Read loudly through your script as if you were Peter Finch in the movie "Network," exhorting your viewers to lean out the window and shout, "I'm mad as hell, and I won't take it anymore."

You'll probably feel uncomfortable exaggerating your reading in such ways, and you won't notice any immediate improvement. But keep working. Little by little your voice will grow fuller, and you'll enhance your natural, casual style of delivery.

Intimate Vocal Energy

Your vocal attitude helps your listeners and viewers decide how important your stories are. A lazy voice suggests that your information lacks importance. A forceful, but affected, voice suggests that you are exaggerating the importance of your information. A thin, halting voice suggests that you lack confidence in your information. A soft, purring voice suggests that you want to call attention to yourself rather than your information.

As a radio or television reporter, you're a storyteller who must use your voice to infect your listeners and viewers with the value and urgency of what you have to say. Your voice must influence your listeners—persuade them, affect them emotionally, or simply make them listen to what you have to say.

If you are to become capable of drawing your listeners into your story to experience the event with you, you'll need to develop vocal energy, an attitude of voice that contains a hint of excitement. Your voice must show that you are eager to share the story.

You can cultivate many techniques to stimulate vocal energy, principally volume, pace, emphasis, and enunciation. But remember that the substance of your stories and the settings in which you tell them should help you determine which techniques are appropriate and to what extent you can use them. Radio, for example, provides a different environment than does television. Both are casual, informal media, but television is more so.

Contrast the reading styles of Paul Harvey and Tom Brokaw. Paul Harvey relies solely on his voice to involve his radio listeners in his narrative, and he uses almost every vocal device available to generate interest. His volume spans the VU meter range from near shouts to quiet chuckles. His pace shifts from gallops to struts. His vocal emphasis calls up unexpected pauses, deliberate inflections, abrupt shifts of pitch and volume, planned repetition, adept changes of pace and, of course, almost flawless articulation.

Tom Brokaw, as a TV anchorman, draws on his physical presence, his setting, and myriad video devices—chroma keys, computer graphics, digital effects, and superimposed words and images. So, he can assume a calm, unruffled vocal attitude. He complements rather than dominates what we see on the screen. Yet, he utilizes some of the same vocal devices that Paul Harvey does, only in unobtrusive ways. His physical presence—bodily attitude and facial expressions—engender confidence in his credibility, but so does his voice—unhurried but firm. His facial expressions shift almost imperceptibly from soberness to smiles. His voice slips easily from thoughtfulness to quiet humor. His articulation is less than precise but still clear.

You could imitate Paul Harvey or Tom Brokaw, but you'd be mistaken to try. Each has developed a style that fits his personality and his medium. You should do the same.

Experiment with volume intensities and distances from the microphone. Find out at what level and distance you seem to be clearest and most forceful. Don't talk so loudly that you lose your vocal warmth, but don't talk so softly that you lose your vocal vitality.

Read at a slightly faster pace than you normally do. Force yourself to the threshold of stumbling articulation, then back off a little. See if you can accustom yourself to a style of reading the least important ideas rapidly, then slowing down to deliberately articulate the most important ones.

Attack the lead sentence of each story with a strong voice and deliberate pace, then increase your reading pace as you glide through the supporting facts, and slow to a measured pace to give the last four or five words of the story a conclusive sound.

Be aware of the pace of voices that precede yours—anchor's, field reporter's, newsmaker's—and consciously approach your first sentence differently. You can rescue a droning actuality if you jump in quickly after the newsmaker's last words with a rapidly articulated thought. You can relieve the tension of a trip-hammer field report if you pause briefly and read your first sentence forcefully and deliberately.

You can emphasize important ideas or words by increasing your volume, pausing or changing your reading pace, or repeating a key word or idea. You can attack a negative word with greater force, for example: "Emergency crews are asking residents NOT to leave their homes." You can pause briefly after the important word: "Emergency crews are asking residents not . . . to leave their homes." Sometimes you can emphasize the important word if you pause briefly before you say it: "Emergency crews are reminding you . . . not to leave your homes." You can emphasize the key phrase if you consciously slow your pace: "Emergency crews are reminding you—do NOT . . . LEAVE . . . HOME." You can emphasize the key phrase if you repeat it: "Emergency crews say you should not . . . should not leave home."

Experiment with various kinds of vocal emphasis and decide which fits the idea most naturally. Often, you can combine techniques to get the emphasis you want.

Enunciation in broadcasting is neither as precise as that of an orator nor as casual as that of a carnival barker. It is somewhere in between. If you enunciate too precisely, you'll sound like you're reading rather than talking. But if you mumble or slur over words, you'll force your listeners to strain to hear what you're saying.

Your reading should be crisp but comfortable. You'll be permitted to say tuh-night instead of too-night, for example, but you'll probably irritate your listeners if you say uh-sess-ree instead of ack-sess-uh-ree (accessory). Your listeners must understand you, and sloppy enunciation usually diverts attention from ideas.

You'll often have trouble with words of more than two syllables. Write down the words you stumble over, and practice articulating them syllable by syllable. Begin slowly, then gradually increase your pace until you can sense the words emerging more clearly. Sometimes, you can help yourself through a difficult word if you pause slightly just before you try to enunciate it. Inhale a quick breath just before you attack the word: "The protest leader says his group does not intend to inhibit . . . dissemination of news."

Pronunciation

Mispronounced words or names will damage your credibility more quickly than any other reading flaw. Listeners won't always detect factual errors. They won't always notice omissions. They may not recognize distortions. But if you mispronounce familiar words or names, not taking time to check on the correct pronunciation, they'll wonder if you checked your other facts.

You should know that Halley's Comet is HAL-ees, not HALE-ees or HALL-ees. In some areas, Weber is pronounced WEE-burr; in other areas, it's WEB-urr; in Germany, it's VAY-burr.

Some names are difficult because their owners do not pronounce them phonetically. For example, some people named Chenoweth pronounce their name shuh-NOFF; others pronounce it CHEN-oh-weth. The Keynesian economic theory is KAYN-zee-uhn, not KEYN-zee-uhn.

Foreign names are particularly difficult unless you're familiar with languages. When the Shah of Iran was deposed, and the exiled Khomeini returned to Iran, reporters called him ko-MAY-nee and kuh-ho-MAY-nee before they discovered it was ho-MAY-nee. Neuchatel, Switzerland, and Neufchatel, France, are both pronounced new-shah-TELL. Negros Island in the Philippines is pronounced NAY-gross, not NEE-grows. Kenya, in east central Africa, is KEN-yuh, not KEEN-yuh.

Pronunciations vary from locale to locale. For example, the city of Houston in Texas is HYOO-stun, but the county of Houston in Georgia and Houston Street in New York are pronounced HOW-stun.

Some broadcasters mispronounce common words. Nuclear sometimes comes out NOO-kyoo-ler instead of NOO-klee-er. Coup sometimes comes out COOP instead of COO. Coyote often becomes coy-YOH-tee when it should be KIGH-oht or kigh-OH-tee. Data frequently emerges as DAT-uh when it should be DAY-tuh.

Pronunciation changes with usage. For example, it's now acceptable to pronounce February as FEB-yoo-air-ee as well as FEB-roo-air-ee. And it's acceptable to pronounce ombudsman as OM-buds-mun as well as OM-boods-mun.

Dictionaries should be available in every newsroom so you can check pronunciation. Each day the wire services transmit pronunciation guides for names that may be unfamiliar but appear frequently in news stories. At least once each year, local wire service bureaus transmit pronunciation guides for common regional names. Some newsrooms have copies of the *NBC Handbook of Pronunciation* or CBS's *World Words*.

Be cautious. Don't assume a pronunciation you've heard is correct. Check.

READING FROM TELEPROMPTERS

You'll always have a script in hand, whether you're reading from it or a teleprompter. Rather than having it distract your viewers, use it, making it seem to be a natural prop.

Teleprompters are not infallible. Sometimes, script paper snarls in them, and the operator can't keep it moving up the screen. Sometimes, the paper slides to one side or the other, and you can't see complete words on the left or the right. Sometimes, the camera may be too far away, and you can't see the words clearly.

the tape and analyze your performance. What parts of the story did you deliver well? What parts did you deliver poorly? What can you do now to improve your delivery for your next ad lib story?

4. Attend a speech or a meeting. Observe the actions of the speakers and their listeners. Make notes on what you see. Write a story that "shows" what happened at the event by describing how the participants—speakers and listeners—acted and reacted. Record your story. Analyze it. Did you create a picture of the event? Did you *show* your listeners what happened?

5. Record a news story by reading at a more rapid pace than you normally read. Then read the same story at a deliberate pace that allows you to over-enunciate each word. Repeat the exercise at least three times. Read the last version at your normal pace. Was it clear? Did you stumble over any words? Can you substitute easier words for those you tripped on? Did you emphasize some words or phrases erroneously? Repeat the exercise to see if you can improve your reading.

6. If you have a teleprompter available, practice reading stories from it. Record your performance, then analyze it. Look for eye movements. Are they obvious? Look for the movements with which you intended to create visual transitions between stories or from you to other newscasters or reporters on-camera. Were they natural? Look for indications of your concentration on others within the scene. Were you attentive or inattentive to them?

Notes

1. Claudia Dreifus, "David Brinkley: News Talks to One Person," *The Press* (June/July 1981): 49.

2. Charles Kuralt, "The View from the Road," *The Red Smith Lecture in Journalism* (Notre Dame, Indiana: University of Notre Dame, August 1986): 5.

3. Edward R. Murrow, a speech to the Radio-Television News Directors Association, reprinted in *The Reporter* (13 November 1958): 32–36.

4. Tony Schwartz, "Are TV Anchormen Merely Performers?" *The New York Times* (27 July 1980): Section 2, p. 27.

5. Edwin Diamond, "Television's 'Great' Anchors—and What Made Them Rate," *The New York Times* (23 March 1980): D35.

12

ETHICS AND THE LAW

If you're a really good journalist, you can set your biases and your prejudices aside and you recognize it; that's part of the professionalism of our business. If there's anything that marks us as professionals rather than artisans or tradespeople or something, it's that ethical judgment that we can make and know that we must hew to this line. We know that we've got a pressure of our own prejudices over here, so we've got to balance it over here when we report and write and edit. We know that we can do that.

—WALTER CRONKITE, "And That's the Way It Was,"
Broadcasting (1 December 1980): 56.

Journalistic ethics are the moral choices reporters make regarding stories they cover and reveal to the public. They are reporters' attempts to use their powers wisely and in the interests of their listeners and viewers.

Ethical questions confront reporters in almost every story they cover: Have I been thorough enough to be sure my story is accurate? Have I restrained my personal feelings about this issue? Am I being fair to the people involved in this story? Will I compromise my integrity if I accept a free ticket to a football game? Will my participation in a community service group influence my presentation of news about that group? Can I offer this story to the wire service without conflicting with the interests of the station I work for? Have I been sensitive to the feelings of the people who were hurt by this tragedy? Have I dealt with my sources honestly? Have I allowed my friendship with my sources to influence my judgment? Am I justified if I offer to keep this source's identity secret? Have I been an observer or a participant in this event? Have I allowed my competitive spirit to push me into breaches of ethical conduct? Have I followed the pack, or have I relied on my own judgment?

These and myriad other questions will face reporters during their careers, but they'll rarely find firm answers to any of them. They can get guidance from supervisors and station policies, but they must ultimately base their choices on their own values. They must decide what is right or wrong, better or worse, good or bad in any ethical dilemma to satisfy their own sense of morality.

Organizations of reporters and editors such as the Radio-Television News Directors Association and the Society of Professional Journalists have written codes of ethics to provide general guidance to their members. Some news departments have written statements of principles to guide their employees; the CBS Broadcast Group, for example, has written a news standards manual of more than 60 typewritten pages to cover subjects that range from insulating public affairs broadcasts from advertising pressures to handling requests for outtake material.

Journalists also discuss ethics often—in professional meetings, in staff meetings, in individual conversations. Their judgments are not always the same. Each circumstance imposes its individual criteria to influence the decisions of reporters and editors. In this chapter, we'll talk about some of their decisions.

ACCURACY

Reporters generally accept the principle that accuracy is one of their primary obligations. They know they must tell their listeners and viewers the truth, and they know that the truth is sometimes difficult to determine. But most of the time they check and recheck until they're reasonably certain they've found the truth.

But the stress of time affects the work of every reporter. Despite the journalistic adage "Get it first, but first get it right," reporters sometimes mistakenly air stories they haven't checked sufficiently due to time pressures to meet their broadcast deadlines.

The president of the Radio-Television News Directors Association, Ernie Schultz, wrote about one such incident in 1981:

> At 9:44 p.m. on Monday night, June 19, 1981, a call came in to the switchboard at WRC, the NBC affiliate in Washington, D.C. The caller asked for the radio newsroom. Instead, the call was switched to the NBC television network desk. The caller identified himself as "James Taylor," assistant to Washington, D.C., Mayor Marion Barry, Jr. He said he was calling from the mayor's command post to report the mayor had been shot. The network desk promptly passed the call to the local desk in the television newsroom, where it was taken by Wendy White, producer of the late news on WRC-TV.
>
> White says the caller again identified himself as an assistant to the mayor, calling from the command post. He said the mayor had been shot outside his home, was in critical condition and was then on his way by helicopter to the hospital at Andrews Air Force Base. The man who called himself James Taylor gave White a telephone number he said was the number of the mayor's command

Retired General William C. Westmoreland brought a
libel suit against CBS over a documentary entitled
"The Uncounted Enemy." The documentary alleged
that Westmoreland had known about the falsification
of body counts during the Vietnam war.

post in case she wanted to call back and verify the report. White called the number, got "Taylor" who then added some further details to the report. At 9:46 p.m. WRC-TV went on the air with a live bulletin reporting that Mayor Barry had been shot.

Other stations monitored that bulletin and began checking the report of the shooting. WDVM-TV news staffers called Andrews Air Force Base where, they say, an Air Force sergeant confirmed that the hospital was preparing to treat the wounded mayor. United Press International moved the story along its wires, and a third TV station, WJLA, then carried the story.

But the mayor had not been shot. The call to WRC had been made, not from the command center, but from a public phone booth on Pennsylvania Avenue, outside the Federal Trade Commission building. WRC and the other news outlets that carried the report had been victims of what one reporter called "a very sophisticated hoax."[1]

The hoax spread beyond Washington, D.C. CBS Radio and NBC Radio in New York adjusted their 10 P.M. newscasts to include the "story" that Mayor Barry had been shot. ABC's West Coast edition of "World News Tonight" inserted the story into the late feed to western states.[2]

Newspeople decided later they had asked too few questions and not enough of the right questions to verify the report.

No reporter is immune from error, but all reporters should try to substantiate their information as thoroughly as possible before they air it.

FAIRNESS

Fairness in reporting has many facets. It refers to thoroughness—a reporter's willingness to look at all of the relevant aspects of stories and to give each the weight it deserves. It refers to sensitivity—a reporter's empathy for the people he or she reports about and the people he or she reports to. It refers to taste—a reporter's awareness of the invisible line that separates useful information from sensationalism. It refers to judgment—a reporter's ability to distinguish between irrelevance and evidence. It refers to honesty—a reporter's determination to talk straight to his or her superiors and sources, to openly assess and answer their questions, and to keep his or her promises.

Thoroughness is especially important in reporting for broadcast because our listeners and viewers seldom hear everything we say. Many of them take away different impressions than we intended in our stories.

One television reporter adopted a football analogy to describe the action at a city council meeting. He started with a group of council members in a huddle, the council president calling signals:

> The president signaled 'break,' and the members
> peeled out of the huddle to take their positions at
> the council table's line of scrimmage. Under the
> center, the council president barked a quorum present
> and called for a motion. The council member split to
> the left, moved toward the center of the line and
> called the question. The president rifled the call
> for a vote over the arms of the defenders into the
> end zone. Score, 6-to-2. Two council members on the
> right grinned as if they'd just performed a super
> spike.[3]

The reporter's analogy was interesting to viewers who understood football. But several viewers who didn't know that a "spike" was the act of slamming the ball to the ground called the television station to complain about the reporter's lack of taste. They thought he was guilty of sexual innuendo. His failure to provide a clear sentence (or to define his terms) allowed his viewers to interpret him erroneously.

A radio news director assigned a reporter to interview residents in a run-down area of the city. The residents were angry because a local automobile dealer had orders to evict them from the homes he owned. He wanted to raze the dilapidated dwellings so he could build new automobile display buildings and maintenance shops on the site. The reporter got some interesting emotional comments for her story. Some of the residents were old and living on Social Security payments alone. Some were unemployed welfare recipients. Some were single parents with as many as six children. None thought they could find affordable housing in any other neighborhood.

The radio reporter tried to telephone the automobile dealer to get his side of the story, but the dealer's secretary told the reporter her boss was in Europe on a business trip. So, the reporter decided to air the story based on the residents' complaints alone. At the end, she tagged her story with a sentence designed to explain why the story was incomplete: "Auto dealer so-and-so has been unavailable for comment."

Many listeners interpreted that statement to mean the dealer was evading the reporter and unwilling to reveal his motives. But in reality he would have been eager to give her his point of view if she had asked. He also said later that he had left his son in charge of the business and he was authorized to speak on the owner's behalf.

The reporter may have been justified in her decision to air the story immediately, but she mistakenly assumed that the automobile dealer was the only source who could talk about his company's point of view. At the least, she could have told her listeners that she couldn't reach auto dealer so-and-so "because he's in Europe," but she'd ask him for his side of the story as soon as he returned.

Radio and television news stories are often brief, but reporters must take as much time as they have available to make certain their stories are complete.

A REPORTER'S EMPATHY

Sometimes, experienced reporters and photographers seem to have two personalities: at times, they seem to be caring, compassionate, thoughtful, and considerate; at other times, especially under the pressures of collecting facts, of illustrating events, and from competitors, they seem to be uncaring, brash, impolite, and even ruthless. Listeners and viewers frequently attribute the Mr. Hyde facets of reporters' personalities to persistent demands to sensationalize news in order to attract audiences.

Some broadcast newspeople argue that they have no right to censor or filter news that contains elements of sensationalism. Others argue that they have a responsibility to think of the effects of their pictures on their viewers.

One such story in Philadelphia attracted national attention in 1987. On January 22, 1987, Pennsylvania Treasurer R. Budd Dwyer called a news conference. He had been convicted of racketeering, mail fraud, and conspiracy, and reporters expected him to announce his resignation before the court sentenced him the following day.

Instead, Dwyer read a long statement insisting that he was innocent, then pulled a .357 Magnum from an envelope, put the barrel in his mouth, and pressed the trigger.

All three Philadelphia network affiliates showed videotapes of the incident, but only the ABC affiliate, WPVI, showed the shooting, and then only on its noon news program (the suicide occurred at 11 A.M.). The networks broadcast the story across the nation. NBC showed part of the videotape, but eliminated the most graphic scenes. ABC and CBS showed still pictures only.[4]

Philadelphia Inquirer reporter Fred Cusick interpreted Dwyer's suicide as an act of revenge: "He didn't want us there as passive witnesses. He wanted to make us feel the pain, too. He aimed his act at those of us he felt had treated him as 'a piece of meat' and 'feasted' on him. In the end, he hated us and needed us, and he used us."[5]

Dwyer apparently believed reporters had abused him. In his written statement, he said, "Please tell my story on every radio and television station and in every newspaper and magazine in the U.S."[6]

Dwyer's wife, Joanne, believes the way reporters told the story of the suicide also abused his family and friends:

> My husband's death was a tragic death, but the reporting should have been based on issues rather than the idea of portraying a sensational story. Somehow the issues were often overlooked, and I believe this is the tragedy of reporting, where we do not see beyond the surface. Journalists do not go beyond a story, when in fact there are underlying issues that are more important than the facts themselves.
>
> The effects of this type of journalistic reporting are so long-range and so hurtful to so many innocent people that it kind of has a snowball effect to the point that all anybody will remember is not the facts or what was behind the event, but just the incident itself. It has a long-lasting effect on family and friends—they are forever devastated, which nobody realizes.[7]

Many television viewers complained, too, about the impact on their emotions of the stark video footage of the suicide. Some complained because the pictures appeared at times when their children were watching.

That on-camera suicide was an extreme incident. Nevertheless, broadcast reporters should be asking themselves daily how their reporting of less sensational stories affects their newsmakers and their audiences.

Newsmakers who are unaccustomed to reporters' interviews may inadvertently commit errors because they're intimidated by tape recorders or electronic cameras. Blind listeners and viewers might be falsely encouraged by a story on research into artificial eyes when such research is merely in its fledgling stage. Victims of nonfatal, but painful, accidents will likely be angered by reporters who ask, "How do you feel?" People accused of wrongdoing may be unfairly jeopardized because reporters write stories that assume they're guilty before they come to trial. Many viewers are offended by pictures of blood stains, even though victims are not included in the pictures; information provided by reporters stimulates their imaginations.

Radio and television reporters should not judge their news stories on their factual content alone. They must think about how the people they portray and how the people they report to will react to and be affected by what they hear and what they see.

TASTE

Taste can refer to language, pictures, racial slurs, sexist designations, or details in stories that may needlessly damage reputations.

Standards of taste vary from city to city, and perhaps that's why the Supreme Court has said obscenity, profanity, and indecency should be "measured by contemporary community standards." The Federal Communications Commission (FCC) has used that phrase, too, in its rulings on indecency. So, reporters must think about what their particular audiences will find acceptable or objectionable.

We have no specific guidance to tell us what language is objectionable. The FCC did provide some specifics in 1978 when it adopted a Supreme Court ruling against WBAI in New York City, which had broadcast a monologue by comedian George Carlin that the court said contained "seven dirty words" that were indecent.[8]

But in 1987, the FCC made its policy hazy again when it ruled that three radio stations had aired "indecent" programming when they broadcast statements about sexual and excretory functions, lyrics of a song that were sexually explicit, and a disc jockey's comments that contained sexual allusions. At that time, the FCC defined indecent language as "material that depicts or describes, in terms patently offensive as measured by contemporary community standards for the broadcast medium, sexual or excretory activities or organs."[9] And the commission said such material could not be broadcast when children "might reasonably be expected" to be in the audience.

The FCC specified that material deemed indecent could be broadcast only between midnight and 6 A.M. But some broadcasters and public interest groups challenged that provision, and the U.S. Court of Appeals in Washington ruled in mid-1988 that the time restriction was unconstitutional. Federal Judge Ruth Bader Ginsburg wrote, "Indecent but not obscene material qualifies for First Amendment protection whether or not it has serious merit."[10]

The broadcast networks and some stations have given their reporters more specific guidance. For example, the CBS news standards manual says, in part,

> When statements (by non-news personnel) with respect to a news event or issue include objectionable language, the inclusion of such statements in broadcasts will depend on factors such as (i) the importance of the news event or issue, (ii) the importance of the statement taken as a whole and its degree of newsworthiness and relevance to the news event or issue, and (iii) the degree of objectionability (i.e., certain objectionable language would be acceptable while other extreme language would not.)[11]

Most broadcasters follow similar policies. For example, if objectionable language fits naturally into a newsmaker's account, they'll leave it in, even though it might sound profane in the parlance of someone else. In most cases, however, newscasters and reporters avoid profanity.

Broadcasters try to avoid sexist and ethnic slurs. They no longer describe women as "shapely brunettes" or "rangy blondes." They avoid sexist adverbs and apply the designations brunettes or blondes only when they need such descriptive nouns to identify women more specifically.

Broadcasters apply racial tags only when they add meaning to stories. They consider race important when it helps to describe a suspected felon, when some newsmaker is the first of his or her race to achieve a particular distinction, or when race is an issue in a story. But the radio reporter who wrote, "A 21-year-old Blanding woman died yesterday after lightning struck her," was more sensitive than the radio reporter who wrote, "Lightning killed a 21-year-old Indian woman from Blanding yesterday."

A REPORTER'S JUDGMENT

Reporters must continually judge how to react to ethical problems that confront them. They must ask themselves if their reactions are in the interests of their listeners and viewers or in their self-interests. They must ask how their audiences will perceive their actions. They must ask themselves whether they are allowing their sources to manipulate them or whether they are accepting information that will be valuable to their public. They must weigh the relative merits of information that can harm newsmakers against the value of that information to their audiences. They must balance their friendships with their sources against their obligations to listeners and viewers. Almost every day, they must answer ethical questions and satisfy themselves that they've reacted in ways they won't regret.

Here are some factual case studies of ethical problems radio and television reporters have faced:

Case One. A television reporter has cultivated a trusting relationship with a deputy county attorney. The attorney is a good source for the reporter and knows the reporter will be thorough and accurate with the information he provides. He also knows the reporter will verify the information before he airs it.

The deputy county attorney is also a friend of the county attorney's executive secretary and knows the county attorney has been sexually harassing her in his statements, suggestive comments, and orders to perform duties unrelated to her office.

The deputy county attorney invites the reporter to a meeting at which he, the executive secretary, her attorney, and her parents will decide whether to bring legal action against the county attorney, and he wants the reporter's advice about whether they should make the story public. Should the reporter attend the meeting?

Case Two. A radio reporter received a tip that a prominent professor had been found dead in a local hotel. He called the hotel, got the investigating officer on the telephone, and learned that the man had apparently fallen in the bathtub, hit his head on the tub rim, and bled to death from a deep wound in his head. The officer also told the reporter the man had moved into the hotel a week earlier after an argument with his wife, and it appeared the man had been drinking heavily before the fall. The officer said he was certain the death was accidental.

The reporter wrote his story, including information about the professor's career as a distinguished teacher of anatomy and his activity in state politics. But he decided to delete the information about the family fight. He did tag the story with this sentence, however: "Police say the professor appeared to have been intoxicated." Was that fact important to the story, or should he have deleted it?

Case Three. Some state legislators have proposed a tax on advertising that would adversely affect radio and television stations, newspapers, and magazines published in the state. A television station manager decides to organize a political action committee among his employees to ask them for contributions, and to use the money to conduct a public campaign against the tax.

The station manager asks his news director to ask her staff members to contribute to the fund and also to assign stories that will show the negative effects of the tax on the station's news and public affairs programs. He tells her to make it clear that the enactment of the tax will force him to cut budgets and jobs in every department in the station. Should she ask her staff members to contribute? Should she ask staff members for the kinds of news stories he wants?

Case Four. A six-year-old girl has been kidnapped from a rural town near the border of the state. Police find her across the border in a small town in a neighboring state. She tells them the man picked her up near the elementary school she attends and offered to show her a playground with giant swings and slippery slides. She says he dropped her at a convenience store in the neighboring town and gave her a quarter to call her parents.

Radio and television stations report the kidnapping, and when police find the child, they identify her and picture her being reunited with her parents. Some stations interview her and her parents and air segments from the interviews.

Twenty-four hours later, police tell you the girl has been abused sexually. They say they've arrested a suspect and charged him with kidnapping *and* aggravated sexual abuse of a child. Your station has already named the child and pictured her. In light of the new information, will you still name her? Will you still air her picture?

Case Five. A father has taken his three sons hostage at the home of his father-in-law. He is apparently estranged from his wife, and she and her sons have been living with her father. The woman and her father were not at home when the man took his sons hostage. The man has told police he has a bomb strapped around his waist. Police say they found an explosive in a milk box near the house and another in a metal can. They assume the father is armed with other explosives.

Reporters gather at the scene. Microphones, cameras, and tape recorders are evenings, but said nothing about having rehearsed the questions and answers. On the evening the final segment aired, the reporter led into the tape with a statement that she had confronted the church leader with "some tough questions about his religion." A critic asked, "How tough can questions be when the reporter allows the newsmaker to rehearse his answers?"

In Boston, a television producer, along with one of his reporters, planned an April Fool's joke. Near the end of the 6 o'clock newscast on April first, the reporter broke in with a "bulletin"—the Great Blue Hill in Milton, Massachusetts, had erupted and was spewing lava and ash on nearby homes. She said a geological chain reaction from the volcanic eruption of Mount St. Helens had triggered this incident.

The producer then showed video footage of the Mount St. Helens' eruption and included statements from the governor of Massachusetts and the president of the United States saying they were worried about a "serious situation." He did not identify any of the video tape as "file video." The "bulletin" ran 98 seconds, at the end of which the reporter held up a hand-lettered sign that read, "April Fool." But by then frightened residents had called police and civil defense officials to ask how they could be evacuated. The general manager fired the producer the following day.

Keep your credibility. Be truthful with your listeners and viewers. Avoid any suggestion that you might have manipulated the news.

UNDERCOVER REPORTING

Investigative reporters face some of the most difficult ethical questions confronting journalists. They must decide when it is ethical to gather information under a false identity or using fake professional credentials. They must decide when it is ethical to use hidden cameras or hidden microphones.

Some stations have investigated questionable marketing practices by buying merchandise, testing its quality, then comparing their findings with the merchants' advertised claims.

For example, television reporters have posed as ordinary consumers to buy large quantities of beef advertised as top-quality meat available at low cost because it is being sold in bulk. Then they've asked butchers and meat-packing experts to examine it and report on its actual quality and value. They've used hidden cameras and microphones to record merchants' oral claims about their products, and they've confronted merchants unexpectedly with evidence that their claims were exaggerated.

Some of these reporters have justified their methods by showing that they drove unscrupulous merchants out of business and thus protected consumers against further abuses. Others argue, however, that such tactics are deceitful, and they brand as dishonest reporters who utilize them, despite the potential public benefit of their findings.

Television stations have used hidden cameras to record public officials admitting they have broken laws, to record illegal sales of drugs, to unmask "bookie joints" or "boiler rooms" operating behind the disguises of legitimate businesses, to shoot identification photographs of people who have avoided cameras. Chicago investigative reporter Pam Zekman of WBBM-TV says she uses hidden cameras to enhance credibility because, if people can see a lot of pictures and documents, they can better form their own conclusions.

Radio and television reporters have posed under false identities to collect information about conditions in hospitals, nursing homes, and prisons, to reveal shakedowns and bribes from public officials, to get information from police that wouldn't normally be available to reporters.

A producer and an assignment editor from WOWK-TV in Huntington, West Virginia, wanted to find out how easy it would be to register to vote more than once under their state's new voter registration law. The law allowed residents to register by postcard if they got their signatures notarized.

Producer Douglas Barthlow and Assignment Editor Roger Sheppard filled out several voter-registration postcards. They used their own names and Social Security numbers, but they listed different addresses in different voting precincts and had different people notarize their applications. They said they wanted to test the system to see if fraud were possible. Their general manager, Leo MacCourtney, said, "From the beginning, it was our intention to turn everything over to the prosecutor's office as soon as the test was discovered."[16]

But one county clerk noticed the repetition of names and called in a prosecutor. He charged the two with perjury, but he later dropped the charges, saying they hadn't violated the law because they didn't try to vote.

ETHICAL LIMITS

Almost every day, broadcast reporters face ethical decisions that range from correcting errors and reacting courteously to newsmakers to intrusions on grief-stricken victims and respecting the rights of accused persons to fair trials.

Each reporter, photographer, editor, producer, and news director must make individual decisions at certain times and reach joint decisions at others. All must be satisfied that they acted reasonably, considering both the interests of their listeners and viewers and the impact of their stories on people in the news.

Station managers influence the ethics of news personnel, too. General managers of large-market stations will probably refuse to allow news staff to deliver commercials, but general managers of some small-market stations may insist that news personnel deliver commercials and even sell commercial time. Some managers insulate news personnel from station sales representatives and advertisers. Others may spike (i.e., block) stories that threaten businesses that advertise on the station. Some executives may instruct their newspeople to observe and report events from the sidelines. Others may demand that their newspeople inject themselves into events to report as if they were participants.

Each radio and television news employee must decide whether he or she is comfortable with the ethical limits imposed by superiors and whether he or she can work within the ethical environment of a particular station.

LIBEL AND SLANDER

Broadcast journalists need to understand the legal limitations on their work, and the legal concepts of defamation are some of the most difficult. The law seems to change frequently. The courts reexamine concepts with each new case, and journalists find they cannot predict how judges or jurors will react to any specific combination of facts.

But reporters cannot be timid. They shouldn't abandon stories simply because they fear the consequences. They need to (1) understand the law as well as they can; (2) report as thoroughly as they can; and (3) consult their news directors or their stations' attorneys if they are in doubt.

Libel and slander are defined as defamation of character—harm to the names or reputations of persons or products. Libel is written defamation; slander is spoken defamation. In most cases, broadcasters are subject to libel suits rather than slander suits because they read most of their material from scripts and because the courts regard the technology of broadcasting as equivalent to the technology of print.

In general, four elements must exist to bring libel action against reporters and their stations. (1) The accusers must show that their reputations have been harmed; (2) they must demonstrate that they were identified by name or inference; (3) they must show that reporters made the harmful information public; and (4) they must convince judges or jurors that reporters failed to exercise proper care in verifying the information and broadcasting it.

Careless reporting probably leads to more libel actions than any other factor. Reporters who accept information and broadcast it without verifying it may be vulnerable. If a city employee tells you that the mayor has diverted public money into his private business enterprise, you need to find out if the employee's claim is true. Even if the employee makes the claim on audio tape or videotape, and you air the taped accusation, you are still vulnerable if you can't prove it. If you read a wire story that contains the libelous information, you are vulnerable because you are the one who made it public. Truth is your protection against liability; if you can't prove the truth of the information you've made public, you are unprotected.

Reporters should not assume they can broadcast harmful information and be protected simply because they do not name the person defamed. If the person is identifiable because of his or her title, job, or description, or if the group of suspected individuals is small, reporters may still be vulnerable. If you broadcast a story about an actor who quits a repertory theater company, complaining that he can't work in a group in which "most of the male actors are fairies," any actor in the group who does not fit the derogatory description can file a libel suit.

Reporters who discover they have erred and broadcast libelous information should retract their stories promptly and prominently. An apology may convince a judge or jury that they did not act maliciously. It does not guarantee protection, but it may help.

Reporters are protected under a principle called "qualified privilege" if they broadcast libelous statements they recorded or wrote down during open legislative sessions or court hearings. The statements of legislators during a floor debate, or the claims of witnesses during a trial, are part of the public record; reporters may broadcast them without fear of retribution.

Public officials and public figures have more difficulty proving they have been libeled than do private persons. In general, public officials or public figures are people who have voluntarily and actively thrust themselves into positions of public attention because they want public support or approval. The courts assume that such people as elected officials, candidates for office, actors, newscasters, comedians, singers, and writers are asking the public to accept them, so they should expect their actions to be open to public scrutiny.

Revelations about the private lives of public people may be subject to libel action, however. Reporters should ask themselves if the private actions of public people relate to the work they do or impair their ability to do it.

Although the courts have subtly changed their interpretations of what constitutes a public figure, they have generally relied on the 1964 decision of the Supreme Court in *The New York Times* v. *Sullivan* case. The court said then that public officials could recover damages only if they could prove that they were defamed with "actual malice," that is, that the libel was made public with knowledge that it was false or in reckless disregard for the truth.

INVASION OF PRIVACY

Broadcast journalists should become acquainted with laws that restrict their access to information that is considered private. The right of an individual to privacy is a relatively new principle. The Constitution doesn't mention it. Attorneys began to discuss it only as recently as 1890, when Louis Brandeis and Samuel Warren wrote in the *Harvard Law Review* that the Supreme Court should recognize the right to privacy.

The principle evolved slowly, but now almost all states recognize some privacy rights. Nevertheless, privacy statutes and practices vary widely. You should check to see what legal attitudes are in your state.

Varied courts have accepted four kinds of privacy: intrusion or trespass, appropriation of one's name or likeness, placing someone in a false light, and disclosure of private facts.

Intrusion or Trespass

Public places are considered open forums, so events that occur on streets, sidewalks, and in parks should be accessible to reporters and photographers. In general, you can photograph and talk about anything or anyone within the view of the public.

You will need permission to take pictures in private places, however. Home-owners or renters may invite you into their homes or apartments, but that is not necessarily permission to take pictures inside. Even when you have permission from police officers or firefighters to enter private property such as a business that has been burglarized or a warehouse that has burned, that does not constitute permission to take pictures. The Supreme Court has said, "Newsmen have no constitutional right of access to the scenes of crime or disaster when the general public is excluded." [17] In most cases when police or fire officials give you permission to enter a crime or accident scene on private property, property owners will not sue for invasion of privacy, but if you feel uneasy about a potential suit, you should ask for permission.

Appropriation of One's Name or Likeness

This principle has generally been applied to the use of a person's name or likeness in advertisements or commercials, but entertainers and celebrities often protect their performances against what they consider to be exploitation in news. Hugo Zacchini, a performer who billed himself as the "Human Cannonball," sued Scripps-Howard Broadcasting Company because, without permission, one of its Ohio stations taped and broadcast on its evening news his performance at a county fair. Zacchini contended that his "professional property" had been violated. The court agreed: ". . . it is important to note that neither the public nor respondent will be deprived of the benefit of the petitioner's performance as long as his commercial stake in his act is appropriately recognized." [18]

False Light

This principle is related to libel because when reporters or photographers place individuals or groups in false light, they tell only half-truths about them or infer that information about them is untrue. But they may err unknowingly.

False-light offenses occur most often when pictures and scripts deliver conflicting information. For example, a reporter and photographer could be assigned to a land-abuse story. The reporter could decide to cover a public hearing detailing abuses and ask the photographer to illustrate with video coverage of land developments. The photographer shoots pictures of legitimate, non-abusive tracts and includes pictures of signs that display the names of developers. The reporter might write a story that calls attention only to unnamed illegitimate developers. If they air the conflicting videotape and script, they will have cast the legitimate developers in a false light.

Disclosure of Private Facts

This principle attempts to prohibit revelation of sensational information that is not newsworthy. It does not prohibit any public happening, sensational or not, only material that is normally private and irrelevant to the basic story. If you were to tell your listeners and viewers that city council members had met in secret to plan a deceitful campaign to convince their constituents that a tax cut would force major cuts in city services, that would be newsworthy and legitimate. But if you were to tell your listeners that you witnessed police picking up one council member during a raid on a gay bar, that is probably irrelevant to the council member's vote on tax cuts. If you were to tell your listeners and viewers that a forgery suspect had been arrested (though not formally charged) on suspicion of altering a payroll check 40 years earlier, you will have inferred his guilt on the forgery charge.

HOW TO AVOID LAWSUITS

Washington, D.C., attorney Bruce Sanford, who represents the Society of Professional Journalists, among others, has written a brief guide titled "How to Avoid Libel and Invasion of Privacy Lawsuits," which is reprinted below:

> 1. Avoid slipshod, indifferent or careless reporting. Whenever a statement could injure someone's reputation, treat it like fire. The facts of a story should be confirmed and verified, as far as practicable, and in accordance with customary professional procedures.
> 2. Truth is a defense, but there may be a vast difference between what's true and what can be proven to be true to a jury. When in doubt as to whether a story is accurate, check it out. Remember a retraction is not a defense to a libel action but serves merely to mitigate or lessen damages.
> 3. There is no such thing as a "false opinion," so you have greater leeway with expressions of opinion than statements of fact. Base your comment or criticism on facts which are fully stated and which are true.
> 4. Watch out for the "routine" story of minor significance. It frequently doesn't get enough attention and, probably for that reason, accounts for more libel cases than all of the investigative reporting and human interest stories combined. Make reports of arrests, investigations and other judicial or legislative proceedings and records precisely accurate.
> 5. Try to give "the other side of the story." A good reporter sticks to the facts and not to some bystander's opinion of what might be the truth if the facts were known.
> 6. Take particular care with quotations. The fact that a person is quoted accurately is not in itself a defense to a libel action, if the quoted statement contains false information about someone.

7. Never "railroad" a story through, but instead edit it carefully to make sure it says precisely what you want to say. Don't use sly or cute innuendo to suggest some misbehavior that you don't describe explicitly. If you're going to defame someone, do it right.

8. Avoid borderline cases of invasion of privacy since the law of the right of privacy is still developing. Egregious insensitivity to the tender and non-newsworthy parts of a person's life may earn you only the wrath of a jury.

9. Don't make unauthorized use of names and pictures for advertising or other commercial purposes. Don't use unidentified pictures to illustrate social or other conditions, when pictures of people who expressly consent, including professional models or staff members, will suffice and are readily obtainable.

10. If an error has been made, always handle demands for retractions which come from a lawyer for a potential plaintiff with the advice of legal counsel. A well-meaning but unnecessary or poorly-worded correction may actually prejudice a publisher's or broadcaster's defenses in a subsequent lawsuit.[19]

FAIRNESS DOCTRINE

At this writing, the FCC is not enforcing the fairness doctrine, but, because Congress may enact it into law, broadcast reporters should be aware of its content. In addition, many broadcasters react as if the doctrine still exists because they endorse its spirit. You should remember that the fairness doctrine dealt only with issues, not with people; equal time regulations still govern the attention you give to political candidates.

The FCC wrote the fairness doctrine into broadcast regulations in 1949 to encourage discussion of controversial issues and to make sure the coverage was fair. The doctrine expected broadcasters to choose issues that were important to their listeners and viewers, expose them to public debate, and assure that all of the responsible opinions on those issues be aired. In short, the FCC designed the doctrine to enforce balanced coverage.

Balance, however, does not mean *equal time*. The doctrine specified no demand for equivalent time or for exposure of all points of view in the same broadcast or for similar formats for presentation of opposing points of view. It expected only that broadcasters demonstrate balanced coverage in their overall programming. (The doctrine contained the threat of license revocation for any broadcaster who failed to live up to its spirit.)

The doctrine expected broadcasters to be aware of controversial issues in their communities and to initiate discussion of those that seemed most important. But it also expected broadcasters to respond to requests, especially from organized citizen groups, for attention to those issues. It did not, however, attempt to ensure the right of any group or individual to speak, only that stations would expose the prominent ideas surrounding the issues.

A station may find the number of potential issues in its broadcast area too great to allow for coverage of them all. Each station is expected to find the issues most important to its listeners and viewers—tax reform is a prominent issue in many communities; improved mass transit versus expanded highway systems is another; the impact of various kinds of industries on the environment is another.

Any broadcast station or news department that wants to serve its community will continue to find and expose to discussion controversial community issues with the balance the fairness doctrine attempted earlier to enforce.

PERSONAL ATTACK RULES

The FCC has ruled that if an individual or group is attacked during a station's coverage of a controversial public issue, the station must act to give the person or group attacked an opportunity to respond. The FCC defines an attack as one "made upon the honesty, character, integrity, or like personal qualities of an identified person or group." An attack is not merely an accusation; it is a statement that casts doubt on the character of an individual or group. It could be an inference, or a claim, that a person is immoral or dishonest or that a group is acting illegally or deceitfully. It is more than mere disagreement with the beliefs and opinions of others.

And, in the same way the courts have interpreted libel statutes, the FCC says that even though the person or group attacked may not be named, they may be identifiable. If so, your station is vulnerable.

The personal attack rule does not apply to (1) newscasts, interviews, or coverage of events on the spot; (2) statements made by legally qualified political candidates; or (3) attacks on foreign groups or foreign public figures. Editorials and other programs, however, are subject to the rule.

When an individual or group is attacked on your station, the station must notify the person or group attacked within one week, delivering a tape or script of the attack, or an accurate summary of the attack, and offering the person or group a reasonable opportunity to respond.

If your station endorses or opposes a legally qualified candidate, the rule specifies that the station must, within 24 hours, notify the candidate it opposes, deliver a tape or script of the editorial, and offer the candidate a reasonable opportunity to respond on the station's facilities.

If your station broadcasts such an editorial within 72 hours of election day, it must act expeditiously to make sure the candidate it opposes has ample time to prepare and present a response. The FCC does not specify a time limit, but the rule suggests that the station must act in less than 24 hours.

EQUAL TIME RULE

The equal time rule, which the FCC calls the "equal opportunities rule," does not apply to newscasts, interview programs, on-the-spot coverage of news events, or documentaries in which the political candidates appear incidentally or to discuss topics other than their campaigns. To qualify for the exemption, newscasts and interview programs that feature candidates should be regularly scheduled programs.

The rule's intent is to provide exposure to all legally qualified candidates for office. Therefore, news departments can use it as a guide to balanced coverage during election campaigns.

To fulfill the intent of the equal time rule, stations need not inform any candidate that his or her opponent has appeared. The candidates themselves are obligated to ask for equal time, and they must ask for it within a week after their opponents have appeared. When they ask, stations must respond affirmatively to their requests. (Many stations make it a practice to invite opposing candidates to appear without waiting for their requests.) Stations are obligated only to allow the candidates, not their representatives, to appear.

Stations must make air time available to opposing candidates that is comparable in length and time of day to the air time given to their opponents.

The FCC does not expect stations to give attention to every candidate for office. If you can accurately predict, for example, that a candidate from a minor party will fail to get a significant number of votes, the FCC is unlikely to hold you accountable for failing to give that candidate air time.

Broadcast news employees are likely to become targets of the equal time rule if they decide to run for public office. A United States court of appeals ruled in 1987 that television stations must offer equal time to opponents of on-air reporters who run for public office.[20]

CHANGES IN THE LAW

The law changes continually: Congress and state legislatures enact new laws and sometimes repeal old laws. Courts interpret existing laws in ways that supplant former interpretations. Radio and television newspeople must be aware of changes that affect the way they do their work. If they unknowingly violate laws or regulations, they may cost their stations time and money.

Reporters, producers, photographers, editors, and news directors who take time to inform themselves about changes in the rules that govern their work will be valuable employees at their radio and television stations, just as they'll be valuable if they keep up with changing technology and news-gathering techniques.

CHANGES IN BROADCASTING

Modern radio and television and audiences are better educated than they have ever been. They demand more information because they want to find solutions to personal and community problems. They want to vote intelligently so they can elect responsible leaders. They want to be aware of the condition of their world and their relationship to it. They want to satisfy their curiosity about the accomplishments and setbacks of other human beings. And they rely more frequently on broadcast news to provide that knowledge and perspective.

To meet audience demands, broadcast news keeps developing and growing. Creative producers, reporters, photographers, and editors regularly find new ways to illustrate and transmit information. News producers are finding new ways to adapt their sophisticated broadcast technology to the transmission of news. Reporters are more conscientious; they are emerging from their one-time superficiality to provide more content in the news they air. Photographers are more imaginative; they know more about how to reveal facts visually. Editors are more businesslike; they have adapted to the pressures of restrictive budgets and limited resources and have learned how to share their materials with networks and groups of stations organized into cooperatives.

Rewards for broadcast newspeople grow, although the gap between neophytes and veterans widens. Entry-level salaries are among the lowest in any industry, but money at the top level is equivalent to the highest. And the prestige of the best-known broadcast journalists matches or exceeds that of top-flight entertainers and executives.

Young radio and television newspeople soon learn that, if they are dedicated to their work and willing to learn, they can advance rapidly. And they find that their road to success no longer leads exclusively to the major national networks; they find that the centers of news in the United States are no longer Washington, D.C., and New York City. Some find their ultimate careers at local radio and television stations, some in cable news systems, some with wire service and independent news networks, some in small-community, low-power radio and television stations.

The potential of radio and television to transmit news seems limitless. Broadcasters still need to explore the effects and the power of information that is transmitted primarily through the senses, but as they learn and adapt their knowledge to their work, they will heighten the value of radio and television news for their audiences.

Exercises

1. Check with radio or television news directors in your area. Ask if they have established ethical standards or guidelines. Are they written down, or are they communicated orally? If they are written, ask for a copy. If they are spoken, make notes on what areas they cover. Evaluate them. Do they cover what you think are requisite practices? What is missing among them? If news directors have no station guidelines, do they endorse codes like those of the Radio-Television News Directors Association or the Society of Professional Journalists? Do they distribute those codes to their news employees?

2. Contact the president of the local professional chapter, or the president of the local campus chapter, of the Society of Professional Journalists. A news director

or newspaper editor will know the name of the professional chapter president. The head of a journalism school or communication department will know the name of a campus chapter president, if a campus chapter is organized. Ask for a copy of the current annual issue of the society's "Journalism Ethics Report." Study it. Prepare to lead a discussion of two or three of the most important ethical issues that appear in the report.

3. Talk to two or three radio or television reporters. Ask about the ethical problems they, or other reporters, have encountered. How were they resolved? Did the solutions satisfy them? Would they react in the same ways if they faced those problems again? What would they do differently on such occasions? Prepare to lead a discussion to determine how your peers would resolve those same ethical problems.

4. Watch television newscasts or listen to radio newscasts for a week. Look and listen for stories or elements of stories you think are in poor taste. Write a paper discussing at least one such story. Why did you think the reporter, producer, photographer, or editor erred? Did the story serve any useful purpose? What would you have done if you had faced a similar incident?

5. Interview two radio or television station managers. Ask for their impressions of the fairness doctrine. Would they like it renewed, or do they dislike it? How do they determine what are controversial issues of importance to their communities? In what kinds of programs (interviews, documentaries, call-in programs, panel discussions) do they air such issues? How do they decide which points of view need attention? Write a paper detailing your findings. Include a discussion of how well you think those stations live up to the intent of the fairness doctrine.

Notes

1. Ernie Schultz, "Anatomy of a Hoax," *Radio-Television News Directors Association Communicator* (August 1981): 6.
2. "Six Darts in Search of a Laurel," *Columbia Journalism Review* (September/October 1981): 27.
3. Roy Gibson, KUTV, 12 January 1982.
4. Fred Behringer, "Dwyer Suicide Called 'Statement' to Press," *Ethics Under Fire: 1987– 88 Journalism Ethics Report* (National Ethics Committee, Society of Professional Journalists, Sigma Delta Chi): 4.
5. "Aftermath of a Suicide," *Washington Journalism Review* (April 1987): 8.
6. Behringer, ibid.
7. Fred Behringer, "Widow Praises, Criticizes Press, Calls for More Ethical Standards," *Ethics Under Fire,* op. cit., p. 5.
8. *FCC* v. *Pacifica Found. Inc.,* 438 U.S. 726 (1978).
9. The Reporters Committee for Freedom of the Press, "Agency Won't Define 'Indecency,' " *The News Media and the Law* (Winter 1988): 47–48.

10. Reuters, "Court Overturns FCC Rule Limiting Indecent Radio Talk to After Midnight," *Deseret News,* 30 July 1988.

11. CBS Broadcast Group, *CBS Television Stations News Standards* (May 1976): 28.

12. "ABC World News Tonight," 5 December 1983.

13. "Inside Story: The Anchor," PBS, 3 February 1984.

14. "ABC World News Tonight," 10 July 1972.

15. Robert M. Steele, "Video Ethics: The Dilemma of Value Balancing," *Journal of Mass Media Ethics,* 2, no. 2 (Spring/Summer 1987): 7.

16. Eric Newhouse, "Region 4 Regional Report," *1985–86 Journalism Ethics Report* (National Ethics Committee, Society of Professional Journalists, Sigma Delta Chi, 29 October 1985): 30.

17. *Branzburg* v. *Hayes,* 408 U.S. 665, 681 (1972).

18. *Zacchini* v. *Scripps-Howard,* 45 LW 4954 (1977) at 4958.

19. Bruce W. Sanford, *Synopsis of the Law of Libel and the Right of Privacy* (Washington, D.C.: Scripps-Howard Newspapers and Scripps-Howard Broadcasting Company, Baker & Hostetler, revised, 1981): 4–6.

20. *Branch* v. *FCC,* 824 F.2d 37 (D.C. Cir. 1987).

Text Credits

Page 1: CBS Inc. has allowed the publication of this excerpt from William S. Paley's "Press Freedom" address which was originally presented on June 6, 1980, at the AP Broadcasters Convention. **Pages 2, 209, and 238:** Excerpts from Edward R. Murrow's speech to the Radio/TV News Directors Association, November 13, 1958, reprinted courtesy of Mrs. Janet Murrow and Mr. Casey Murrow. **Pages 5 and 235:** Excerpts from Elmer Lower, "A Quarter Century of Television News: From Talking Heads to Live Moon Landings," *Television/Radio Age,* August 28, 1978. Reprinted with permission from *Television/Radio Age.* **Pages 8 and 112:** Charles Kuralt/Eric Sevareid interview, on the CBS EVENING NEWS WITH WALTER CRONKITE. CBS Inc. has allowed the publication of these excerpts which were originally broadcast on December 13, 1977, over the CBS Television Network. © CBS Inc. 1977. All rights reserved. **Page 16:** Excerpt from Jerry C. Hudson, Director of the School of Mass Communication, University of Tennessee, "Broadcasters Want Experience, Skills, and Liberal Arts," *Journalism Educator,* Winter 1987, pp. 36–38. Reprinted with permission. **Page 49:** Excerpt reprinted with permission of United Press International, Copyright 1985. **Page 53:** Excerpt reprinted with permission of United Press International, Copyright 1985. **Page 82:** Roger Mudd, on the CBS EVENING NEWS WITH WALTER CRONKITE. CBS Inc. has allowed the publication of this excerpt which was originally broadcast on January 23, 1978, over the CBS Television Network. © CBS Inc., 1978. All rights reserved. **Page 89:** David Brinkley, NBC Nightly News, December 28, 1977, reprinted courtesy of NBC News. **Page 93:** Sydney Harris, *Deseret News,* April 26, 1973. Reprinted from the *Chicago Sun-Times,* 1989. **Pages 109–110:** Charles Peters, "Tilting at Windmills," *The Washington Monthly,* July/August 1978, p. 4, reprinted by permission of The Washington Monthly. Copyright by the Washington Monthly Company. **Page 114:** Thomas Griffith, "You Have to Be Neutral to Ask the Questions," *TIME,* September 13, 1976, p. 2. Copyright 1976 by Time Inc. Reprinted by permission. **Pages 140–141:** Emery King, WBBM-AM Radio. CBS Inc. has allowed the publication of this excerpt which was originally broadcast on February 4, 1977, over the CBS Radio Network. **Pages 141–143:** Scott Simon, "All Things Considered." This report was originally broadcast on National Public Radio's news and information magazine, "All Things Considered," on February 5, 1977, and is printed with the permission of National Public Radio. Any unauthorized duplication is prohibited. **Pages 151–152:** Howard Berkes, "Morning Edition." This report was originally broadcast on National Public Radio's news and information magazine, "Morning Edition," on February 20, 1986, and is printed with the permission of National Public Radio. Any unauthorized duplication is prohibited. **Page 178:** William Leonard, "TV News of the Future—as Seen by Network Chiefs." Excerpted from the November 20, 1978, issue of *U.S. News and World Report.* Copyright, 1978, U.S. News and World Report. **Page 181:** Gary Nunn and Alan Walden, NBC Radio News, August 18, 1987. Reprinted by permission from NBC Radio Networks, A Division of Westwood One Inc. **Pages 182–183:** Gary Nunn, Tom Aspa, and Fred Kennedy, NBC Radio News, August 18, 1987. Reprinted by permission from NBC Radio Networks, A Division of Westwood One Inc. **Page 184:** Bill Whitney and David Horowitz, CBS News. CBS Inc. has allowed the publication of this excerpt which was originally broadcast on August 18, 1987, over the CBS Radio Network. **Page 185:** Ann Taylor and Jay Barbaree, NBC Radio News, August 17, 1987. Reprinted by permission from NBC Radio Networks, A Division of Westwood One Inc. **Pages 185–186:** Ian Hunter, ABC Entertainment Network, August 19, 1980. Reprinted courtesy of ABC Radio News. **Pages 187–189:** Ted Robbins, KALL-AM, April 2, 1985. Reprinted by permission of KALL 910 AM, Salt Lake City. **Pages 189–190:** Alex Sullivan, KNX-AM. CBS Inc. has allowed the publication of this excerpt which was originally broadcast in 1977 over the CBS Radio Network. **Pages 192–193:** Bill Lynch and Barry Peterson, CBS News. CBS Inc. has allowed the publication of this excerpt which was originally broadcast on August 24, 1987, over the CBS Radio Network. **Page 194:** Douglas Edwards, CBS News. CBS Inc. has allowed the publication of this excerpt